CW00418219

The Wars of Alexander's Successors

323-281 BC

THE WARS OF ALEXANDER'S SUCCESSORS

323-281 BC

VOLUME 1: COMMANDERS & CAMPAIGNS

BOB BENNETT
& MIKE ROBERTS

Pen & Sword
MILITARY

First published in Great Britain in 2008 by
Pen & Sword Military
an imprint of
Pen & Sword Books Ltd
47 Church Street
Barnsley
South Yorkshire
S70 2AS

ISBN: 978 1 84415 761 7

Typeset in 11/13 Ehrhardt by Pen & Sword Books Ltd

Printed and bound in England by Biddles Ltd

Pen & Sword Books Ltd incorporates the imprints of:
Pen & Sword Aviation, Pen & Sword Maritime, Pen & Sword Military, Wharncliffe
Local History, Pen & Sword Select, Pen & Sword Military Classics, Leo Cooper,
Remember When, Seaforth Publishing and Frontline Publishing.

For a complete list of Pen & Sword titles please contact:
Pen & Sword Books Limited
47 Church Street, Barnsley, South Yorkshire, S70 2AS, England
E-mail: enquiries@pen-and-sword.co.uk
Website: www.pen-and-sword.co.uk

Contents

Acknowledgements

Though both authors have always had a love of ancient history, the seed of the book germinated after reading Robin Lane Fox's magisterial *Alexander the Great*. We felt an abiding curiosity as to what had actually happened after Alexander's death and that his lieutenants merited much more attention than they had received. Failing to find the necessary information, we decided to do the job ourselves.

Our first personal acknowledgement must be to Bob's old Latin teacher, Mr Polack, who is sadly no longer with us. He kindly agreed to translate the appropriate fragments from Polynaeus which was the one key source we could not find in translation. Then there is Jeff Champion, who we have not met but who read the book on our website and, though hoping to publish a similar work, selflessly recommended it to Pen and Sword Books. There we have been fortunate to have as a commissioning editor, Philip Sidnell, who has been willing to give us a chance to get published and has supported us every step of the way.

Special thanks must go to our family and friends who have tolerated us putting so much time over so many years into this project. Bob's mother has been very enthusiastic and supportive over the last few months. Finally, our thanks go to our wives, Janet and Sue, and our children, Katie, Joe, Philip and Steve, whose intermittent interest has always been a morale booster.

List of Illustrations

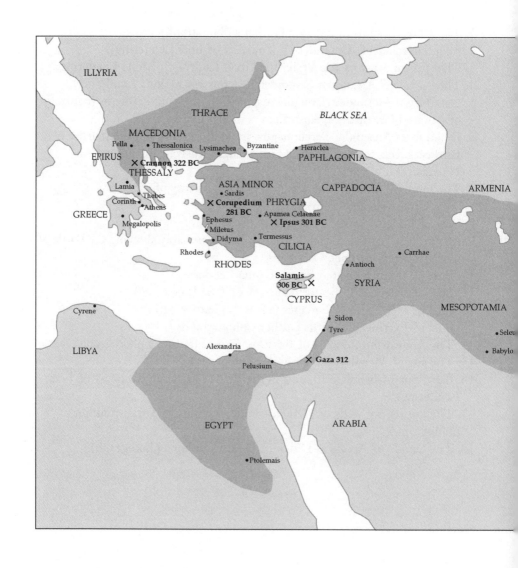

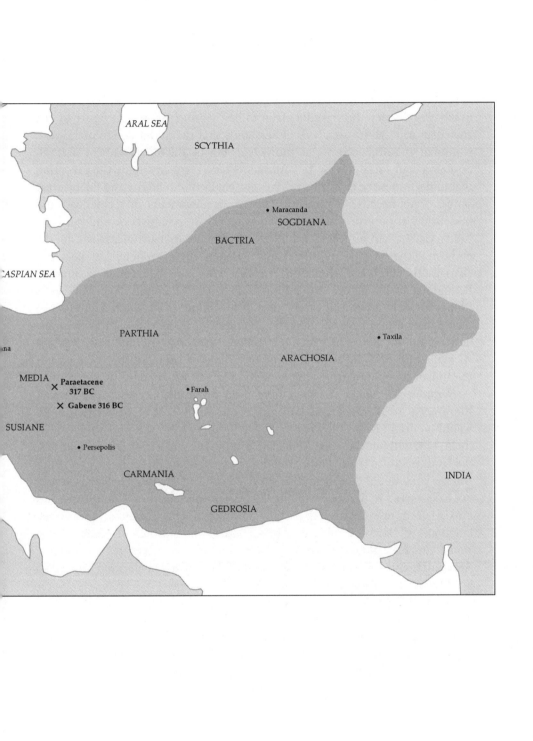

Introduction

When Alexander III of Macedon crossed into Asia in 334 BC, with an army of nearly 40,000 men, he staked a claim to be the most significant figure of the ancient world. Mature analysis understands that the grand design of History is ultimately influenced not by individuals but by the movements of natural, economic and social forces. Yet, Alexander's career seems to be the exception that undermines the rule. The progress of civilisation, the rise and fall of great states, occur because of climatic change, developments in technology and trade; they are not determined by kings, generals, scientists or philosophers. Julius Caesar, Archimedes and Plato are the great instrumentalists in the orchestra; their virtuosity affects and enlivens the symphony but does not change its nature or direction. In this company Alexander is unique. Something in his nature drove him to do what Xenophon, Agesilaus, even Philip, his own father, and surely most of his followers considered impossible. These men would have thought the conquest of Asia Minor, or at most the destruction of Persepolis, enough achievement for any lifetime; but for Alexander all this, the acquisition of the whole of Iran and the northwest of the Indian subcontinent was not enough to satisfy his appetite.

Without Alexander it would have been different. Certainly the Persian Empire was weak, ramshackle and ripe for a take-over. The western satrapies would no doubt have fallen to aggressive invaders from the west whoever led them, but, without the great Macedonian's unique and extravagant ambitions, the lands east of Mesopotamia would not have felt any direct impact. A rump Iranian state would doubtless have survived east of Babylon; Hellenism would not have spread to the shores of the Caspian or the valleys of Transoxania and into what is now modern Pakistan. The remarkable fusion of the Greek kingdoms of Bactria would never have come about and the rich trade of Asia would not have flowed unrestrictedly to fuel the great centres at Antioch, Alexandria and Ephesus, where the light of Hellenistic civilisation burned so brightly for centuries after Alexander's death.

But if this Macedonian princeling is honoured for a titanic influence that justified self-elevation to Olympus, he did not do his work alone. The extraordinary conqueror of Darius was kept company by lieutenants who lived on a scale almost as Homeric as his own. The story of these men during Alexander's life would make them sufficiently worthy of notice; without their bravery and talent he could not have filled the years between 334–323 BC with the incredible achievements he did. Yet, it was the fact that many of these same individuals dominated the world for forty years after his death that puts their true significance into perspective. Alexander died young, after achieving so much, whilst many of these comrades kept burning the fire of ambition until in their seventies and eighties. They rarely died in their beds and in the case of two they were cut down in battle near the age of eighty.

Out of their struggles emerged dynasties that rang down the passage of time. Some were temporary with progeny despoiled and kingdoms dismembered on the founder's violent death. One made a bid that looked set for two decades to reunite the whole of Alexander's empire only to founder in cataclysmic reverse. Even so, his grandson emerged to create a dynasty that ruled Macedonia itself until the final Roman deluge brought down Alexander's kingdom at Pydna in 146 BC. These were no puny actors on the stage of history and though it is a temptation to look at each individually, their fortunes began together and their destinies were so intermingled, it is hard to separate them.

These, the first of Alexander's Successors; the *Diadochi*, have not received a fair share of attention from historians. General works exist, but frequently the years from Alexander's death to 280 BC are treated as an introduction; a settling of the sands that reveals the finished world of Hellenistic kingdoms.

Interest is drawn always to the monarch whose feats were so great and for whom the chronicles are extensive and detailed. Ragged, incomplete and questionable, the sources from which the story of the Successors has to be constructed has clearly discouraged the attempt. They stand in the rain-shadow of another's mountainous achievements. The pattern of Alexander's career is clear and clean-rooted in the work of his father, moving along its extraordinary course to culminate in the tragedy of premature death. For the Successors there is no such easy appeal. All is confusion, with the rise and fall of these potentates apparently at the whim of random fate, dying in battle or assassinated with no neat driving force to fit them in place and time. Theirs is a struggle to survive and cement their power without the glamorous, and perhaps unlikely, vision of Macedonian-Iranian partnership that Alexander is sometimes credited with in his later years. Alexander broke the mould of the Classical world; he thought outside the restraints of his upbringing and claimed a prestige of godhead that leaves the student feeling he was unlike other men of his, or any, age. This makes him difficult to grasp; he bestrides the world too high to be knowable in ordinary terms, though the attempts to do so have consumed forests of paper over the centuries. But his Successors are exemplars of human fallibilities and seem more contemporary for it.

Unbound, rootless and irresponsible, they are familiar, if far from wholly admirable. Seleucus with his loathing of paperwork, Lysimachus and his reputation for parsimony and Ptolemy with his inclination to ruinous domestic arrangements; they are graspable in a way that the all-conquering Macedonian Achilles is not.

The soldiers who invaded Persia in 334 BC were pursuing an idea that Alexander had inherited from his father Philip II. The Asian war had provided the context of the king's policy in the last years of his life, though the idea itself had a longer gestation. Since the Battle of Cunaxa, the march of 'The Ten Thousand' and Agesilaus' campaigns in Asia Minor, the invasion of the Achaemenid empire had been canvassed, most urgently through the voice of Isocrates. Yet, over his short, extraordinary reign, Alexander would transform the concept into one uniquely his own, so that it would seem to future generations that the genesis of the crusade against Persia began with him.

What is true of the policy is also true of the instrument that accomplished it. The army that crossed the Hellespont on the heels of Alexander was largely the one reformed and used to such good effect by his father. Certainly, without the political, military and ideological groundwork laid by Philip it is impossible to imagine the achievements in Asia. And, like the idea, the army that accomplished it would be changed and made his own by Alexander over a decade of conquest. From top to bottom it would wear a different face in 323 BC from that at Pella, the Macedonian capital, when a twenty-two-year-old Alexander first set his foot on the road to Asia.

Nowhere is this more apparent than in the hierarchy of command. Officers of the highest rank at Alexander's death will be looked for in vain in the early battles against Darius, while many who filled the greatest offices in 336 BC were long gone when the young king expired in Nebuchadnezzar's palace at Babylon. Death in bed or battle, honourable retirement and natural wastage can explain some, but far from all, the changes charted by the chroniclers of the reign.

Alexander's accession to his father's undivided inheritance had depended on, amongst other things, the adherence of Philip's great officers. One of the most important gained much from his efforts. Years before, Philip had commented about him that 'the Athenians elect ten generals every year, but I have only ever found one, Parmenion'.[1]

Parmenion was in his sixties when the invasion of Persia began and the authority and prestige of his name was unassailable. Second only to Alexander in the army of invasion, in combat he commanded the left of the battle-line, while on the right the king headed the decisive thrust. In the three great battles at Granicus, Issus and Gaugamela, his contribution was vital to Macedonian success. His importance was both indicated and ensured by the positions held by members of his family who between them controlled the most militarily powerful and prestigious units in the army. His son, Philotas, was general of the Companion cavalry, the elite horsemen who had the credit as battle-winners in Alexander's campaigns. Nicanor, another of Parmenion's sons, led the Hypaspists (Shield-bearers) the infantry elite of the Macedonian national army. Nor was this the extent of the family's influence, a nephew and a son-in-law of Parmenion also held important commands. Between them, they represented a faction of great importance within the king's peripatetic court.

Parmenion's own military experience was enormous; indeed, he had campaigned in Asia when leading Philip's initial expeditionary force. His efforts had smoothed the way for the main invasion and it is not surprising that he frequently found himself in independent command. After Granicus, while the king marched south to Caria and Pamphylia, Parmenion led the other half of the army along the Royal Road through the heart of Anatolia.

Darius, after his last defeat in battle, withdrew to Media as the Macedonians plucked the fruit of victory in Babylon, Susiane and Persepolis, but his respite was short lived. The invaders came after, chasing him out of Ecbatana and deep into Iran. While Alexander continued the chase, Parmenion went no further and stayed in the city chosen as the treasure house for the vast Achaemenid booty that he was entrusted to bring up from Persepolis. He would never meet Alexander again.

Three defeats in the field and growing indecision undermined Darius' authority and he died at the hands of his own councillors. Alexander delayed to campaign by the Caspian Sea but was soon again on the trail of the Bactrian and Sogdian assassins who had proclaimed Bessus as the new Great King. The Macedonian army left the lush green country north of the Elburz Mountains and turned south to the borders of Seistan. Here the country was harsh and supplies difficult to obtain so the soldiers were relieved to find the satrapal capital, Farah, well stocked with grain. There they rested and there also took place an event that totally changed the face of the organisation that had won so much and come so far.

Much of the detail of the Philotas affair remains mysterious, and the context uncertain, but the ruin of the family of Parmenion is only too dramatically clear. Their power had already suffered some erosion; Hector, a younger son, had died by drowning in Egypt and Parmenion was deeply upset by the event. A second casualty was Nicanor, the commander of the Hypaspists, who barely a month before had died during the chase after Bessus. Alexander had not had time to stop to attend to his funeral but left Philotas behind with a small contingent of soldiers to mark his passing. Between them, Parmenion and Philotas still held the most prestigious commands in the army but they were separated and increasingly isolated. That Philotas was proud, arrogant, and extravagant was not unusual amongst a bevy of generals to whom ostentation was second nature, but he had little grace to accompany it and an inability to dissemble his feelings that he and his father had not got more for their contribution to the overthrow of Persia. His showy lifestyle was legendary; Leonnatus might have silver studs in the soles of his boots but Philotas kept hunting nets that, when fully extended, stretched for twelve miles.

The bare bones of the bloodletting at Farah are simply told. Dymnus, a Macedonian of no great note, allegedly hatched a plot to kill the king and confided the details to his lover. This young man was terrified and, to ensure his own safety, revealed the details to Philotas. He, though having many opportunities to tell Alexander, chose to say nothing and Dymnus' lover, now even more alarmed at the lack of developments, informed a royal page, who straight away told the king. Dymnus was killed before he could be questioned and Philotas came under suspicion for his failure to inform on the plotters. It seems Alexander initially accepted his explanation that he had not considered the information worth serious attention but on consulting with his other senior officers, notably Craterus and Hephaistion, reversed the decision. Philotas was arrested, tried and stoned to death by the assembled army. With the execution of Philotas, the elimination of Parmenion became a necessity in case family ties demanded he revenge his blood. The old general had a large army in Media and it required subterfuge to compass his end. An assassin was employed who was well known and trusted by the victim; he coaxed him away from his protective screen of bodyguards and officers and struck him down.

At a blow, the most powerful party in the army had been eliminated. After this, no other family or faction had the prestige or authority to effectively oppose the will of Alexander. All this was made more certain by the arrangement made to fill the gaps left at the head of the military hierarchy. The Companion cavalry were not entrusted to one individual but split between Hephaistion and Cleitus the Black. The former, a total intimate of the monarch, was complemented by a grizzled old sweat whose sister had wet-nursed Alexander and whose promotion was a sop to those worried by the violent removal of veterans who had served Macedonia so well in the past.

In no sense had all sources of tension been removed at Farah.[2] Other realities ensured Alexander's court would remain a hotbed of intrigue and discontent. It was in a camp at Samarkand that a crude and bloody affray became the catalyst for further change. With the death of Darius, Alexander had decided to clothe himself in the prerogatives of the great kings of Persia. Ideology arrived to complicate the divisions of family, faction and generation. Alexander needed, and was no doubt inclined, to take on the trappings of oriental kingship to underline his authority with his new Iranian subjects. In the process, he alienated many of his officers who saw nothing of worth beyond the norms of their own culture.

Proskynesis became the touchstone of this fractious time. Diadems and Persian skirts might be grumbled about but endured, but when the price of communion with the king was being forced to follow this act of prostration practised by 'slavish Orientals' the bubble had to burst. The combatants in the weary and bitter sniping that accompanied the argument were numerous. Aristotle's nephew, Callisthenes, was one who would suffer for his views; tough old hands like Polyperchon received short shrift for their whingeing and even the glamorous but feather-headed Leonnatus would receive a rebuff; but the most dramatic victim was none of these. In the aftermath of the bloody war in Bactria and Sogdia, nerves were frayed all round and the officer who fatally loosened his tongue in this atmosphere was Cleitus the Black. Perhaps, having saved his king at Granicus from a sword cut that would have decapitated him, he assumed an entitlement to thoroughly explore the boundaries of *lèse-majesté*. At a party when everyone had drunk to excess, the general of the Companions, with offensive directness, expressed the resentment of many over what they saw as Alexander turning his back on the triumphs and traditions of old Macedonia. After a ludicrous pantomime of postured aggression, tragedy unfolded with Alexander spearing Cleitus to death.

The story of Alexander's remorse for his action is well known, but less noticed is the crucial military reorganisation the event allowed. Half the Companion cavalry were without a general, but, instead of filling the post, Alexander took the opportunity of dividing the whole force into six independent squadrons, each commanded by young officers who were contemporaries and friends whose loyalty and malleability could be assumed as those of Philip's old officers could not.

Accident, execution and murder had ensured much of the old Philippic character of the Macedonian army had been eliminated, with new names well established or coming more to the fore. The greatest of these was Craterus. A nobleman from Orestis, his father had served Philip but he, himself, is not heard of till the new reign. Emerging first into the light of history at Granicus, he was then already a senior commander in charge of one of the six *taxeis* of the Macedonian phalanx. That he was not educated with Alexander and already held so high a post at the beginning of the Persian war suggests he may have been a few years older than his king.

In what was almost a year before the Persians gave battle at Issus, Craterus' importance had markedly increased. In combat he now had authority over the whole left of the phalanx, not just his own *taxis*. At the siege of Tyre his contribution is recalled; once even sharing charge of the enterprise with Perdiccas, when the king and Parmenion were absent.

Already, when Parmenion was elsewhere, it was clear Craterus had become Alexander's most dependable subordinate. When the former was permanently left behind in Media, Craterus took over his role in the royal army and brought up the baggage and heavy troops while Alexander led his picked force of Companions, Hypaspists and light infantry on ahead.

The fall of Parmenion and the emergence of Craterus had been the pivotal features in the first half of Alexander's decade of conquest, but the spectacular advancement of men who, for a number of reasons, stood particularly close to the king was the hallmark of the years in Bactria, Sogdia and India. One of these stood out not just for his significance after the king's death but as the only one whose known career stretches back before the Asian war began and into the time of Alexander's father.

Perdiccas' background is only sketchily known; his immediate antecedents, like Craterus, came from Orestis but his pedigree was considerably bluer, including a family connection with the Argead line itself. This was a lineage that earned him a place in Philip's royal bodyguard and put him on the spot, not only to witness that king's death, but to be part of the group who apprehended and killed the assassin, Pausanias. In the new reign he is well attested holding high command in the campaigns before the Hellespont was crossed. He led a battalion of pikemen drawn from his own Orestae in the Illyrian war. During the attack on Thebes his men won the day, being sent forward by the king to exploit a gap in the defences. He led his men at Granicus in the heart of the battle-line and at the siege of Halicarnassus, where Memnon of Rhodes was putting the break on Alexander's astonishing progress. Perdiccas also fought at the head of his men at Issus and shared command with Craterus at the siege of Tyre. At Gaugamela his phalangites were involved in a bloody fight in which he himself became a casualty. His stature even before the affair at Farah was high. With the subdivision of the Companions, Perdiccas was given a *hipparch* of these troopers, command of whom represented the most prestigious office in the army.

After the hardy warriors of Sogdia and Bactria had finally succumbed,

Alexander directed his eyes south to India. It was appropriate, when the invaders entered the new world of the subcontinent, that the group of new men who had been brought forward by Alexander should emerge into the full light of historical fame; men of the king's generation who had spent most of their adult life outside of Macedonia. Their careers had been founded in Asia and with their arrival the last vestiges of the pre-Alexandrian organisation fell away. The likes of Leonnatus, Ptolemy, Lysimachus, Peucestas, Pithon and Seleucus are heard of only occasionally before, usually in the role of bodyguards and friends, but with the invasion of India they take on the kind of responsibilities that foreshadow their significance after the conqueror's death.

They had grown up with Alexander, some had suffered exile for him and that they had not risen earlier is one more indication of the residual power of men from Philip's reign. Most were aristocrats connected with the princely houses of Macedonia who could have expected promotion in due course, but it was in the distant East that they emerged as great men in Alexander's empire.

When the Khyber Pass was breached and Alexander and Craterus rampaged through the Swat hills, Perdiccas marched with Hephaistion along the main highway with instructions to bridge the Indus and crush any opposition they found on the way. The man with whom Perdiccas shared the venture in the Punjab was unique amongst the men around the king. He had been Alexander's lover for many years and his was the central relationship of the conqueror's adult life. Since boyhood he had been his confidant and Alexander took great pleasure in public emphasis of their relationship. When the king laid a wreath at the tomb of Achilles at Ilium, Hephaistion did the same at that of Patroclus, paralleling their affection to that of the loyal lovers of the Trojan War. While Parmenion lived Hephaistion had not held high command - not that evidence exists to suggest Parmenion or Philotas blocked Hephaistion's advancement – but his climactic rise to the heights of official power came when the hand of Philippic tradition had been removed and Alexander felt free to use his patronage in an unrestrained fashion.

The years in the East revealed his intention to rule as heir of the Persian kings. Hephaistion was made *chiliarch*, essentially a vizier which, as a Persian invention, implied he was deputy to his ruler in a very special way. Parmenion may have been the second-in-command of the army of conquest while he lived, but Hephaistion's role meant he was second in authority to the king in everything in the state. That patronage brought him to the fore, and that he suffered in the normal way of royal favourites, should in no sense suggest

Alexander acted perversely, as Hephaistion proved to be competent in the military tasks his promotion inevitably brought him.

Perdiccas' relationship with Hephaistion seemed excellent and was founded on a shared understanding of Alexander's policy of the intermingling of Iranian and Hellene in a new imperial ruling class, although this was anathema to many. These two did their job well in 327 BC, overawing opposition along the road and throwing a pontoon bridge across the Indus river. It had taken time – one city withstood thirty days of siege before it fell – but in bringing in local allies and securing a bridgehead in the Punjab they had achieved much when Alexander arrived and led his vast army over the Indus.

The marriages that were celebrated with such mixed feelings at Susa, the ancient capital of Elam, paint in a most graphic manner the pattern of authority in the Macedonian Empire a short year before the conqueror's end. Hephaistion and Craterus held special place; only they shared with Alexander the distinction of brides from within Darius' own family. The king and chiliarch married daughters of the dead Great King and Craterus wed one of his nieces. For the rest, the likes of Perdiccas, Leonnatus, Ptolemy, Lysimachus and Seleucus, Alexander found brides from the front rank of the Iranian aristocracy that had ruled the provinces as satraps or held the great ceremonial offices at court. But the hierarchy of command that had evolved since the death of Parmenion was not destined to last.

Discontent surfaced at Susa amongst many veterans who, while they might accept Persian wives, found it difficult to stomach when 30,000 young Persians, who had been trained to fight as Macedonian-style phalangites, arrived to show off their paces to Alexander. They had no vision of partnership of conqueror and conquered, only a fear of being displaced by foreigners. Such feelings festered as Hephaistion led the main army down to the Persian Gulf while the king made an excursion cruise near the mouth of the Tigris. At the town of Opis, Alexander, in front of all the army, tried to discharge the veterans. Confirmed in their worst fears, they realised it was only in solidarity that they could resist relegation to impotence. They began to demand that if any should be demobbed all should. This was not in Alexander's plans; he still needed his phalanx and only wanted to be rid of the older men. The mutiny failed with ringleaders executed and the king sulking in his tent until he got his way.

These inflexible characters with contempt for anything non-Macedonian had their counterparts in the officer corps; in particular, Craterus. So he had to be the first to depart the court with instructions to return to Europe and replace Antipater as viceroy there. With him and 10,000 old soldiers (many of whom had fought not only in Asia, but with Philip in the old reign) went others of the same kidney: the old warrior Polyperchon, Cleitus the White, and other generals whose mind set would not adjust to a new world.

While it seemed the king now had key men about him who would follow his lead in everything, the cornerstone of his arrangements was suddenly removed. The departure of Craterus was followed closely by the loss of Hephaistion. The army had reached Ecbatana, where, for the first time in three years, Alexander allowed his men a substantial period of time for leisure and recuperation during the campaigning season. Festivities with athletics and artistic competitions were arranged to divert the army but they were not enjoyed by the chiliarch who had picked up a fever. What at first had not seemed serious was aggravated by the sudden consumption of boiled chicken and too much wine (and, perhaps, inadequate doctoring). After eight days, the king's lover and deputy died.

Inconsolable, Alexander refused food and drink for days and for a time seemed to lose his mind, but the loss was not purely personal. For the empire, it meant that in a matter of months the two most important men, after the king, had gone. The chiliarchy had been an office created to fit Hephaistion, but even without him a dependable deputy and second-in-command was necessary for the efficient running of the army and government. The post was soon given to Perdiccas. The esteem he already enjoyed was shown when he was entrusted with transporting Hephaistion's corpse to Babylon. With Craterus absent, Perdiccas was the obvious choice. Other reconstruction was also required as Alexander prepared for new wars; changes of which the importance would only be felt in the context of the struggles after Alexander's death. Perdiccas' position was strengthened when Eumenes, a partisan, was given his command in the Companions, while his brother, Alcetas, and brother-in-law, Attalus, retained key commands in the phalanx.

The combination of Alexander and Perdiccas had no opportunity to flower; time was against the young king. As the new chiliarch took up his responsibilities at Babylon he found fresh plans for conquest afoot. A great fleet was planned and Iranian recruits were being increasingly integrated into the royal army in preparation for the invasion of Arabia. He shouldered much of this work as well as efforts to construct a huge ziggurat to commemorate Hephaistion.

Alexander III of Macedon, called 'the Great', never did see Arabia Felix. The months of preparation in Babylonia and Phoenicia were the last in a life of only thirty-three years. In June 323 BC he sickened after a drinking party.

Summer in Babylon is notoriously unhealthy and what was probably malaria proved too much for a constitution that had been badly used up in the previous fifteen years. In perpetual motion since the age of sixteen, always at war and frequently wounded, that he succumbed was hardly surprising.

Alexander displayed his taste for high theatre to the end. As he lay on his sickbed near to extinction, the army, officers and men, filed past to take their leave of the man who had dominated both the known world and their own lives for so long. The effort brought Alexander's death closer and so reduced the time available to make clear his views on the succession. Considerable confusion surrounds the injunctions he left to his generals. Was it really possible that after struggling so hard to impose a stable formula for the government of his multiracial empire Alexander should invite civil war as his death rattle?

Chapter 1

Babylon

*When they asked him to whom he bequeathed his kingdom, he answered
'to the best man', but added that he could already foresee great
funeral games for himself provided by that issue.*[1]

Perdiccas was the most important Macedonian leader remaining at Babylon on
the death of Alexander in June 323 BC. He had received the royal ring[2] from
the conqueror on his death bed and his office as chiliarch implied that in the
king's absence he would command. In no sense was the reality of the post-
Alexandrian world that simple; the source of his high position was the king
and now he was no more. While Perdiccas might just be confident of
maintaining his position at Babylon, two men, both of them miles away, had
stronger claims on Alexander's inheritance. Craterus, with his 10,000 veterans
in Cilicia, could advance greater credentials for supreme command, and the
affection in which he was held by the ordinary Macedonian soldiers made him
a formidable rival. Even further away was Antipater, who overtopped them all
in venerable service to the dynasty of Philip and Alexander. He governed the
Macedonian homeland and the European provinces, his military resources
were great and he was unlikely to take kindly to receiving orders from young
men he had not seen for years.

Alexander left no heir when he died but one of his wives was six months
pregnant, which only served to further complicate the situation. No absolute
constitutional procedure existed to cover the problems that faced Perdiccas
and the generals at Babylon, but traditions and hallowed custom constrained
what the army would accept. Coups by strong men not directly in line for the
throne were by no means uncommon in Macedonian history. Philip himself
had taken the throne from his nephew this way and pretenders had
proliferated at the beginning of the fourth century. But Alexander's very
success had made the magic legitimacy of his line so great that usurpation by
even a princely claimant like Perdiccas was much more difficult, especially
when there was a possibility of a male heir.

Alexander's two wives were both Iranian. Roxanne was the daughter of
Oxyartes, whom Alexander had overcome at the Sogdian rock, and Stateira

was nothing less than the daughter of Darius himself. It was Roxanne who was pregnant and the unborn heir was an important factor in the deliberations at Babylon. Yet, legitimate heir or regent, the accession had to be ratified by the Macedonian people in assembly.

This caused problems, for the Macedonian empire now stretched from Epirus to the Oxus and an assembly of the people could have been held almost anywhere. In reality, it had to be held in Babylon, notwithstanding Craterus in Cilicia and Antipater in Macedonia. The power was with the bulk of the army in the East, which not surprisingly arrogated national authority to itself.

It is difficult to imagine a more highly charged gathering in the history of the ancient world than the one which Perdiccas now convened. It would decide the fate of the greatest empire the world had yet known, one that made the Egyptian, Hittite, Assyrian and Babylonian empires look puny and was larger even than the Persian empire at its greatest extent.

The assembly was held in one of the five great courtyards of the palace built over two centuries before by Nebuchadnezzar and surrounded by the fabulous Hanging Gardens. Nearby was the extraordinary Ishtar Gate, which now stands in the Pergamum Museum in Berlin. The colourful tiles of mythical animals which covered the gate would have decorated the walls all round the soldiers as they gathered for the assembly, only a few yards away from the throne room where their dead leader was lying in state in oriental splendour.[3]

As chiliarch, Perdiccas controlled the setting of the stage in the arena where the Macedonian officers and men now gradually congregated and he intended to use this advantage to effect. Ostentatiously on the rostrum he had arranged the robes, diadem and throne of Alexander and, to emphasise the continuity of power he claimed from the dead king – the royal ring was placed on the throne in clear view. Everything was arranged to reinforce the impression that he had received the mantle of power direct from Alexander's hand. Perdiccas' position ensured he was able to set the agenda and address the assembly first. Unfortunately, his proposals seemed indecisive and indecision was the last thing the army was prepared to tolerate. What he suggested was that they withhold an irrevocable decision on the succession until Roxanne's child had been born and instead merely appoint an interim ruler. He outlined that the chosen man would become regent if the child was a boy and monarch if it was a girl. All this left far too much up in the air for the inclinations of the assembled soldiers and this initial over-elaboration from Perdiccas was, in part, responsible for the chaos that ensued over the next hours and days.[4]

Feeling that Perdiccas had lost the ear of the assembly, others now began to put forward their proposals. Nearchus, the Cretan admiral, author and boyhood friend of Alexander (just a few days before he had been reading his history to the dying king) suggested that there already existed a rightful heir in Heracles, Alexander's son by Barsine. Barsine had been Memnon of Rhodes' widow and had borne Alexander a son who was not, however, acknowledged as legitimate. This idea was greeted with a cacophony as the assembled soldiers beat their spears against their shields, the traditional Macedonian way of expressing disapproval. Their opposition is not hard to understand; here was this Greek telling Macedonians to acclaim a half-Persian bastard as king. Not only this but the Greek's self seeking was transparent. He had married the half-sister of Heracles at Susa and clearly had ambitions to be the power behind the throne.

Next to address the boisterous and confused gathering was Ptolemy, who argued that, as no one person had the complete confidence of the army, a committee of Alexander's closest advisers should rule the empire with differences decided by a majority verdict. It is difficult to believe that Ptolemy intended this as a serious proposal that would either work or be accepted. He was merely trying to undermine the prominence of Perdiccas; a ploy to emphasise that others of the king's friends were as worthy as the chiliarch to wield supreme power. The effect of his intervention served only to try further the patience of the assembly, which made it abundantly clear that any rule by committee was unwanted.

Perdiccas was by now deeply concerned about the way the meeting was developing. Three proposals had been placed before the assembly and none had gained sufficient support and with every moment that passed his position was being eroded. Before more damage was done, the Perdiccan party attempted to re-establish control of the meeting. Aristonous, one of the seven bodyguards, reminded the assembly that Alexander had given his ring to Perdiccas and that his intentions were clear that the chiliarch should take over the mantle of command. Whether Aristonous was prompted by the chiliarch or used his own initiative is unknown but his intervention received an immediate response. The soldiers had at last been offered some sign of certainty on the leadership issue and, in this suddenly-unpredictable world, they looked set to grab it with both hands. There were shouts for Perdiccas to assume the throne but, according to Quintus Curtius, he hesitated to accept. This description of his reluctance to seize the crown may have more to do with Roman politics of the first century AD, than Macedonian practices of the fourth century BC.[5] It is difficult to believe that Perdiccas, having once almost thrown away his advantage by indecision, would continue to prevaricate when directly offered command. Whatever the details, it looked as though a clear outcome had been arrived at; but it was not to be, as another actor now entered the stage to throw the Macedonian ship of state way off course, just as it seemed to have found its direction.

Meleager has not been kindly treated by history. He is depicted as an incompetent rabble-rouser who, in a bid for personal power, nearly caused a civil war around the very death bed of Alexander. Yet this is only part of the story as he had a long and distinguished military career. He had held important commands from the beginning of Alexander's reign and had certainly served under Philip. He led an infantry battalion on the Danube when his young king was crushing the Triballians and Getae. At Granicus his *taxis* of the phalanx won distinction, alongside Craterus, Perdiccas and Coenus. After revisiting Macedonia to recruit reinforcements, he had returned in time to participate at both Issus and Gaugamela in his capacity of phalanx commander. In India his unit was part of the force that Hephaistion and Perdiccas led to clear the crossing of the Indus, and at Hydaspes he played his part in overcoming the formidable opposition put up by Porus. His contribution to the Macedonian conquests is remarkable for its sheer consistency; he appears to have had the same post throughout Alexander's reign. For some reason, however, he was not marked out for greater things, never being promoted to lead a cavalry unit or given independent commands. His reaction to seeing the likes of Leonnatus, Ptolemy, Pithon and Seleucus receiving these rewards when they had but a fraction of his military experience can only be imagined.

He was not a close confidant of the king and the only incident that throws light on their relationship does not suggest any meeting of minds. It occurred after the Indus had been crossed in 327 BC. Alexander had befriended a Punjabi potentate, called Omphis, whose cooperation had been rewarded with a gift of 1,000 talents. At a supper party shortly afterwards, Meleager, his tongue loosened by drink, had remarked that at least in India the king had found a man worth a 1,000 talents. This suggestion that Alexander was ungenerous to his long-serving Macedonian followers was not the comment of a man who sympathised with or understood his monarch's thinking on the treatment of the peoples he had conquered. Equally, it does not suggest Meleager possessed much in the way of tact as a similar remark had cost Cleitus the Black his life in a drunken brawl not long before.

Meleager, now, dramatically intervened in the assembly at Babylon. Initially, when he addressed the throng he did not put forward his own claims, but expressed the pent up resentment and bile he felt against the likes of Perdiccas, who had risen so far above him through the patronage of Alexander.

These men, he suggested, were not of the ilk to be trusted with their great king's legacy and that the common Macedonian warriors were the real heirs of the conquerors' lands and treasures. Clearly, this was no proposal of policy; it was an incitement to riot and nearly had that effect. What had, up to then, been a meeting drifting in the direction of chaos bubbled over into mutiny and several voices started to cry out that they should loot the royal treasury as they themselves had won this bounty by their own hard fighting. What had begun as an orderly assembly had become a mob of unruly warriors; the Macedonians had never been easy to handle, Alexander himself had discovered this on a few notable occasions. His surviving officers were to be put to a similar test and found wanting.

When the whole body of the meeting seemed on the point of breaking up, more voices from the floor started shouting another name, that of one who they claimed as a perfectly good Macedonian monarch ready and waiting there in the royal court itself. This was Arrhidaeus, a son of Philip and half-brother of Alexander, a man they were all familiar with but who had not previously been considered even remotely appropriate for the crown. His disqualification for preferment was not age, being a few years senior to Alexander, but the fact that he was mentally impaired. He was the offspring of Philip and a Thessalian mistress, a mere dancing girl according to gossip. As an infant he had seemed normal enough, which gave rise to stories that his adult condition was not a natural one. Olympias was implicated as the administrator of the drugs which induced his parlous state, so that he could not become a rival to her son for the throne of the kingdom her husband had created. The truth is impossible to ascertain; it is possibly a later legend created to blacken her name but it fitted well with the mythology of the 'barbaric' Epirote witch who kept a snake as a pet and mated with the gods.

Arrhidaeus' insignificance is attested by the lack of notice by the histories until his unlooked for eruption into power politics on the banks of the Euphrates. The only exception to this silence was the Carian affair which took place during Philip's reign. The king had wanted to forge an alliance with Caria for the purposes of his forthcoming Persian war. To this end he offered the hand of Arrhidaeus to the satrap's daughter. Alexander, almost unbelievably, felt that he was being disinherited in favour of his half-brother and sent a secret envoy to offer himself in place of Arrhidaeus. The Carian's reaction to this offer is unrecorded although he must have been astounded by his apparent good fortune. He had little chance to celebrate, however, as Philip discovered Alexander's meddling. Not surprisingly, any wedding was called off and the king was furious with his son for ruining a nicely-judged diplomatic coup. As punishment for his behaviour, several of Alexander's friends (including Nearchus and Ptolemy) were banished from Macedonia. As for Arrhidaeus, he simply disappeared from view again.[6]

Alexander obviously did not bear any grudges towards his half-brother as on his accession, when he dealt mercilessly and efficiently with any potential rivals to his position, Arrhidaeus survived. Alexander may well have been fond of him as it is difficult to otherwise account for his decision to trail him around Asia in the train of his conquering army. Whatever his mental limitations, Arrhidaeus was a royal Macedonian and the call for his elevation received a warm response from the rank and file, who were now even more in the mood for a simple and definite solution. Meleager realised that this might be a heaven-sent opportunity both to ensure high position for himself and undo the plans of Perdiccas. To achieve these aims he would have to gain control of Arrhidaeus and, with commendable speed, he sought out the prince and brought him before his subjects, who were already trying to acclaim this other son of Philip with as much enthusiasm as they used to cheer Alexander.

The Perdiccans, with Pithon this time as their spokesman, tried to regain their momentum by proposing Leonnatus as joint guardian with Perdiccas of the unborn child of Alexander, hoping the former's princely standing combined with the prestige of Perdiccas would appeal to a broad cross-section of the assembled Macedonians. The time for sensible debate was, however, long gone. Meleager and his supporters had put on their armour and were pushing Arrhidaeus onto the royal throne, acclaiming him as King Philip III. The high-born commanders could have no illusions that they had managed to lose control of a situation in which they had held all the advantages; not only had the army collapsed into a mob with factions looking set to spill each others' blood, but it was clear that the personal safety of Perdiccas and his supporters was now in jeopardy. By divisions and indecisive leadership they had precipitated the chaos that looked to be their undoing.

These aristocratic generals were hard-headed, cool individuals; life under Alexander had taught them that even the highest could fall from grace. The present situation, though, thoroughly unnerved them; it looked as if the men they had led so often in battle were contemplating murdering them in cold blood and following the lead of an incapable monarch. In desperation, Perdiccas, most of the senior officers and 600 followers retreated to the room where Alexander's body was waiting, embalmed in preparation for his funeral. They locked the doors but were pursued by a mob of soldiers who had no difficulty breaking the locks. As Quintus Curtius relates:

In a rage, Perdiccas called aside any who wished to protect Alexander's corpse, but the men who had broken into the room proceeded to hurl javelins at him, keeping their distance. Eventually after many had been wounded, the older soldiers removed their helmets so that they could be more easily recognised and began to beg the men with Perdiccas to stop fighting and to surrender to the king and his superior numbers. Perdiccas was the first to lay down his arms, and the others followed. Meleager then urged them not to leave Alexander's body, but they thought that he was looking for a way to trap them, so they slipped through another part of the royal quarters and fled towards the Euphrates.[7]

It was no coincidence that the high command had sought sanctuary in Alexander's funeral chamber. They had hoped to shame the soldiers, to dissuade them from assassinating Alexander's friends and advisors under the dead king's eyes. In this they succeeded, at least long enough for them to escape, but it had been a close-run thing. While the discomfited generals fled through the corridors of Nebuchadnezzar's palace the army had split in two. The infantry had remained in the assembly ground with the most militant following Meleager, while the cavalry moved off to encamp elsewhere. Alexander had been dead only a few hours, yet his followers were already fighting amongst themselves.

Meleager's position, though he had temporarily won the day, was fraught with difficulties. The new king in the emotional atmosphere of the assembly had appealed to Macedonian patriotism, but in the clear light of day the confused and shambling figure who now occupied the throne seemed an insult to the corpse of Alexander. More seriously, the cavalry had shown that they were not prepared to take their lead from Meleager. The horsemen were well-born men of substance whose class instincts inclined them to the aristocratic friends of the dead king. Realising his power base and his options were rapidly decreasing, Meleager agreed to a truce. His next move had an air of desperation about it. He browbeat the unhappy and reluctant king to authorise the arrest of Perdiccas. The chiliarch had remained in his normal lodgings, not moving to the cavalry camp where he could have expected complete protection. It may have been overconfidence or he might have wished to avoid becoming completely associated with one faction, in the hope of persuading the infantry over to his side. Meleager's aim of destroying any opposition by removing its head was rudely shattered when even the men selected to detain Perdiccas lost their nerve. The chiliarch, with only a small bodyguard of pages but with a considerable show of personal eloquence and authority, managed to turn back the party who had come to arrest him. But, realising to stay within the walls of Babylon was to court assassination, he withdrew to the cavalry lines, from where he led them into the plains outside the city.

Meleager woke to find that his rival had quit the city. This act showed that Perdiccas was determined to fight it out, if necessary, and sowed doubt and dissension amongst the ranks of the already-confused and distrustful infantry. They were being challenged to a civil war they did not want and, when the cavalry blockaded the supply routes into Babylon, for the first time their own comfort and security was being threatened. The rift between cavalry and infantry was not sustainable; these men had been through too much together. If it seemed to Meleager that he might benefit by gaining complete control of the city precincts, he was rapidly disabused. Many were looking for someone to blame for their predicament and he was clearly first choice.

Interestingly, all the sources suggest it was largely through the good offices of Greeks, not Macedonians, that the divisions in the army were reconciled. Perhaps the fact that they were, to some extent, detached, not committed to either side, allowed them to assume this role. Eumenes, who had been secretary to both Philip and Alexander and who we will hear much of later, was particularly prominent, but also mentioned as emissaries were Pasas, a Thessalian, and the Megalopolitan, Damis. They had remained about the court when the horsemen and generals had fled, but it is probable that they personally inclined to Perdiccas because he represented continuity with the days of Alexander that had been so fruitful for them all. When they went to Perdiccas they almost certainly informed him how isolated his rival was becoming and that, if an agreement was made, he would find himself in an extremely powerful position with many of the infantry eager to transfer their allegiance. If Meleager had any reluctance to come to an arrangement, it was overcome by the fact that, after only three days, the blockade was already threatening famine in the city. News of his attempted arrest of Perdiccas had also become common knowledge, incensing many who were hoping for reconciliation.

Negotiations soon achieved a compromise that appeared to take into account the key demands of both sides. Philip Arrhidaeus was confirmed as king, while Roxanne's expected offspring was, for the moment, conveniently forgotten. Perdiccas remained in his post of chiliarch, effectively commander-in-chief of the whole army. As guardian for the new king, who clearly could not rule for himself, he had achieved the position he had originally sought, with the only drawback that Meleager became his deputy. Antipater was confirmed as commander in Europe and Craterus given the undefined title of Protector of King Philip. No mention is made in the arrangement for Ptolemy,

Leonnatus, Pithon et al, underlining that from the Perdiccan side it was only a step on the road to complete control. There was no intention of letting the agreement stand. They would never have accepted Meleager taking precedence over them in a final settlement. But, even if there had been any possibility of real reconciliation it was soured by personal antipathy between the two principal actors. Perdiccas regarded Meleager as vain and unstable, not a man he could deal with on a permanent basis.

Perdiccas had regained the initiative that his mishandling of the army assembly had put at risk, and he had no intention of losing it again. He had Arrhidaeus in his control and, crucially, knew that the phalangites would not fight to retain Meleager and his supporters in their positions of power. He surely would not have risked what was to follow unless he was certain of this.

A Macedonian purification ceremony was arranged for the whole army, to purge them from the recent conflict and ensure complete reconciliation amongst the units that had, a few days before, been at each others' throats. Meleager agreed as, ostensibly, it was traditional ritual behaviour after a particularly traumatic event. To refuse to co-operate could only expose lack of confidence in his own support. With mixed feelings, the generals and men of Alexander's army marched out of their encampments to a large plain outside the walls of Babylon.

Lustration, a highly-charged religious rite, consisted of a bitch being disembowelled and its four quarters and entrails placed at the boundaries of the parade ground for all the battalions to march between. The soldiers and officers were fully armed, in their best parade regalia, and to most it was a relief to bury the past with this display of corporate unity. Few of the thousands gathered in ordered ranks knew of the hidden agenda, written by the Perdiccan faction, for this day of reconciliation, but all were aware of the tension in the air as armed men who had so recently been enemies came face to face. Curtius again describes the scene:

> By now the columns were coming together and only a small space separated the two lines. The king began to ride towards the infantry with a single squadron and, at Perdiccas' urging, he demanded for execution the instigators of the discord ... threatening to attack with all his squadrons plus his elephants if they refused. The infantry were stunned by this unforeseen blow, and Meleager lacked ideas and initiative as much as they did. The safest course in the circumstances seemed to be to await their fate rather than provoke it. Perdiccas saw that they were paralysed and at his mercy. He withdrew from the main body some 300 men who had followed Meleager at the time when he

burst from the first meeting after Alexander's death and before the eyes of the entire army he threw them to the elephants. All were trampled to death beneath the feet of the beasts and Philip neither stopped nor sanctioned it.'[8]

It has been suggested that this act of calculated brutality came as a shock and warning that Perdiccas was ambitious for supreme power at the expense of his colleagues. This is self-evidently ludicrous as the regent would not have risked the confrontation without the connivance of the rest of the officer elite, who could guarantee support from the cavalry if it came to a fight.

Meleager was certainly alarmed by these events. His position was clearly crumbling beneath his feet when the infantry acquiesced in the orders of Perdiccas (albeit through the mouth of the puppet Philip). Although he had not been called out to be dealt with by the elephants (to go this far would have been courting a hostile reaction), his life was very much in danger when the ceremony finished. He attempted to find sanctuary in a local temple but Perdiccas was in no mood to allow religious scruple to interfere with his plans. Meleager was assassinated by the regent's agents without ceremony.

For a week, Meleager had been at the centre of the world stage before being removed permanently, but much of his troubles he had brought on his own head. He had overreached himself without having considered the consequences, and so signed his own death warrant. Had he remained content to keep in the background, it is likely that his experience and talent would have ensured a major satrapy or command. Instead, allowing his frustration at Alexander's promotion of younger, less-experienced men to sour his judgement, he paid the price.

In the shadow of Alexander's hardly-cold corpse, one of the most dramatic tableaux of the ancient world had been played out, but far from ushering in a new and stable era it was the first of many extraordinary events in a forty year period most notable for instability.

With the almost-unanimous support of the army, officers and men alike, Perdiccas abandoned Alexander's half-organised campaign against Arabia, as well as the other grandiose plans of building and conquest that were said to have been found in the king's papers.[9] The organisation and exploitation of the vast tracts that had already been conquered was a large enough task to be confronted for the present. This the first of the great imperial settlements and, though it would be much changed in the coming years, it created a framework of which at least one part would last for three centuries. The province of Egypt was allocated to Ptolemy whose descendants would rule that rich and civilised land until the dynasty ended with Cleopatra in the very different world of Mark Anthony and Octavius at the end of the first century BC. Ptolemy was only one of a number of great officers and potential rivals whose standing demanded significant reward. Perdiccas tended to rid himself of those men whose presence he feared at court by granting them distant satrapies. Leonnatus was one of these, being high-born kin of Eurydice, Alexander's grandmother. He was given Hellespontine Phrygia as his province, the key that commanded the route from Europe to Asia.

Lysimachus, another of Alexander's bodyguard, was granted Thrace, a province beset by internal strife which he needed to overcome before he emerged as one of the major powers in the decades to come. Peucestas was reconfirmed in Persia as was Antigonus Monopthalmus (the One-eyed) in Greater Phrygia, and the rest of the satrapies were either confirmed or redistributed.

Perdiccas had triumphed in Babylon but a fortnight's frenetic activity had left much of the larger problems of the Macedonian empire unresolved. The most important consideration was what the reaction of Antipater and Craterus would be to the elevation of Perdiccas to the regency. These magnates had not been forgotten at Babylon; both had been designated joint commanders for the monarchy in Europe, but whether this was acceptable to them had not been explored. Perdiccas probably hoped they would end up fighting each other in the west, while he had time to establish himself in Asia. However, before any significant moves could be made by any of the principal actors, other repercussions of Alexander's death were to throw the Macedonian empire into turmoil and dramatically affect the alignment of these rival generals.

Chapter 2

The Perdiccas Years

Perdiccas...was outstanding in war and of exceptional intelligence; his powerful character allowed him to face any danger with confidence, while his boastfulness which made him seem contemptuous of all Macedonians, aroused envy for his success. Hatred followed envy; people could not stand him being and being called superior to them.[1]

The story of Antipater's life is the story of Macedonia itself. He was an indispensable part of the glorious reigns of both Philip and Alexander and witnessed the rise of his homeland from a backwater to the greatest power in the world. He was born, probably, in 398 BC, over fifteen years before Philip II; his was a life begun in the era of Xenophon and Socrates, when the Spartan victory in the Peloponnesian War was a very recent memory.[2]

Macedonia had played only a peripheral role in the history of the Hellenes, a state on the barbarian marches, regarded as more akin to its Thracian and Illyrian neighbours than the communities of Greece. An economically and politically backward tribal agglomeration, whose royal house had only been recognised as Greek in the previous hundred years, it had seemed only too frequently incapable of defending its national integrity. In the early fifth century BC, the Persians had overrun the country and, in the century of Antipater's birth, Macedonian monarchs were often puppets of powerful Greek city-states, Persian satraps or tribal warlords of Thrace and Illyria.

In the first four decades of his life Antipater experienced at first hand the faction fighting, assassination and foreign invasion that contrived to keep the Macedonians divided and impotent. He witnessed no less than eight kings of Macedonia, with five pretenders vying for the throne at one point. Kings were exiled, cut down by relatives or defeated by foreign invaders with bewildering rapidity.[3]

But Philip had changed all that and in the year 342 BC the heights to which Antipater had reached in his monarch's estimation were made abundantly clear. He was installed as regent while Philip marched east on a campaign intended to last a few months but which actually took years. In the last decade of Philip's life Antipater headed the domestic administration far more often than his monarch.

What we know of Antipater's character paints a consistent picture. He was a serious man, not only eschewing drinking, a great Macedonian pastime, but gambling too. A short man, he was not given to humour and notoriously mean; whilst he may not have dripped charisma, his character suited the hard and demanding job of governing Europe as others tasted the glory of conquest. In the aftermath of Philip's assassination, the speed with which Alexander took control was a cause of some satisfaction for Antipater. Ruthless disposal of rivals was just his style and he unstintingly supported Alexander as the man whom he considered would continue to deliver the success and prosperity that had been the hallmark of Philip's reign.

In May 334 BC, when the invasion army was ready, Antipater was recognised as the viceroy for the European territories in Alexander's absence. He held post for three generations of the Argeads, but now his task was very different from the one he had performed so ably for Philip. The vast distance Alexander's war would take him from Macedonia meant that, for all intents and purposes, Antipater was an independent dynast. In the years after Alexander's departure the viceroy's rule was ruffled only by abortive threats from Memnon of Rhodes, commanding Darius' fleet, and a quickly resolved war with Agis III of Sparta. Yet he did not administer a totally united kingdom. When Alexander departed for Asia he left behind, in the person of his mother, the seeds of bitter troubles for his viceroy. The relationship between Antipater and the queen had always been fraught but it developed into mutual loathing as Olympias sought to erode Antipater's position with her absent son. She managed to blacken the name of Antipater's son-in-law and even secured his execution but she could never shake Alexander's faith in his viceroy's loyalty. To her increasing chagrin, the further Alexander moved away from Europe, the more her influence declined. Eventually, Olympias fled to Epirus where she ruled until she once more bloodily erupted on the Macedonian stage when both her son and implacable enemy were dead.

In 324 BC, Alexander took a decision that is initially hard to understand. He decided to replace the old master of Macedonia and Greece with Craterus. The context of this highest level switch in personnel is the political world of the Greek cities. Since his return from India, Alexander had received numerous embassies from Greece listing grievances against Antipater's rule. The policy of ruling through moneyed oligarchs or Macedonian garrisons had enjoyed considerable success but it stored up problems for the future. And there were large numbers of embittered Greek exiles and mercenaries who constituted a threat to stable government.[4] To settle the problem it was decided to restore Greek exiles to their home cities. The Exiles Decree was promulgated at the Olympic games of 324 BC, and there were 20,000 potential beneficiaries there to hear it. This cut at the heart of Antipater's policy, threatening the power and property of his friends and allies. Craterus, with no axe to grind, could be expected to see the change of policy through.

The response in different parts of the Greek world differed, but for the Athenians, in particular, it was anathema. Since the 360s they had been colonising the rich and strategically placed island of Samos. A return of the Samian exiles would end their rule and drastically disadvantage their friends on the island. Furthermore, the Aetolians were in the same case with an Arcananian city they had absorbed. Athens' treasury was now full as only months before Harpalus, Alexander's ex-treasurer, on the run, had deposited much of his ill-gotten fortune there.[5] In July 324 BC, Leosthenes had been elected one of the ten Athenian generals and with long contacts in the mercenary world, where many were left unemployed with the disbandment of the satrapal armies, he was able to muster a considerable force at Cape Taenarum in the Peloponnese.

Samos and the Exiles Decree, the existence of ready money, a veteran army on tap and the Aetolians eager to fight made for a tinderbox of rebellion. However, a spark was needed to finally ignite the conflagration. In the following year, 323 BC, the news of Alexander's death provided the stimulus as no other event could have. The first rumours of the conqueror's demise had been scarcely credited. Many wished to believe it was true and Demades' fine turn of phrase, 'the stench of the corpse would have filled the world long before', captures both the venom of anti-Macedonian opinion and the disbelief that this titan could so meekly pass away.[6]

With Alexander's death established, there was little opposition to a course of rebellion. The Athenians had recently radically overhauled their military system; now, all citizens were conscripted for two years, receiving weapon training and being posted to the frontier forts. Defences were refurbished and a full treasury allowed the rebuilding of the fleet. Soon more than 400 warships were ready, the only problem being the lack of oarsmen and marines to man them all. Demosthenes, that old anti-Macedonian veteran, who had spent a lifetime haranguing against Philip and Alexander, was a prime mover in the effort to find allies. Corinth, Sicyon, Elis, Messene and Argos were all recruited. While this diplomatic activity was taking place, Leosthenes received from Athens fifty talents to pay and equip his men and made his move. No opposition was encountered and he reached Aetolia in safety, where he found his allies had 7,000 warriors ready to march. Other peoples of central Greece sent contingents, sensing there was never going to be a better opportunity to throw off the Macedonian yoke.

Antipater could eventually hope for help from Asia but, for now, he had to act within his own means. He had allies in Boeotia but they were weak and isolated with only the small Macedonian garrison from Thebes to support them. Soon, even these were discounted as Leosthenes moved to the pass of Thermopylae, then marched southeast in conjunction with the Athenians and crushed the outnumbered Boeotians, before quickly marching back to his post at Thermopylae.

Against this tide of war, Antipater could only field 13,000 infantry and 600 cavalry. As he crossed the border into Thessaly, more bad news arrived. The list of enemies was growing daily; Doris, Locris and Phocis had joined the coalition. He faced a solid band of enemies stretching from Aetolia to Athens. North of Aetolia, the Malians, Achaeans of Phthiotis and Oetaeans, whose lands surrounded the Malian Gulf, had all declared against him.

Antipater had banked heavily on the Thessalians but these impressive horsemen, though they first joined the Macedonians, transferred to Leosthenes when they reached Thermopylae, where they heard news that their home cities had gone over to the Greeks. Leosthenes, with the unexpected arrival of the Thessalians, no longer needed to confine himself to the defensive. Antipater still had faith in his phalangites and accepted battle somewhere north of the pass. The Greeks won a famous victory, and with the situation desperate for the old marshal he took his battered army to Lamia, the one city in the area that had stayed loyal. Antipater's opponent stayed on the heels of the Macedonians and set his victorious men to attack the town. But the town was strong and the coalition army started taking considerable casualties before settling down for a siege. Then Leosthenes was killed in a skirmish in the trenches and Antiphilus, another Athenian, took over; from this time things seemed to begin unravelling.

Antipater, though blockaded through the winter of 323/322 BC, could see a chink of light. During the middle of the winter, news came that Leonnatus was on the way to Lamia's relief. It was spring of 322 BC when Leonnatus bought his makeshift force, with many raw recruits picked up on the march, down through Thessaly, following the road Antipater had travelled the year before. Antipater tried to rendezvous with him to face Antiphilus but failed, so Leonnatus faced the Greeks alone.[7] The Greeks fielded 25,500, slightly outnumbering Leonnatus' 21,500. It was in cavalry the coalition had the significant edge because of the 2,000 first-rate Thessalian horsemen and these had immediate success. Leonnatus' squadrons were dispersed and he received a fatal wound. With the end of this gallant but foolhardy general the contest ended.

The Greeks claimed victory but it was not so simple. Antipater took command of Leonnatus' leaderless warriors, added them to his own army and encamped amongst the hills north of Melitia. Now, at the head of the remnants of two defeated but sizeable armies, the regent could look forward to renewing the war with more confidence, though the enemy could still dominate the countryside with their markedly-superior cavalry. The only option open to the old man was to keep to the hills and retreat north towards Macedonia. He moved from one entrenched camp to another while Antiphilus' army dogged his heels all the way.

While the land forces of the Greek coalition were overthrowing all who stood in their way, at sea another struggle was taking place. The Athenian admiral, Evetion, had bottled up Antipater's fleet in the Malian Gulf and with another detachment blocked the Hellespont to Macedonian reinforcements. But then Cleitus[8] had arrived with the Macedonian Asian fleet and crushed the coalition navy in three sea battles.[9]

For Antipater, as he carefully conducted his retreat north, the news of this success was a real fillip. Even more heartening was the promise of further help from Asia. Craterus and his veterans were on the road to Europe. The most distinguished of Alexander's generals had, at long last, determined to succour Antipater. The army he led included 6,000 phalangites, veterans of all the king's campaigns, and 1,500 tested cavalry with the quality to face the Thessalian horse. Craterus led them over the Hellespont, without incident, and marched directly to link up with Antipater in Northern Thessaly.

The regent now found himself, for the first time since his incarceration at Lamia, with resources sufficient for him to take the initiative. He had concentrated 40,000 first class infantry, 3,000 light infantry and 5,000 cavalry and with him was Craterus, the Macedonian with the greatest military reputation of all. The Greeks discovered these new odds and withdrew their army to a defended position. Antipater offered battle, repeating the challenge several days running while the Macedonian cavalry denied them supplies. Forced to fight or starve, Antiphilus accepted battle. The climactic fight took place near Crannon in early August 322 BC. It is as obscure in detail as it was decisive.[10] Despite the success of their mounted arm, when the phalanxes clashed the allies had no answer to the Macedonian sarrissas (pikes). The Macedonians held the field at the end of the day. The balance had swung. Now the road from Asia was open and Antipater, by surviving, had secured his country's pre-eminence in the Balkans. News from the south indicated that Antiphilus could hope for little in the way of reinforcements and, without them, his future was bleak. It was agreed to approach Antipater for a truce. He exploited the tensions within the coalition for all its worth bringing the war to a close on his own terms. He refused to talk with the allies as a whole but insisted that each city send representatives to negotiate separately. Once their fragile solidarity had been ruptured, the edifice of Greek co-operation collapsed. Only the implacable Aetolians and Athenians, the two prime movers of the coalition, stood firm.

Antipater set up pro-Macedonian governments or garrisons in the key Thessalian towns as he moved south. He was unopposed at Thermopylae so headed south against his two remaining enemies. The Athenians realised that further resistance was futile. Demosthenes had already taken the precaution of fleeing the city; the rest prepared for the worst and sent a delegation to Antipater's camp to ask for terms.

Phocion and Demades led the delegation as men with reputations of pro-, or at least not anti-Macedonian predilections. Phocion, of unimpeachable reputation, had known Antipater for years and indeed these two men shared the unique distinction of always being addressed by Alexander with a personal greeting in correspondence. Demades was a man of a very different stamp. No one had ever claimed high probity for him but, at least, he had no great history of opposition to Macedon and had led the move to deify Alexander at Athens. Like Phocion, his political attachments were to the class of rich aristocrats whose oligarchic inclinations made them temperamentally sympathetic to the Macedonian leadership. All this cut little ice with Antipater who demanded unconditional surrender and threatened to attack when they prevaricated.

A second embassy including Xenocrates, head of Plato's Academy, served only to further irritate the old marshal who considered his restraint in not wasting Attica was being abused. Finally, the Athenians realised further delay was futile and humiliating terms placed the Athenian government in the hands of a narrow property-based oligarchy and Macedonian soldiers in the fort of Munychia at Piraeus. The nadir of Athens' fortunes was complete when the Samian question was decided against her and the exiles restored.[11] Athens was despoiled economically, politically and finally spiritually, as the day chosen to march the Macedonian garrison into the Munychia was during the Eleusinian mysteries, a date traditionally associated with the city's greatest triumphs.

The war had taken almost two long years to win and it had tested Antipater's temper. Not only Athens felt the effects of his rancour. Many cities were forced to accept garrisons, pro-Macedonian oligarchies were installed in others and the army crossed the Isthmus of Corinth into the Argolid to intimidate the communities there before returning north to Macedonia.

The return to Pella saw Antipater marry his eldest and favourite daughter, Phila, to Craterus. This cemented an alliance that had not only won the Lamian war, but which now clearly represented one of the most important foci of Macedonian loyalty in an increasingly uncertain world. Other daughters were offered to Ptolemy and Perdiccas to grease relations with the potentates of Asia and Africa. Yet, while diplomacy took up much of the interest of the viceroy and his new son-in-law in the first months of 321 BC, they still had an enemy to deal with. The Aetolians remained obdurate. Leading protagonists in the war that had shaken Antipater to the core, they would prove inveterate enemies of Macedonia for many years to come. Antipater's solution was conceived on a grand and brutal scale; he intended to round them up and forcibly resettle them in the interior of Asia.

But it was easier planned than done. The country was invaded but most towns and villages were found deserted. The inhabitants, with their children and possessions, moved into the inaccessible mountains. The terrain favoured the locals against the heavily-equipped invaders. Craterus, taking the lead, tried to starve them out by occupying the country for the whole of the winter. He could wait them out, a patient strategy which was beginning to bear fruit when events in Asia came to the rescue of the beleaguered Aetolians.

As in Europe, in Asia too, the heirs to the king's power had found it easier to claim Alexander's authority than to sustain it. The Greek communities in eastern Iran followed the example of mainland Greece and took the opportunity to break into open revolt. In the Iranian satrapies many thousand of Greek mercenaries had been left, as garrisons or settlers, in the towns that had been taken from the Persians or been founded by the invaders. These unruly warriors were not content with the stations at which they had been posted. The interior of Iran was a hard alien land for those used to the softer comforts and greater amenities of the Mediterranean. The compensation of being the new rulers of the region did not make up for the taste of olive oil and the sight of the sea. It was not the life they had fought so hard to achieve. The Bactrian garrison had already revolted once when Alexander was in India. Now, with his death, many more took action, banding together, overthrowing loyal officers and preparing to march back to Greece. For the moment, the subject peoples watched these antics but Perdiccas was concerned that, if these men were allowed to desert their forts and cities, there would soon be insufficient troops left to control the vast tracts of land east of the Tigris. The mutineers had elected a Thessalian, called Philon, as their leader and had moved in numbers to Media by the time the new regent was able to respond.

The man Perdiccas chose to head the expedition against the rebellious mercenaries was Pithon, who had been one of his strongest supporters at Babylon and had been appointed satrap of Media as his reward. One of Alexander's seven bodyguards, he had an aristocratic background and considerable military skills but was also a rash and inveterate intriguer. Pithon marched directly into battle. Though outnumbered heavily, he had taken the precaution of bribing one of the rebel officers to come over when the battle began, with the inevitable result of a Macedonian victory. Despite Pithon's misgivings about the waste of high-quality recruits, the rest of the rebels were massacred, as Perdiccas had ordered, and Pithon led his men back to the regent's encampment.

Perdiccas now sought to consolidate his position in Anatolia. He had hoped that the Babylonian settlement would have ensured good order there, particularly with his protégé, Eumenes, ensconced in the key satrapy of Cappadocia. Antigonus and Leonnatus had been instructed to help impose Macedonian rule on this region, which was still largely independent.

Antigonus, from the beginning, paid no heed at all but Leonnatus marched his army down from his headquarters on the Dardanelles and joined Eumenes. It transpired his ambitions had little to do with campaigning in Anatolia but centred on gaining control of Macedonia. He wished to have Eumenes as an ally and suggested they went together into Europe. This was, one suspects, far too speculative a policy for the Cardian to hitch himself to and he had no hesitation in fleeing Leonnatus' camp to return to his sponsor in Babylon.

Perdiccas' reaction was to mobilise in preparation to do for him what his lieutenants would not. He knew he still needed the brilliant Greek in the area and a successful campaign against a 'barbarian' prince was just what was required to keep the army up to scratch and cement the soldiers' allegiance to their new commander in chief.

Eumenes' value to Perdiccas is not hard to understand. Even amongst the collection of talented individuals who struggled for power after Alexander's death, he stands out as remarkable. As a general his career shows he was possibly the most brilliant of them all. As a scholar, diplomat and administrator only Antipater rivals him in the range of his interests and experience. Starting his career as secretary and ending it leading Macedonian armies in battle, he alone of the immediate successors merited a biography by Plutarch. A singular honour considering the company he keeps in that writer's pages. His worth to the regent was not just his obvious talents but that, as a Greek in a Macedonian environment, he was more dependable than other officers whose national pedigree might tempt them to establish factions of their own, independent of Perdiccas' interest.

Although only ten years or so older than Alexander, he quickly rose to be Philip's chief secretary and was retained in this position by Alexander. It was in this post that Eumenes accompanied the army on the great invasion of Asia. His tasks as chief secretary of the peripatetic military court of the conqueror are now impossible to exactly determine but he would have kept the numerous records and reports that were produced by a literate administrative and military elite. He was responsible for organising the diary and itinerary of Alexander, who combined the role of commander-in-chief, high priest and chief justice. Many of the tasks of ordering the smooth administration of the newly-conquered lands would have fallen to Eumenes and he had a large input into the shape and direction of imperial policy. The only area where he had little influence was that of finance, which was administered separately.

But these onerous bureaucratic tasks would not have excused him from military duty and he must have impressed Alexander because he was eventually elevated to take military command. No details emerge of his activities in the wars until the conqueror left Darius' former lands and entered the exotic domain of rajas and elephants. Here, in India, the Cardian secretary was given charge of 300 mounted men, under the overall command of Perdiccas, to follow up the victory at Sangala.

Eumenes disappears from view again until the army had returned to the Hydaspes, doubtless kept busy in the mammoth task of organising the supply fleet and baggage train. He was appointed as one of the ten Greek trierarchs who, with fellow high-ranking Macedonians and oriental comrades, were given the task of equipping and commanding warships to escort the fleet down the uncharted and dangerous rivers of India. Alexander desperately needed more money to procure supplies and guides, to outfit his naval expedition under Nearchus and to provide for the army that would accompany him across the Makran Desert to Persia. He asked all his friends and officers for loans and contributions and, although others were reluctant to contribute, it is the story of Eumenes that is left to us. Alexander asked his secretary for 300 talents but only 100 were forthcoming and even this sum was grudgingly given with frequent protests of poverty. Alexander became frustrated with his Cardian friend's prevarication and one night he sent some of his servants to set Eumenes' tent on fire to expose his treasure. This was successful to a greater degree than Alexander had intended as 1,000 talents of gold and silver were melted down in the conflagration, as well as most of the royal documents and correspondence Eumenes kept. With embarrassment on both sides, Alexander took no more than the 100 talents and furthermore ordered his generals and satraps to replace with copies as many of the lost documents as possible.

When Perdiccas succeeded as chiliarch, the most powerful man in the army, his office as a senior hipparch was given to Eumenes, a promotion that indicates the increasing ties between them. But Eumenes was a powerful man in his own right, as witnessed by the Susa weddings. He married Artonis, the daughter of Artabazus, an old Achaemenid courtier and satrap of Bactria. Her sister was Barsine, who had married Memnon of Rhodes before she became Alexander's mistress and mother of his son. This made Eumenes step-uncle of the king's sole, but illegitimate, male offspring, a kinship that indicated how much Alexander respected his talents. The death of Alexander changed everything as the immediate succession crisis became an almost exclusively Macedonian affair. In fact, he played a major part in bringing together the two halves of the Macedonian army in the agreement that gave Perdiccas the regency.

His reward was the satrapy of Paphlagonia and Cappadocia, where the royal army now marched to install him. A local Persian official called Ariarathes was the real power in the land and this formidable octogenarian had to be overthrown if Eumenes was to take up his command. When the regent led out the army on this campaign, the royal court accompanied him, as it would in all his travels in the few years of his power. There had been changes, however, in its composition for Philip Arrhidaeus was not now the only king, as Roxanne had given birth to a male child who was unsurprisingly acclaimed as Alexander IV.

The regent's army debouched north over the Taurus Mountains into Ariarathes' kingdom in the summer of 322 BC. The journey had been uneventful as Craterus had already left the area, allowing Perdiccas an unobstructed passage across the plains of level Cilicia and through the mountain pass at the Cilician Gates. When battle was joined the outcome was inevitable; Ariarathes' army was crushed, 10,000 of his men were killed or captured and the king himself impaled by Perdiccas, who was annoyed by the considerable trouble and expense the old man had caused.[12] The rest of Cappadocia was easily subdued and Eumenes established in his new province. With the proper conquest of this large area of inland Anatolia, the new regent theoretically headed an empire of even greater extent than that ruled by Alexander.

The problems of the Anatolian interior had not all been solved by the campaign in Cappadocia. Neoptolemus the satrap of Armenia, the province to the northeast of Eumenes', had not proved able to pacify his new subjects, so Perdiccas ordered the Cardian general to go and help him with this war. Neoptolemus was a member of the Molossian royal house and a close relative of Olympias, a connection that assured him a place amongst Alexander's intimates. The new satrap had been given a sizeable army to establish his rule, including several thousand Macedonian infantry. Even so, his campaign was no success. Plutarch refers to 'Armenia which had been thrown into confusion by Neoptolemus', which, if it tells us nothing of what had occurred, makes it abundantly clear the region had been far from pacified.[13] In 322 BC, Eumenes joined Neoptolemus in Armenia and it is from this point that the feelings of bitter personal enmity arose between them. Neoptolemus resented the implication that he could not subjugate his satrapy by himself. He and his men made it clear they would take no orders from Eumenes and the Cardian had no option but to return to his own province. Here he raised 6,000 cavalry from the Cappadocian squirearchy and returned to Armenia, but Neoptolemus again refused to cooperate and by the end of the campaigning season of 322 BC Eumenes once more returned to Perdiccas.

These had been useful months for the regent; he had established his key lieutenant in Cappadocia and had shown his Macedonian followers that he, too, could be a conquering leader in the mould of Alexander. However, news had arrived that Antipater and Craterus had finally suppressed the Greek rebellion and were now acting in concert. With their talent, reputation and considerable armies, they represented a potential opposition far stronger than anything Perdiccas had encountered previously. The results of the Lamian War had not, however, been totally unfortunate; at least, Leonnatus was no more.

In fact, it soon became clear this might not be the only consolation. A visitor had arrived that indicated the intention of the generals in Europe might not be invariably hostile. Nicaea, the daughter of Antipater, had come to marry the regent. The offer of dynastic alliance was not unsolicited because, soon after Alexander's death, Perdiccas had asked for the marriage. He had been concerned about Craterus' intentions and hoped by marrying Nicaea to ensure that Antipater would not join any alliance against him. Because of the Lamian War, no progress had been made in this matrimonial exchange until now. Antipater clearly wished to revive the arrangement but now the situation was not the same and the implications needed careful consideration.

An alliance with the powers on Perdiccas' western flank would have advantages but no doubt the two great generals from Europe had ambitions east of the Hellespont. Perdiccas was by no means sure that an agreement which redrafted the Babylonian settlement, to the detriment of himself and his supporters, was not too high a price to pay for an alliance with Antipater and Craterus. His confidence was high and as he had travelled from Mesopotamia to Pisidia with no significant opposition, who was to say he might not continue his triumphal march to Pella, itself? Whatever the details of his thinking, the upshot was that Nicaea was kept waiting at court with no definite sign of the regent preparing to take her for his wife. If this was frustrating and humiliating for both father and daughter, what followed was almost intolerable. It was the emergence of a rival in the form of Cleopatra, sister of Alexander the Great, perhaps the greatest matrimonial prize of the age.

Cleopatra was a mature woman of thirty-two years who had already been married to one king, Alexander of Epirus, whom she wed in 336 BC at the momentous ceremony where Philip was assassinated. Cleopatra had acted as regent of Epirus for her young son after her husband's death on campaign in Italy. Olympias had joined her daughter there in 331 BC and ruled with her until 325 BC when Cleopatra returned to Pella. Since then she had become involved with Leonnatus, who intended to marry her to improve his claim to the throne of Macedon. These machinations had been brought to an end with his death but there could be no misapprehension that this was a powerful queen whose hand in marriage could bring great advantage. She had now set up her court in Sardis, the capital of Lydia, which had been the administrative centre of the Aegean and Hellespontine provinces of Asia since Persian times.

The evidence suggests that Olympias was behind the intrigues of her daughter; she was continuing her feud against Antipater and intended to buy support with the hand of Cleopatra. Now that Craterus was firmly bound to her enemy, and with Leonnatus dead, the only man who had the power to help her was Perdiccas. The regent fell into a complete quandary with this multiplicity of matrimonial choices; whichever way his decision fell, it would involve both dangers and opportunities. Marriage to Cleopatra would link him with the dynasty of Alexander and be of inestimable help if circumstances should allow him to aspire to the crown of Macedon, itself, but it would certainly embroil him in immediate conflict with Antipater and Craterus, who would interpret the act as a claim to their European lands. But to marry Nicaea implied an acceptance of his sharing the empire with her father and brother-in-law. Perdiccas looked to his councillors for advice and Eumenes was a key figure as the regent's most trusted confidant outside his own family. The Cardian, though, had his own axe to grind. He had known Olympias and Cleopatra for some years at Philip's court and evidence indicates they were politically close, an affinity bolstered by a mutual dislike of Antipater. He certainly argued hard for a marriage with Cleopatra and it has been suggested that he and Olympias had jointly arranged the arrival of the widowed queen with the intention of bouncing Perdiccas into her marriage bed. Alcetas, the regent's brother, led the opposition to this policy, partly no doubt through personal rivalry with the Cardian, but more importantly for fear of his own position. His fortunes were inextricably bound up with those of his brother and he was well aware of what he might lose if a conflict brought on by the alliance with Cleopatra went against Perdiccas. Eventually, the regent decided his brother's more cautious policy was the soundest course, and he ordered his marriage to Nicaea to be arranged.

But now more women took centre stage and these included not only Nicaea but two other royal females who had travelled from Macedonia to Asia (despite Antipater's attempt to stop them), intent on furthering their ambitions. This pair was yet another formidable mother and daughter combination with direct ties to the royal line. The elder princess was Cynane, a daughter of Philip, by Audata, an Illyrian, whom he had taken as queen after his victories over her people in 358 BC. Cynane had been married to Amyntas, the son of Perdiccas III, whom Philip had disposed of to gain the throne and whom Alexander had eliminated as a potential danger to his crown, in 336 BC. The child of this union was Adea, now a teenager of marriageable age, who accompanied her mother to claim a destiny which the particular legitimacy of her lineage entitled her to. Years earlier it had been arranged that, when mature enough, Adea should marry Philip Arrhidaeus, and now this formerly-insignificant princeling was king they intended to enforce their claim. If Perdiccas felt any relief that, at least, it was not him they wished to wed, it was no real consolation for the imminent arrival of this party, who might threaten his control of the puppet monarch. Even though the princesses did not seem to be attached to any of the major factions, what was inevitable was that they and their retainers would have ample opportunity to influence the king once ensconced in Philip Arrhidaeus' quarters. This year of Macedonian queens was wearing the regent's patience thin and, before the latest of these royal women arrived, he allowed his brother, Alcetas, to persuade him into a bloody and final solution of this particular problem.

He gave him a free hand to ambush and kill the two women on the mountain road they were travelling from the coast. The plan, in fact, only half succeeded and the result was the worst possible for the regent's position and reputation. Alcetas and his soldiers attacked the princesses' caravan and Cynane was murdered before the Macedonian soldiers realised whom it was they were attacking. Once they recognised the young Adea they refused to hurt her and escorted her on the rest of her journey. Now the truth was known, the army was horrified at the complicity of their commander-in-chief in the death of a member of the great Alexander's family. It was hardly two years since his death at Babylon and affection for the dynasty amongst the soldiery had, as yet, little eroded. Rebellion was in the air and Perdiccas had no option but to agree when Adea asked the support of the Macedonian warriors in pressing her claim to be Philip's queen. His rash attempt at assassination had completely backfired; Adea married the 'half-witted' king (taking the name Eurydice) and his own standing with the army suffered a severe blow. The Cynane affair sowed seeds that the regent did not reap until the following year in Egypt. Eurydice had shown herself cool and resourceful and she would continue to exhibit these qualities as she rode her fortune over the next few years. Since the demise of Meleager, Philip Arrhidaeus' reign had been peaceful and orderly under the tutelage of the regent, but his new wife would once more take him into the troubled waters of power politics.

Perdiccas had not shown a sure touch in his handling of the domestic arrangements of the court and army but at least he had not faced any direct challenge to his authority. Now, this would all change. The storm burst from a direction that would not have been a complete surprise to Perdiccas, but the act of rebellion perpetrated was totally unexpected. Ptolemy was the culprit and his crime the theft of Alexander's corpse. The Egyptian satrap had never hidden his lack of support for Perdiccas' regency; he had murdered Cleomenes, who had been left as his deputy, and had annexed Cyrene without reference to his overlord. Perdiccas had no illusions about Ptolemy's antagonism, but the problem of dealing with him justified condoning these minor misdemeanours, which were generously interpreted as reasonable initiative from the commander on the spot.

This latest outrage, however, could not be overlooked. Alexander's corpse had lain by the waters of the Euphrates for over two years while his funeral carriage was being constructed. It was built under the supervision of one Arrhidaeus (not, as one source notoriously suggests, the mentally impaired king[14]) and was regarded as one of the wonders of the age. Arrhidaeus' relations with Perdiccas had deteriorated to the extent where he felt he had no future under the regent and he looked elsewhere to capitalise on his great asset: the possession of the dead king's corpse. Making an alliance with Ptolemy, he arranged that the cortege be transported up the Euphrates valley and across to Damascus, where a rendezvous with a force sent by the ruler of Egypt had been arranged. Perdiccas, distrusting Arrhidaeus' intentions, sent his generals, Polemon and Attalus, with an army to arrest them. This countermeasure was not attended by any success and the funeral caravan was rushed across the frontier into Egypt. The original destination of the body is a matter of some debate. The most reasonable notion is that the marvellous vehicle carrying the body was to be transported across Asia amid much pomp and circumstance for the interment to take place at the Macedonian royal cemetery at Aegae. Against this, it is suggested that the dead man had left instructions that his remains should be taken to Egypt, because of his special relationship with Zeus Ammon of Siwah. But, even had this been the case, it is difficult to believe his followers would have countenanced this permanent exile. These rumours were an attempt to whitewash Ptolemy's actions and have no real credibility; what the Egyptian satrap had sanctioned was a straightforward hijacking.[15]

This was no minor infringement of Perdiccas' prerogative, but a direct rejection of his authority and it was clear that Ptolemy's possession of Alexander's mortal remains was an implicit claim to the inheritance of his empire. The paraphernalia of Alexander's dynasty were important icons to the Macedonian warriors who had conquered the world under his leadership. Perdiccas had understood this emotional attachment to his cost when his plot against Cynane had been discovered; he could not allow such desecration to go unavenged.

Since Alexander's death, his generals had not actually taken up arms against each other. The peace may have been fraught and fragile but it had existed; now war between Macedonians had begun and it would continue almost without interruption for four decades. It was in the regent's interest to keep the scope of this conflict as limited as possible, to contain the war to the Egyptian front, but this he completely failed to do.

The regent had failed to build on his marriage to Nicaea and cement a friendship with Antipater and Craterus; instead he had allowed the question of Cleopatra to fester on. The widowed queen was not only encouraged to keep her household at Sardis, but Perdiccas made her satrap of Lydia and put the previous incumbent, Menander, under her direct command. Eumenes continued to act as go-between; he knew that any improvement of relations with Antipater could only be to the detriment of his influence at the court of the two kings. Notwithstanding his marriage to Nicaea, Perdiccas was now showing disturbing indecision over this matter and it was inevitable that his father-in-law should put the worst possible interpretation on his behaviour. A decline in Alcetas' influence, following from his instigation of the disastrous Cynane episode, allowed Eumenes to persuade the regent to rethink his commitment to an alliance with Antipater. There is no evidence that Nicaea, herself, ever complained of her situation and there are no suggestions that Perdiccas either formally denied her position as his wife or thought of doing so.

The appointment of Cleopatra as satrap had incensed opinion in west Asia Minor. Menander was not the sort of man prepared to suffer in silence and he encouraged the idea that Perdiccas intended to repudiate Antipater's daughter and take up with Cleopatra. Asander, the satrap of Caria, would also soon show he no longer had confidence in the Asian regent's authority. Another, not unconnected, misfortune compounded deteriorating relations between the European and Asian camps. Antigonus, the satrap of Greater Phrygia, was impeached by Perdiccas for his refusal to help Eumenes conquer Cappadocia. To save his skin he fled to Pella, where he passed on these reports that the regent was Antipater's enemy and, not content with his oriental empire, intended to intervene in Europe. News that Eumenes had travelled to Sardis with presents for Cleopatra (and, by implication, a formal proposal) only provided more ammunition for those with an interest in driving a wedge between Perdiccas and Antipater. The effect at Pella was that what had first been a suspicion, originating perhaps from agents of Ptolemy, now seemed a certainty and the viceroy of Europe and his son-in-law prepared for war.

It was to be war on two fronts; a Hellenistic world war involving almost all the surviving officers who had campaigned so long under Alexander. Antipater and Craterus were currently involved in a campaign against the Aetolians but it was soon wound up, freeing their forces for an invasion of Asia in the spring of 320 BC. Speed was of the essence, now that the die was cast, if they were to forestall Perdiccas from crushing Ptolemy before they could enter the fray. It is unlikely that Antipater or Craterus had much personal respect for the body-snatching satrap, but he was their most powerful ally and had to be supported.

With the approach of the campaigning season, the regent had much to decide, both to ensure the defence of his possessions and to accomplish the elimination of his treacherous subordinate in Egypt. He chose to deal with Ptolemy personally, with the main army, whilst Eumenes was left to defend the Hellespont against invasion. This, at first sight, might seem a dangerous disposition as Antipater and Craterus had a larger and better army at their disposal than the enemy on the Nile, but the temper of his Macedonian troops dictated strategy. While Perdiccas was confident his army would fight against Ptolemy, he had grave doubts about their preparedness to enter battle against such revered commanders as Antipater and Craterus. Time was to show this would be a real problem for Eumenes. The regent conjectured that after a triumphant campaign against Ptolemy his popularity with his Macedonian soldiers would allow him to deal with these other enemies.

Under Eumenes were the armies of Neoptolemus in central Anatolia, and Alcetas in Pisidia, but both these officers were inclined to refuse the regent's orders to support Eumenes. Perdiccas' brother excused his conduct on the grounds that his Macedonian soldiers had too much respect for Antipater to possibly fight him and allegedly had such affection for Craterus that they would undoubtedly defect the moment they saw him. While Eumenes led his own troops to the Hellespont, the whereabouts of Neoptolemus were unclear; he had left Armenia but news had not arrived as to where he had reached on his line of march and his intentions were ambiguous. For the moment, strengthening the defences and garrisons at the crossing points to Asia occupied Eumenes' mind in this, his first independent military campaign of any magnitude. A severe induction: to fight two of the greatest of Alexander's marshals with an army whose loyalty was bound to be highly questionable.

He was not allowed to await his enemies in a prepared position at the Hellespontine crossings, because a threat from elsewhere drew him away. Part of his enemies' plans for invasion included a sea-borne attack on the provinces far to the south of Eumenes' position. To this end, Antigonus had taken a small army to Caria. Asander, the satrap, came over to him immediately and Menander was only too happy to cooperate. Perdiccan control in the Aegean provinces looked set to be completely undermined and, with Alcetas undependable, Eumenes had to respond himself. By the time he arrived in the south, news reached him that Antipater and Craterus had crossed into Asia, thanks to treachery amongst the Hellespontine garrisons. With two armies converging on him, Eumenes decided to withdraw into the interior of Phrygia and only avoided being ambushed by Antigonus' men through a timely warning from Cleopatra.

His position was such that Neoptolemus' forces were a vital ingredient if he was to have any chance of facing the enemy with success. Eumenes' Cappadocian troopers soon located the difficult Molossian prince, even in the vastness of west Anatolia. Approximately ten days march east of the Hellespont, the two supposed allies encountered each other.

When Eumenes ordered Neoptolemus to join him it became clear that he, like Alcetas, had no intention of accepting Perdiccas' injunction to obey his orders. His behaviour showed that his plan was to join the invaders from Europe who, he felt, were more likely to be victorious now the main army had left with the regent. The Greek general found his nominal subordinate with his army drawn up in battle array. It was apparent he would need to fight his own men, before he even reached the enemy. The stakes were such that the whole Perdiccan edifice in western Asia might collapse without Antipater and Craterus having to strike a blow. But the encounter in Phrygia ended well for Eumenes, with Neoptolemus forced to flee with a few of his horse. The rest of his leaderless men had no option but to join with Eumenes, whose troopers had captured their baggage train. They were an important addition but one whose loyalty was always questionable.

Only days after this action, ambassadors arrived from Antipater and Craterus. The two hoped they could subvert the Greek from his loyalty to Perdiccas with promises that he would 'enjoy possession of his present satrapies, would receive additional troops and territory from them'[16]. The Cardian felt no need to desert his leader, who he expected to triumph in Egypt, but he was quite prepared to spin out negotiations rather than risk the lottery of combat. He proposed himself as a go-between to bring about peace between Craterus and Perdiccas, on the basis of them sharing equal power in Asia, while presumably - though his intended role is not mentioned - Antipater would remain as viceroy in Europe.

The desire to talk before they fought was not uncommon with these Macedonian armies in the early years of the succession wars. The ties between old comrades were not sundered without some trauma and a real desire to avoid the shedding of Macedonian blood can be detected. But here the aims of the two sides were too far apart and it only needed the catalyst of Neoptolemus' arrival in Antipater and Craterus' camp to force the issue. The Molossian brought little in the way of real fighting strength from the wreck of his army but he had news that compensated for this weakness. He assured his new allies, who had just crossed from Europe, that, though Eumenes was marching towards the Hellespont in apparent confidence, his men would never fight against the likes of them. With these assurances, the invaders broke off their desultory peace negotiations and decided on pursuing the war in earnest. To this end, they split the army. Antipater was to march southeast and take the Cilician route to Syria, where he might assist Ptolemy by threatening Perdiccas from the north. Craterus was left to deal with Eumenes and secure Asia Minor. Neoptolemus joined Craterus as his second-in-command, and without further delay they led the troops forward to find Eumenes and bring on the decisive battle.

The first great battle between Alexander's marshals was fought only three years after the death of the man they had all served, and it is no surprise that the first time blood was spilt between them the shadow of their dead king hovered over the event. Eumenes even dreamed of two Alexanders fighting each other the night before the battle.

Eumenes was a juggler with a good many balls in the air and the stress was playing on his mind. He had hardly been able to retain the loyalty of his Macedonian followers in the face of Neoptolemus' disloyalty. Now, with the arrival of Craterus, he knew he would not persuade them to directly attack a man who they had allegedly always seen as their champion and comrade.[17] The key to his tactics was to not allow his Macedonian infantry to hear that the general opposed to them was Craterus until Eumenes had been able to use his preponderance in cavalry to decide the fight. The army that he was facing was formidable. The core was made up of 20,000 infantry, most of whom were Macedonian phalangites, veteran foot who could only be halted by their peers.

The weakness in the Macedonian formation was in cavalry. Craterus could field only slightly over 2,000 horse and though it was intended the infantry would gain the victory, the senior generals took their posts on the wings with the horsemen. Craterus led something over half these cavalry on the right wing, the position of honour, while Neoptolemus led the troopers on the left.

The Perdiccans could also field 20,000 infantry, but by no means of the same calibre as those opposed to them. A few thousand were Macedonian phalangites who had been with Neoptolemus, but the rest were mercenaries from Asia Minor and light infantry from Mesopotamia and Iran. And Eumenes knew he could not keep the identity of the enemy general permanently a secret from his Macedonians and when they found out it was probable they would desert. He depended on his superiority in the cavalry arm, with his 5,000 horsemen, to win the day. To ensure the reputation of Craterus would not impact on the men directly opposed to him, Eumenes placed on his left wing only 'barbarian' European and Asiatic horsemen under two foreign generals, Phoenix of Tenedos and Pharnabazus.[18] On the right, Eumenes led the largest number of cavalry as it was here he intended to win the fight.

To keep his men from knowing who was approaching, Eumenes used both subterfuge, claiming it was merely Neoptolemus with some local cavalry, and the terrain, as he manoeuvred to keep a hill between the two armies, masking Craterus from sight. He attacked with his cavalry wings while the main bodies of the armies were still out of sight. This tactic carried considerable risks but the question of security was of such importance that he could not allow communication between the two armies before the battle began. That the Cardian achieved this feat is one of the triumphs of his career and if he showed brilliance throughout the preliminaries, he also had the luck required in consummating success in battle.

On the right flank, Eumenes, leading his thousands of Cappadocians, achieved his decisive blow. Against him stood Neoptolemus, a man whose personal dislike of Eumenes was completely returned and makes believable the report that the fight on the right was largely decided by a personal combat between the two generals. A Homeric struggle ended when Eumenes dealt his opponent a fatal sword-stroke on the neck. With the death of Neoptolemus, his forces, who had previously been holding their own, lost heart.

On the other wing, Craterus had led his outnumbered troopers forward to confront the enemy with typical *élan* but in the resulting melee he lost his life; an event of great moment that would have a profound effect on the succession struggle. The greatest of Alexander's generals and veteran of all his wars had met his end. With both Craterus and Neoptolemus dead and the horsemen on the flanks routed, the footsoldiers, who had not begun to fight, had little option but to accept the truce Eumenes offered. This time, the Cardian had no luck in recruiting them but tried, at least, to ensure their neutrality for the current campaigning season. Even in this he was to be sorely disappointed as, at the first opportunity, most of the soldiers stole away under cover of night to make their way to Antipater in Cilicia. Even so, Eumenes' victory had been spectacular. He had faced the greatest of Alexander's generals and a first-class army, defeated them comprehensively and personally killed a particular enemy. The victory had retained for the Perdiccan cause control of the crucial Hellespontine crossings. His misfortune was that events elsewhere would undo his work and much of the army he had defeated would return against him under different leadership.

The death of Craterus was the overriding factor for the Macedonians in this encounter. The man's stature was unquestioned by any in the Hellenistic world. In his way, he had been the equal of Hephaistion in the king's eyes and to the Macedonian rank and file this was even more the case. Eumenes had no doubt about the impact of his enemy's death and it is not too machiavellian to suggest the reason he gave the dead general's body a worthy funeral and sent his remains back to his family was because he had some idea of the approbation he would experience for being the cause of Craterus' death.[19]

The war in the north had been schemed and struggled to a successful end by Perdiccas' general but it had still always been a side-show. By his decision to attack Ptolemy in Egypt, the regent had ensured that it would be far away from the Hellenised world of the Dardanelles that the final test of his rule should take place. At the start of the campaign, Perdiccas had had other dispositions to make apart from sending Eumenes north. On reaching Cilicia, he had deposed the local satrap and sent Docimus to Babylon to replace the governor there.[20] In addition, learning of Ptolemy's success in subverting some of Cyprus' petty kingdoms, he despatched a fleet and army under the overall control of Aristonous to secure the island.

For the main army and the court of the kings it was a long march before they would come face to face with their foes. Ptolemy clearly had no intention of risking battle in Syria or Palestine; he would await the invasion in Egypt behind the natural defences of the Nile. Alexander had travelled this route a decade before and even if he had needed to fight at Issus, Tyre and Gaza, Egypt had fallen like a ripe plum. Perdiccas had lived through that campaign and he had high hopes that his rival on the Nile would put up no better resistance than Darius' satrap had. A deeper appreciation of Egyptian history ought to have instilled a little more caution into the ruminations of the regent and his advisers as they met at his campaign headquarters. To the Assyrians and Persians before them, this ancient kingdom had been a source of continual problems, only its riches making the effort to retain it worthwhile.

Pelusium, the traditional gateway to the river kingdom, was reached with little difficulty and no opposition. Perdiccas knew he must utilise the tributaries and canals if he was to move his great column of men and supplies efficiently, and so began to clear some old canals which had become silted up. Either his engineers were inept or agents of Ptolemy were at work, for the Pelusic branch of the Nile flooded the newly-cleared routes and caused havoc in the army's encampment. If this was not a bad enough start, some of his followers deserted to the enemy. It may be that they considered the flood was a sign that the invasion was ill fated, but more likely Ptolemy was sending bribes to the weaker links amongst the regent's supporters. It is suggested that to counter this loss of men, Perdiccas resorted to offering gifts and promises of preferment, but the hard fighting and marching that the army would soon sustain implies the disaffection, for the moment, only affected a few officers and not the rank and file.

The regent answered any sagging in morale by decisive action; he forced-marched by night to a ford on the Nile, at the Fort of Camels. He hoped to cross over with picked troops and surprise the garrison, before the enemy was aware of his movements. Unfortunately for Perdiccas, Ptolemy had been vigilant and repulsed the attack.[21]

Perdiccas may have withdrawn his men, but only in order to try an assault elsewhere. He again marched by night and day to attempt another crossing, this time at Memphis. What is extraordinary, in face of what soon would happen, is that the army the regent led was clearly prepared to perform wonders for him, in desert country with their lines of communication left undefended. At this point in the course of the Nile, fortune appeared, at last, to be favouring Perdiccas, as near Memphis there was an island large enough to encamp the whole army. His men had begun to cross when it became apparent that the river was deeper and the current stronger than had been anticipated. Perdiccas had been with Alexander when he had forded the Tigris and, in the face of similar difficulties, he now tried to put some of that experience to good use. Alexander had placed lines of cavalry up and downstream of the crossing, both to break the current and to catch any men who were swept away. The regent did the same but he used elephants, which he placed upstream, thinking they would be more effective in holding the flow of the water than horses. This manoeuvre worked well for a time, with many men getting over to the island with nothing worse than a soaking. Unfortunately, the first units of soldiers and animals disturbed the sand on the bed of the river and the current carried it off, lowering the level of the river's bottom at the crossing point. Some men were lost and it became clear that the rest of the army could not get over. To avoid dividing his forces, he ordered those who had crossed to the island to return. But disaster struck and hundreds of men and animals were swept away to their death or found themselves on the opposite bank in the hands of the enemy. Two thousand soldiers, in all, were lost; casualties commensurate with a major battle, yet nothing had been achieved. To make matters worse, many of those who drowned had been eaten by crocodiles and were thus deprived of proper rites in death, which did little to improve morale.

They were in desperate straits; stuck in the interior of Egypt, far from any friendly base and with no prospect of taking an enemy town that might offer them shelter and supplies. The soldiers turned against the regent, shouting out that he had led them to disaster. With his authority in question, there was no lack of ambitious officers eager to exploit this opportunity to challenge his leadership. Many followed when a group led by Pithon staged a coup. This exemplar of treachery forced his way into Perdiccas' tent, determined to assassinate his commander. This time there was no loyal bodyguard to defend him nor could his eloquence save him from the swords of his assassins. He died from repeated stab wounds, delivered by Pithon and other officers who had been the beneficiaries of his patronage.

The regent's body was barely cold when word came through of success in the north. Perdiccas may well have escaped assassination, if the news of Eumenes' triumph over Craterus had reached the beleaguered army in Egypt sooner. The delay had been fatal. The end was shabby and inglorious for the man raised to supreme power at Babylon. He had held Alexander's empire together for three years; it had been a precarious unity but no other would achieve it again, and it is questionable whether any of the other successors would have bettered this feat. The reputation he left suffers from a lack of sympathetic sources and evidence indicates that the last campaign is reported from a tradition designed specifically to denigrate him. This from Diodorus:

> Perdiccas, indeed, was a man of blood, one who usurped the authority
> of the other commanders and in general, wished to rule all by force; but
> Ptolemy, on the contrary, was generous and fair and granted to all the
> commanders the right to speak frankly.'[22]

Not the balanced analysis of one who was prepared to understand the
Herculean task of the first heir of Alexander. Hieronymus is generally
suggested as Diodorus' source for the period but this kind of remark suggests
a more specifically pro-Ptolemy informant may have been used, perhaps even
the pen of Ptolemy himself.[23] Whatever the complexities of traditional
attestation, an attempt at a non-partisan critique can only fault Perdiccas'
policy and temperament on two important counts. He could be politically inept
and indecisive and was, in the final analysis, unlucky. His career under
Alexander had been exemplary, his military accomplishments were considerable
and, even if not a leader of the highest political ability, it should not be
forgotten how he dominated the first few crucial years after the great adventure
of Alexander ended on the banks of the Euphrates.

These events, in the early summer of 320 BC, were the culmination of a
considerable carnage amongst Alexander's great officers. The world he had
left may have been rich in opportunities, but it was dangerous for the great and
noble as well as the common soldier. The very top echelon of the conqueror's
friends had been removed in a few years. The group of officers who seemed
from birth, experience and talent most fitted to rule the empire after him had
been wiped out, leaving room for others who had been by no means as
significant while the king had lived. Hephaistion had died a few months before
Alexander. Leonnatus had fallen in a cavalry skirmish in the Greek war and
now Perdiccas and Craterus were dead. These last two had stood head and
shoulders above all the rest, after the king's demise, and the only man left alive
of comparable stature was Antipater, whose age and disinterest in Asia
precluded him from dominating events for any length of time.

New men would come forward in the very near future but, for the
moment, it was the old regent and friend of Philip II who alone had the
prestige and power to offer the hope of a real settlement. Not that this would
have been apparent immediately. He was on the road to Cilicia when he heard
the news of Craterus' defeat and death, and the arrival of refugees from the
battle left no doubt of the extent of the disaster on the Hellespont. There
must have been much in him that wanted to turn back and deal with the
Greek general, who was now securely sitting on his lines of communication
with Macedonia. Most of the infantry from Craterus' army had rejoined him
and he certainly had sufficient strength to face Eumenes' army. That he did

not take this course of action shows that age had not dimmed his capacity to analyse and act at the nub of events. To turn back might ensure the protection of Macedonia, but it would mean he could have no impact on the war in the Levant, which was bound to decide the long-term future of his rule in the Balkans.

Cut off in the middle of Anatolia, he had not heard that Perdiccas had fallen to the swords of his companions and the propsect of his enemy returning victorious with his resources swelled by the wealth of Egypt was real and imminent. When he heard the news is unclear, but probably on arrival in Cilicia, where the events would have been common knowledge in the ports along the coast. The situation was altered at a stroke; Ptolemy had triumphed and the royal army that was returning north from Egypt was led by men who wished for his friendship. He could now continue his journey in the expectation of rendezvousing with the royal court, not fighting a battle with the army that accompanied it.

Not that it was completely without trepidation that he followed Alexander's route past the battlefield of Issus. He could not predict the attitude of the two guardians who had replaced Perdiccas in command. They were lightweights next to Antipater, yet the soldiers of the army he was meeting had been long years away from home and might be less than responsive to a representative from a pre-Alexandrian past.

As it turned out, the danger he had to face was not from powerful rivals but from the chaotic power vacuum that had been left by the death of Perdiccas. The coup at the royal court had been smoothly executed, in the short term, but the cohesion of the ruling Macedonian aristocracy had been cruelly rent and it was far from clear that the new commanders-in-chief would have the authority to undo the damage. The shedding of Perdiccas' blood had been compounded by a purge of those of his supporters who could be found. An army assembly, convened for the purpose, condemned many other notable Perdiccans, including Eumenes and Alcetas, in their absence - the vengeful inclinations of the rank and file being aroused by news of the death of Craterus.

Ptolemy crossed over the river and addressed the assembly of soldiers. Apparently, he was himself offered the regency but declined this poisoned chalice and threw his weight behind the arrangement that saw Pithon and Arrhidaeus acclaimed as temporary joint guardians. This weight was considerable as he was able to arrange the provisioning of the royal army and was, clearly, the only man who could ensure a safe withdrawal from their exposed position.

Once out of Egypt and free of danger, the shallowness of the new guardians' authority soon became apparent. Acceptance of the authority of the murderers of Perdiccas may have been a necessary course when the priority was an arrangement with Ptolemy, but real loyalty to these self-seeking opportunists did not run deep. From the beginning, the army that marched along the coast of Palestine towards Syria could hardly have been said to be led by the guardians; they merely travelled together. The new leadership could not even provide the soldiers' arrears of pay, the first prerequisite in an age when royal authority and tribal loyalty had become an inadequate substitute for the cash nexus.

In this disorderly cavalcade that hurried north from Egypt another figure began to exercise long-held ambitions. This was Eurydice who, for some time now, had been installed as Philip Arrhidaeus' queen. Perdiccas had suffered the marriage but while he was alive she was in no position to challenge his authority. His inadequate successors were another matter and this remarkable woman began to put about the contention that they were not now needed, as her husband was quite up to the task of ruling with her assistance. Finding some support amongst the army, her intrigues swept away what little authority Pithon and Arrhidaeus retained. Unable to contain what seemed incipient mutiny and without the imagination to find answers to this new threat, the guardians were forced to resign their office. The rump of what had been Perdiccas' army rolled onwards, an agglomeration of factions and discontented regiments rather than a disciplined force, towards the rendezvous in Syria where they were to wait for Antipater coming from the north.

The area where the two armies were to meet was a complex of verdant hunting enclosures, constructed by the Persian aristocrats who had ruled there until a decade and a half before. Well treed with a considerable river running through it, this orderly terrain was turned into chaos with the arrival of the leaderless and dishevelled army. In the luxurious pavilions that housed the kings and court, Eurydice was building on prestige lent her by being the only competent fully-Macedonian adult member of the Royal family. The civilian bureaucracy looked to her, in default of any other official authority, now that Pithon and Arrhidaeus had stepped down. These people were not sufficiently important to sustain any long term authority and with the news of Antipater's imminent approach she found other friends who might have the resources on which to base her hopes of power. Attalus, whose wife, the sister of Perdiccas, had been lynched in Egypt, had taken the fleet from Pelusium to Tyre, a town that had become the centre for those Perdiccans who had escaped the debacle on the Nile. Not only did he have the benefits of a great reputation, a fleet and a growing body of soldiers but he also controlled much of the royal treasure that had been taken to that city in preparation for paying the wages of Perdiccas' army. Attalus, either personally or through agents, made efforts at Triparadeisus to restore Perdiccan authority within the army in concert with Eurydice.[24]

While the elephants enjoyed the mud of the river, the unpaid rank and file were becoming increasingly truculent under the summer sun, against which their rough field tents gave little enough protection. The old soldiers took the lead, grizzled pikemen who knew their worth and remembered when ordinary soldiers had flexed their muscles before in India, on the Beas, at Opis and at Babylon. Their officers were powerless to maintain normal discipline and many, no doubt, sympathised with the anger at the non-arrival of their pay. They had run up debts with the merchants, whose caravans always followed the fighting men, and had no sympathy with leaders who pleaded the problem of circumstances in excuse for breach of contract.

Into this mayhem the great viceroy of Europe risked his dignity, not knowing the depth of discontent that faced him. His own army, footsore and many affected by the experience of defeat under Craterus, camped on the far side of the river before he crossed the bridge that led to the tents of the kings and royal army. Friends of Eurydice and Perdiccan agents inflamed the mob that greeted him, howling out its demand for arrears of pay.

A hair's breadth from being ripped to pieces, Antipater was rescued by the intervention of two men who had travelled very different roads to Triparadeisus. Seleucus had trailed back from Egypt uncommitted to the arrangements that put Pithon and Arrhidaeus in charge but unprepared to directly challenge them. He had been as highly placed as any in the army before the Nile campaign and some of his authority with the men remained. As partner he found Antigonus the One-eyed, who had come from fighting against the Perdiccans in Cyprus and in a short period had established some influence with the army. These two stepped in to protect the viceroy and allowed him sufficient time to hurry back across the bridge to the protection of his own camp.

The realisation that they had almost murdered a man who had served the state at the highest level under Alexander and Philip sobered the soldiery. More than this, in the calm light of day they knew that the others who were aiming for power could only promise further civil strife, while Antipater alone had the authority to offer a Macedonian peace. The mechanism of this rapprochement is unclear, but the upshot was that Antipater was soon in undisputed control; perhaps some money was found to ease the matter of unpaid wages. He set about another reordering of the empire and the beast that Alexander had created drew breath under the tutelage of the old regent, giving a promise of stability that was to again prove illusory.

Time would show that, as at Babylon, few of the arrangements made would have any longevity. Ptolemy and Lysimachus were reconfirmed in their satrapies but this was not an act of policy, just a recognition of reality. Seleucus was rewarded for his loyalty with the fiefdom of Babylonia but he and many of the others were to be ousted in the years to come, by the man Antipater designated as his general in Asia.

Well versed in conciliation and manipulation from his years in Pella, Antipater moulded enough unity amongst the most senior of the Macedonian ruling class to create this new settlement but, the need to crush the unregenerate Perdiccans in Asia Minor ensured from the beginning that it would be born in conflict.[25] Antipater's advanced age ensured it would hardly be a year before the central issues of succession to Alexander's power would return to dog the world for forty years.

Chapter 3

The Struggle for Macedonia

Polyperchon whenever he was elated by wine would dance, even though he was
rather old and second to none among the Macedonians either in military
achievement or in general esteem: he danced continually, clad in a saffron
tunic and wearing on his feet Sicyonian slippers.[1]

When Antipater died in 319 BC, he was nominally regent for the whole of
Alexander's empire. But the realm which he had seen grow from its beginnings
was now too vast to be controlled from Macedonia and, in any case, one
suspects Antipater was not much interested in the affairs of Asia, where he had
only ventured once, late in his life. Antigonus had command there, even if
under the overall authority of the regent to whom he referred major decisions.
The old man was content to administer Greater Macedonia and the parts of
Greece where either his garrisons were installed or oligarchic allies were in
control. The two kings, the infant Alexander IV and Philip Arrhidaeus were
with him at Pella, kept in suitable state as the descendants of the dynasty he
had always honoured and served so well, but real power belonged to him. Now,
coming to the end of his life, the need was to determine who would succeed
him.[2]

In the end, this extraordinary steward of Macedonian power nominated
Polyperchon to carry on after his death, deciding against entrusting the task to
Antigonus or any of the other generals currently squabbling in Asia. Their
unscrupulous ambition was already too evident for Antipater to happily trust
them and led him to an appointment that must, at the time, have come as a
considerable shock to many. Polyperchon, like Antipater and Antigonus, had
seen service under Philip and was by no means a young man. In 319 BC he was
already in his sixties with a career of steady achievement behind him. Of his
history under Philip, like that of so many others, we know frustratingly little,
but with the advent of Alexander more is heard of him. During the Battle of
Issus a phalanx commander was killed in combat and Polyperchon was
promoted into his place. Senior command had come late in life, particularly as
his noble lineage was unimpeachable as a member of the royal house of
Tymphaea, one of the hill principalities Philip had finally incorporated into
the Macedonian state. Generational distance from Alexander may answer the

puzzle of his late advancement, but when the vacancy arose a noble of his status could not be overlooked.

Mentioned at the Persian Gates, it is not until the Bactrian and Sogdian wars that he experienced a short period of independent command. Mainly he led his *taxis* of phalangites under Alexander's command, being involved in the desperate campaign in the Swat highlands and mentioned as a contender for the capture of Ora, a city situated on the army's approach to the rock of Aornus.

The most intriguing reference to him during these years occurs at a banquet held between campaigns in Sogdia. Alexander, seeing himself more and more as heir to Darius, was demanding *proskynesis* from his Persian followers. Less than keen on the procedure, Polyperchon is recorded taunting a Persian courtier who, in prostrating himself, had almost touched his chin to the ground. The old commander mocked him suggesting he should bang it harder, only to elicit a furious response from the king who dragged him from his couch and forced him onto the ground to make him do the act of homage he so despised.[3] That there was not a meeting of minds between Alexander and Polyperchon on the imperatives of Alexander's imperial policy is confirmed in the last reference to him in the lifetime of the great conqueror. He was sent home as second-in-command to Craterus when he left with the 10,000 veterans to return to Europe.

Polyperchon's career under Alexander had been by no means inglorious but he had not reached the front rank of generals and was overshadowed by those rising stars, Ptolemy, Pithon, Leonnatus, Peucestas and Seleucus. Absent from Babylon when the king died, his prospects of advancement were completely chained to the fortunes of Craterus. Polyperchon played his part in the successful conclusion of the Lamian War and was the natural choice to be left in command in Greece when Antipater, Craterus and Cassander invaded Asia, in 320 BC, to settle with Perdiccas.

Antipater chose as his successor this soldier, of a similar generation, whose long career of loyal service to the dynasty of Alexander appeared to offer a safe option as guardian of the kings. There was reason to hope that he would live long enough to see Alexander IV safely ensconced on the throne. But to one person the decision was not only surprising but a deep insult and a personal humiliation. Cassander, the eldest of Antipater's sons, had fully expected to inherit his father's mantle. He was about the same age as Alexander the Great but had not shared in the Asian adventures, remaining at Pella with Antipater. It has been suggested that Cassander and Alexander were already bitter enemies from their youth but this is too glib a conclusion to reach from the evidence of later events. Cassander's younger brother, Iollas, accompanied Alexander and became one of the king's cupbearers, an honoured position, which hardly suggests the king was hostile to the family of his regent.

Cassander was a cultured and intelligent man who had been educated at Philip's court with Alexander, attending the classes of Aristotle. He had assisted his father in his role as regent while Alexander was in Asia, and, though we have no details of his activities, there is every reason to believe that he carried them out efficiently, for his father chose him for at least one vital mission. This was to plead the case with Alexander against Craterus replacing Antipater as the ruler in Europe. The mission was a personal disaster as Cassander fell foul of Alexander on more than one occasion and the experience was to have far-reaching effects on his subsequent behaviour. In the event, the death soon afterwards of the king made the purpose of the mission superfluous. Cassander, amongst men he had not seen for over ten years, had no part to play in the machinations at Babylon and returned to Macedonia.[4]

Playing no discernible role in the Lamian War, he was nonetheless at his father's side at Triparadeisus. Though briefly attached to Antigonus, when Antipater returned with the two kings to Macedonia Cassander was again with him and shared with the old man the increasingly onerous tasks of government. He acted decisively at the highest level on the occasion of Demades' embassy from Athens in early 319 BC. The venal Athenian had travelled to Macedonia to plead for the withdrawal of the garrison at Munychia, installed in the aftermath of the Lamian War. Unknown to him, however, treasonable correspondence from Demades to Perdiccas had come into Antipater's hands. Cassander, furious at this revelation, had both Demades and his son executed when they arrived in Pella.[5] The nature of this impetuous act, accomplished without the benefit of trial or proper procedure, was not lost on the ailing Antipater.

The incident served to deepen Antipater's concern about the fitness of his son to rule after him. Cassander's experiences in Babylon and his obvious personal ambition had sowed the seeds of doubt as to his appropriateness to guard and guide Alexander IV to the throne of Macedon. The old man decided to deny him the highest post but, aware of his son's abilities and not wholly immune to the imperatives of dynastic solidarity, appointed Cassander chiliarch to the new guardian of the king.

Cassander was not prepared to be deputy to another old man and determined to fight for what he regarded as his proper inheritance. Dissembling his discontent and anger at his father's decision, he spent the days after Antipater's death arranging an appropriately magnificent funeral for the country's leading citizen. Polyperchon, who was relieved to find that his colleague had so easily accepted a subordinate role, was in for a rude awakening when Cassander discarded the pretence of acting the loyal chiliarch and fled with some followers, under the guise of a hunting expedition, first to Thrace and thence across the Hellespont to join Antigonus.

Before he left, Cassander had prepared his ground, discreetly canvassing for support both at home and abroad. He approached Ptolemy for an alliance and his agents had been in contact with some of his father's numerous old friends in Greece. More importantly, he had staged a spectacular coup by gaining control of the garrison at Munychia, the citadel of Piraeus. A feat accomplished by Nicanor, one of Cassander's most brilliant officers, who had been despatched with all speed to replace the previous commander before news of Antipater's demise reached them.[6]

Antipater's deathbed arrangements for a peaceful transfer of power were already coming apart at the seams. Polyperchon acted swiftly, calling a meeting of those great men of the kingdom whom he considered untainted by sympathy for Cassander. From their deliberations came policies and pronouncements that would have effect in all parts of the Macedonian empire. With Antipater's son receiving aid from Antigonus, it was necessary to find allies in Asia to counter this threat. Using his full authority as guardian of the kings, Polyperchon deprived Antigonus of his office and offered it to Eumenes, along with troops and money in Cilicia. That the Cardian had been condemned by a Macedonian assembly in Egypt was conveniently ignored. If Antigonus could use Cassander to occupy the guardian in Europe, he could use Eumenes to distract Antigonus in Asia.

The other ally Polyperchon courted was much nearer at hand: that wife, mother and grandmother of three successive Macedonian kings, Olympias. She was in her native Epirus, forced there years ago after a dispute with Antipater and hardly likely to favour his son. Polyperchon would have been well acquainted with her from his years at Philip's court. She was invited to return to Pella, to take charge of her grandson Alexander IV and prepare him for the eventual assumption of power. As important as the prestige she would bring to Polyperchon's already-foundering guardianship was possible military aid from her Epirote compatriots. He was a surprised and disappointed man when she spurned his offer after consulting Eumenes, an old friend, who advised her to bide her time until the outcome of the struggle became clear. She remained ostensibly neutral, though from time to time tried to use what influence she had on Polyperchon's behalf.

These diplomatic initiatives had garnered mixed success, but it was a new threat from the south which forced Polyperchon into further radical measures. Antipater had controlled Greece largely through oligarchic cliques who had been happy to see the independence and democracy of their cities restricted if this price bought them Macedonian support for their domestic regimes. Now they were aligning themselves with Antipater's son (who had assiduously cultivated them) to sustain themselves in power. To counter, Polyperchon mobilised the opposition to the oligarchs by issuing a proclamation, in the name of the two kings, which would bring the democratic factions to the fore. Letters were sent ordering the exile of the governments set up by Antipater, extending the franchise to the poorer citizens of these communities and declaring Greece free from Macedonian control. Though it suited his immediate purposes, Polyperchon was unwittingly setting a dangerous precedent for any Macedonian who wished to retain control of mainland Greece.[7]

Having set the political agenda, Polyperchon needed to follow it up with military success. As so often, the city of Athens played the most prominent and dramatic part. Whilst its tradition as the great receptacle of Greek history and culture exaggerated its real political and military importance, the well-defended port of Piraeus, with its impressive naval facilities, made Athens an ally well worth having. The city was thrown into confusion when the declaration of freedom was announced. Much of the populace was enthused by Polyperchon's initiative but concerned over the presence of Nicanor at Piraeus, particularly now the whole of the port was lost to him.

Cassander was fortunate in his lieutenant, who showed rocklike loyalty in a situation where it was by no means obvious that Cassander's cause was sustainable. Olympias had written to Nicanor to persuade him to return the control of the port to the Athenians, but this had no effect. Soon, however, a more pressing threat appeared than the importuning of the old queen. Polyperchon had sent his son, Alexander, to try to evict the allies of Cassander from Attica and news arrived that he was fast approaching. Little is known of the previous history of this Alexander but he was to show considerable military skill and ambition in the next few years and now, in the spring of 318 BC, he took on responsibility as his father's first general and marched with a large part of the available royal army. Once in Attica, it became inexorably caught up in Athenian domestic affairs.

The aristocratic faction in Athens, who had prospered under Antipater's rule, found themselves reaping the whirlwind of Polyperchon's proclamation of freedom. Phocion, in particular, was suspected of having secretly collaborated with Nicanor in the seizure of Piraeus. Alexander's arrival in Attica gave the democratic faction the opportunity they wanted. At the citizen assembly, the old rulers were not only ousted but condemned to death and their property confiscated. These desperate men, finding no support in the city they had ruled for so long, fled to Alexander's camp before the sentences could be carried out. Alexander sensibly decided to defer the decision on their fate to his father as he had more pressing military business to attend to.

In the end, the guardian had no other choice but to rule against the aristocrats as he had no wish that the gates of Athens be closed against him, as well as those of Piraeus. An alliance with the current Athenian government was essential. Cleitus, the satrap of Lydia, recently fled from Antigonus and now in the service of Polyperchon, led Phocion and his colleagues back to Athens in chains.

They were found guilty and their death sentences affirmed; any chance of mercy was stillborn due to the presence of so many they had sent into exile and who had been reinstated as citizens by Polyperchon's decree. Among them was Phocion, the last of the generation who had struggled for power at Athens in the era of Macedonian expansion. Pragmatic attachment to that great power had stood him in good stead for many years but finally when Macedonian power fragmented between factions he ended as one of its victims.

The problem of Nicanor remained. The guardian's son, Alexander, had tried negotiations but these ran into the ground as Cassander's lieutenant played for time and waited for reinforcements. These arrived before the royal army could cover the short distance from Phocis to Piraeus. Cassander himself sailed into the harbour with a fleet of thirty-five warships and 4,000 soldiers provided by Antigonus. Nicanor was mightily relieved to see his commanding officer as he had by now become very concerned about his ability to hold the port against the full might of the royal army.

Polyperchon arrived too late; he found Piraeus almost impregnable. The port was bordered on three sides by the sea and Cassander's fleet controlled these waters. To assault the short land defences would be difficult and the army could not be fed for long in Attica. The city itself was dependent on imported corn and, with the sea-lanes blocked, famine seemed imminent. Polyperchon needed to move and so marched for the Peloponnese, leaving Alexander with adequate forces to blockade Piraeus. He expected a warm welcome as his army crossed the Isthmus of Corinth because news had reached him that many of the communities there had bloodily disposed of Antipater's oligarchic friends, and democratic factions had taken power on the strength of Polyperchon's proclamation of freedom.

Cassander tried to respond to show his friends he was not a spent force by making a descent with his fleet on Salamis. But the citizenry resisted and Polyperchon, sending a naval squadron from the Peloponnese, checked Cassander's move. It seemed, for the moment, that Antipater's son was isolated in his small toehold in Attica, but events at Megalopolis soon turned this around.

Megalopolis was the one major Peloponnesian city that had refused to remove its oligarchs and stayed true to the family of Antipater. Polyperchon could not allow it to hold out against the royal edict with impunity. He brought up the army with its elephants and siege train and soon had the city's impressive defences surrounded. Mining brought down three towers and the defences between, but an assault was baulked by a second wall the defenders had improvised in the breach.

A second attack was led by what remained of the sixty-five elephants Polyperchon had bought down from Macedonia but, against this, the defenders had improvised caltrops which disabled the animals and then picked off the mahouts with a rain of missiles.

Polyperchon virtually called off the siege, taking most of his army and leaving only a token force around the bloodied but unbowed city. The effect of this news was far-reaching and, almost from the instant of Polyperchon's embarrassment, his bubble of success burst. Morale within the ranks of the royal army was deeply affected and some of the mainland Greek cities defected to Cassander. Reverses at Piraeus and Megalopolis initiated an erosion of support that would dramatically change the balance of power in the Balkans.

Even worse was to follow. Polyperchon's problems on land were compounded by greater disasters at sea. His ally, Cleitus, the ousted satrap of Lydia, held the Propontis with his fleet to make sure that Antigonus could not send help across from Asia to Cassander. But Nicanor had been sent to work with Antigonus' navy and, after a fierce naval battle near Byzantium, Cleitus, despite initial success, was caught with his ships beached and annihilated. He was captured by Lysimachus' soldiers as he fled through Thrace and promptly murdered; an inglorious end to an illustrious career.

The attitude of the Athenians was indicative of how far the stock of Polyperchon had fallen with these setbacks. The city leaders realised their ally was in no position to evict Cassander from Piraeus, especially as he now had no fleet worthy of the name to call on. If they were to retrieve the vital facilities of their port, it would be necessary to come to an arrangement with Antipater's son. The terms agreed allowed Athens to retain a large measure of self-government and regain the use of Piraeus. However, Cassander kept his garrison in Munychia and he acquired the right to appoint an overseer of the Athenian government. The man he chose for this essential task was Demetrius of Phalerum, who was to prove invaluable to his cause in the years to come. Demetrius, a philosopher and an adroit political manipulator, offered the citizenry of Athens peace and prosperity as opposed to independence and adventure. Yet, even with such an inspired appointment, Cassander's hold on Athens rested ultimately on the spears of the Munychia garrison.

The triumphant return of Nicanor, parading the beaks of Cleitus' vessels, further emphasised the realities of power to a citizenry reluctant to accept that the great days of freedom and influence were over. Cassander's joy at the return of the victorious fleet was qualified by fears over the nature of his admiral's personal ambition. Nicanor's whole history had been one of loyal service that had proved instrumental in enabling Cassander to get his struggle against Polyperchon off the ground. Yet, this meant nothing to Cassander who believed that Nicanor was, in fact, putting his own men into Munychia in preparation for a coup. It is improbable that this represented any real threat to Cassander; Nicanor was merely re-establishing his authority over the garrison he had commanded since the war had started. But Cassander, trusting no one, had him arrested and brought before an Athenian assembly which dutifully condemned him to death.[8]

Cassander now had the upper hand in Greece and Polyperchon's already fragile position was further undermined by events in the north. His rule in Macedon itself was being challenged and total catastrophe loomed large for the veteran general. The moving force behind these developments was Eurydice, consort of King Philip Arrhidaeus. Antipater had not unnaturally forced her to take a submissive role, as the king's wife, on his return to Macedonia. After his death the ensuing strife gave her further opportunity for intrigue. She was now intent on overthrowing Polyperchon. Left behind in Pella when Polyperchon marched south, she was well placed to take advantage of his recent reverses. She cultivated the most important nobles and administrators left in the capital and, having created a sufficient faction, engineered the deposition of Polyperchon and the proclamation of herself as regent. She was certainly helped by Cassander's remaining friends in Macedonia and, even if there was no prior arrangement between the two, circumstances of mutual enmity to the guardian made an alliance inevitable.

Unfortunately for Eurydice, her actions triggered off the intervention of another queen, none other than Olympias. Hitherto, she had refused to commit herself totally to Polyperchon's cause and had remained in her native Epirus, observing but not overtly interfering with events in Macedonia and Greece. With Eurydice in power at Pella, she saw grave dangers threatening her dynasty. Alexander IV, her grandson, ought in a few years to be in a position to take over the reins of power and no regent or royal cipher could expect to maintain their position against a competent adult king. Eurydice's obvious ambition and ruthlessness was bound to mean that Alexander would never reach the age of maturity.

Olympias' first action was to send an embassy from Epirus to Polyperchon's army offering a formal alliance against both Eurydice and Cassander. This approach not only offered the support of the Epirote army but a lifeline in a situation slipping away from him and reducing him to a state of total inactivity and indecision. Polyperchon was clearly a man of some talent and energy but he seemed at his best when under the direction of others; when final responsibility rested on his own shoulders any sense of purpose sapped away. He was still in command of a formidable army but, since the experience of Megalopolis, had done nothing, seeming incapable of stamping his purpose on events. Olympias was a woman who, whatever her failings, never lacked determination, and with the combination of veteran queen and veteran general the engine of the legitimist party once again sparked into life.

Polyperchon's itinerary from the Peloponnese is unclear but by the end of the winter of 318/317 BC he had joined Olympias and her cousin, King Aeacides (father of Pyrrhus), in Epirus. When they crossed into Macedonia in the spring it was in considerable force as the remnant of the army that Polyperchon had retained was joined by the Epirote army. Eurydice was taken by surprise; she evacuated Pella and retreated northwest towards Illyria whilst sending off appeals for help to Cassander in the south. Pella was entered and the young Alexander IV placed under his grandmother's protection. But Eurydice could not be allowed to remain at large and Olympias chased her down to Euia just over the Macedonian border in Illyria.

Eurydice had assembled a considerable army but, when the soldiers saw the wife of Philip and mother of Alexander coming against them, they would not stand. The unfortunate Philip Arrhidaeus was captured straight away but his wife took to her heels heading for Thrace (and possible refuge with Lysimachus) only to be captured just short of Amphipolis.

Olympias had intrigued for decades to impose her authority in her adopted country; she had confronted her husband Philip, argued with Antipater and had annoyed the preoccupied Alexander with her importuning, but now, finally, she ruled at Pella. Her power was soon untrammelled even by the presence of Polyperchon, the nominal guardian of the kings. The old general, shaken by recent disasters, recognised his inability to resist the will of his formidable ally and returned south to campaign against Cassander.

Unfettered, her reign proved to be short and bloody; the years of frustration, bitterness and humiliation had taken its toll on a personality which at the best of times had been unforgiving. With no limit on her power, she indulged in an orgy of vengeance. Some of the stories associated with her rule should not be taken at face value, as it was at this time that much of Cassander's propaganda about her appeared, as did many of the horror stories about Antipater's son.

Almost as soon as the reins of power were securely in her hands, the elderly queen had the hapless Eurydice and Arrhidaeus bricked up in an outbuilding with only the smallest of gaps for food to be passed through. Such gratuitous cruelty began to cause adverse comment amongst leading Macedonians. The treatment of Philip Arrhidaeus was considered particularly harsh as he had not been responsible for the plots his wife had hatched in his name. And, whatever his mental condition, the blood of the Argeads still ran in his veins. Olympias had always hated him for being a son of Philip and potential rival for Alexander's inheritance. Her attitude towards him had not mellowed with the passing years. But the pressures that Olympias now felt to treat the prisoners more humanely had the opposite effect. The queen chose to rid herself permanently of her grandson's rivals. She found recruiting suitable executioners difficult, her Macedonian subjects understandably reluctant to stain their hands with the blood of a popular and legitimate dynasty. Eventually, Thracian mercenaries were found who had no qualms about despatching Philip Arrhidaeus for sufficient reward. By using foreigners, Olympias hoped to deflect some of the opprobrium from her subjects on to her hired assassins. By Thracian knives, the life of Philip Arrhidaeus was ended. The hapless monarch had been king in name for over six years. In this time he had been toted about the world, used and abused by Meleager, Perdiccas, Pithon, Antipater, Polyperchon and his own wife, Eurydice. Always he had been without influence and, most probably, without the slightest glimmering of an understanding of the world of power politics he so reluctantly inhabited. He had had little peace of mind since Meleager had plucked him from obscurity during the confusion of the Babylonian assembly and now his sad existence was terminated by the very woman thought responsible for his original condition.

Eurydice did not long outlive him. Olympias offered her the choice of suicide by sword, poison or hanging. The widowed queen determined to end her life with the dignity befitting her royal status. She carefully laid out and cleaned the body of her husband, for in death she wanted him to look a king and, perhaps, give belated atonement for the shameful way she had treated him. This task carefully done, she hung herself by her own girdle.

Even with Arrhidaeus and Eurydice gone, Olympias' blood lust was unabated. She continued her vendetta against Antipater's family even though the old man was dead and his eldest son out of her immediate reach. Nicanor, Cassander's brother, was executed and the tomb of another, Iollas (allegedly the poisoner of Alexander), desecrated. A hundred of the most important Macedonians known to be supporters of Cassander were next on the death list. The disposal of political rivals was not uncommon at this period but this brutal purge stands out in its excess. In the long run, these acts of ruthless cruelty did little to enhance her cause, many feeling she had gone beyond the bounds of respectability.

During these upheavals Cassander had remained in Greece and, with

Polyperchon absent, had some success in regaining hegemony in the Peloponnese. Not that all had gone his way, some places were prepared to resist him; indeed, he was preparing to invest the city of Tegea in Arcadia when news of events in Macedon reached him.

Olympias' treatment of his family and friends horrified him but outrage, in itself, was not the only cause for his return. He was well aware that Olympias' rule was now highly unpopular and many would greet him as a welcome liberator from foreign tyranny. Even so, there were good arguments for remaining where he was. Polyperchon's son, Alexander, was active in the peninsula with a strong force and to leave now was to risk losing all the support and influence that he had striven so hard for. Also, the route back home would be difficult and dangerous, with the formidable Aetolians ready to obstruct him. They had been subdued by Polyperchon in 320 BC and been loyal to the elderly guardian ever since. An Aetolian army was occupying the famous pass at Thermopylae, the gateway to the north. Despite this, Cassander knew he was nothing without Macedonia and he patched up a convenient truce with Tegea. Orders were given to his allies to guard against aggression from Alexander while he marched north across the Isthmus of Corinth, to the final confrontation with Olympias.

By the time he reached the vicinity of Thermopylae, Cassander had sufficient knowledge of the Aetolian defences to realise breaching them would be a difficult feat. His aim was Macedonia, not to capture strategic sites in mainland Greece. He had enough agents and allies in the port cities on both sides of the Euboean channel to be able to muster quickly a fleet of small boats and barges. With this makeshift navy, he transported his men by sea and simply bypassed the Aetolians, disembarking his army on the coast of Thessaly. Having overcome one hurdle, he now faced another. Polyperchon was waiting for Cassander in a strong position in the hills of Perrhaebia, on the left flank of Cassander's route through southern Macedonia. Once more, Antipater's determined son did not allow himself to be deflected from his main purpose. He could not leave this enemy unattended, as Polyperchon would then have a free hand to play havoc with his supply lines. Accordingly, he detached part of his army under Callas, to deal with the guardian, while the rest of his troops went straight for the heartland of Macedonia. Olympias was not content to await his arrival; she had other plans. The royal court was moved from Pella and her headquarters set up at Pydna. A town conveniently placed on the coast for a quick escape by sea, if things went against her.

Olympias had taken a large number of non-combatants with her, having left most of the army behind to defend themselves against Cassander as best they could. The general she chose as commander-in-chief was Aristonous, a man of great pedigree. He had been one of her son's seven bodyguards; a signal honour indeed when one recalls the other six; Hephaistion, Perdiccas, Ptolemy, Pithon, Leonnatus and Lysimachus.

Cassander was content to let Aristonous be for the moment; it was Olympias he was after. Either he moved with great speed or Aristonous and the rest of his officers were unable to mobilise their forces in time, as Cassander simply swept through the passes south of Pydna and entrapped the queen. He surrounded the landward side of the city with entrenchments and a stockade while a makeshift fleet was gathered to prevent any help from the sea getting through. Although Olympias was almost in his grasp, it was a considerable gamble he was taking as he faced threats from many directions. Cassander was staking all on cutting off the head of the opposition. In this he was certainly correct, for the response of her supporters was somewhat variable. Again, Polyperchon failed to make any impact on events. When Callas confronted him in Perrhaebia, wholesale bribery soon prised most of the veteran's army away. Polyperchon was humiliatingly forced to look to his own survival, rather than come to the aid of Olympias.

If Polyperchon had proved a broken reed, Olympias still had high hopes of succour from the land of her birth. She had sent to Aeacides, in Epirus, to come and aid her against Cassander and he was once more on the march with the Epirote army. Cassander dealt with this threat by detaching a general, Atarrhias, to close the passes from Epirus to Macedonia. Yet again, Olympias was doomed to disappointment as this help from Aeacides came to nothing. The Epirote army had no stomach for another war with Macedonia which was, in essence, no concern of theirs. Clearly their king's foreign ambitions were out of step with the wishes of his subjects. Neither officers nor men wished to leave their homeland on what promised to be a severe winter campaign and soon after they had started a mutiny broke out. Most refused to go on and Aeacides had no choice but to let them return home, while he led the few remaining men on to help his cousin. What he hoped to achieve with such a negligible force is unclear but to return to Epirus after the massive rebuff he had received was fraught with danger. Sure enough, the returning mutineers promptly staged a coup, exiling Aeacides' infant son, Pyrrhus, who was to become the greatest Epirote expansionist of them all.

Olympias' last hopes were pinned on Aristonous and his fellow officers in Macedonia. While Aristonous was at Amphipolis, on the mouth of the River Strymon, bordering Thrace, there were other generals in the key cities of the country. But none of them made any move to break the blockade Cassander had imposed at Pydna. The next campaigning season found them able to mobilise sufficient forces to pose Cassander plenty of problems and clearly their loyalty to Olympias was not in any doubt. The reason for their inactivity related to the military resources available to them. Apart from a limited number of garrison troops, their potential for taking the field against Cassander depended on calling out the national levy. They were unable to do so because of the time of year; like their Epirote counterparts, the Macedonian farmers would have been reluctant to don their arms with the campaigning season of 317 BC virtually over.

But, if winter made things difficult for Olympias and any chance of help improbable, Cassander had his problems too. Stormy conditions made it hard for him to effectively assault the city and he could not use his ships to attack from the seaward side. Consequently, he was forced to rely on starvation to win a victory. He cannot have been entirely happy to be tied up here; his instinct was to push on and secure Pella but he could not afford to leave Pydna, with its control of the coastal route between Mount Olympus and the sea, unconquered. In any case, an attack on the capital would have been a difficult undertaking in winter weather.

Olympias, in one way, chose wisely when she moved to Pydna for its defences were strong enough to withstand a long siege. But, her position was undermined by the hordes of non-combatants with her. The royal court included her grandson, Alexander IV; his mother, Roxanne; Thessalonice, a daughter of Philip II; and various members of the newly-exiled Epirote royal family. With them were their attendants, all of whom needed feeding and could contribute little to the defence. In addition, Olympias had the elephants that had survived the horrors of Megalopolis; they had crossed half the known world to meet their fate in the miserable cold of a Balkan winter. Under this burden, supplies soon began to run short.

Inevitably, when spring arrived many of her soldiers had had enough and wanted to get out. Olympias, in an almost impossible situation, had to acquiesce with their wishes; they left and went over to Cassander's camp. He treated them kindly, knowing full well that, even with the queen's unpopularity, he still had to win the hearts and minds of the Macedonian populace if he was to succeed her. Success not only depended on the defeat of Olympias but also victory over her generals in Macedonia, who were busy recruiting as the campaigning season had begun. Mindful of this, he sent an army under Cratevas to attack Aristonous in Amphipolis. Cratevas found the region well defended by a large army still loyal to the legitimist cause. Aristonous showed that he had not been a substantial figure in Alexander's army for nothing, as he soundly defeated the invaders on the lower reaches of the Strymon. He chased the survivors into a nearby town, where, after a short siege, Cassander's soldiers surrendered.

Nor was Olympias quite at the end of her resources. She knew she could not hold Pydna but if she could reach her friends in the north something might still be salvaged from the wreck of her fortunes. She tried to escape on a quinquereme that had been made ready in the harbour but Cassander got wind of the ruse and sent his fleet to capture the vessel before the queen had embarked. Hopelessly trapped, she reluctantly agreed to negotiate the surrender of both the city and her person. Olympias had little to bargain with and could only extract from Cassander a guarantee of her personal safety, after agreeing to order her generals to surrender the towns they held. Only Aristonous was reluctant to obey, not altogether surprisingly after his recent comprehensive victory, but agreed when he received written instructions from his queen. The soundness of his qualms were soon proved when, despite assurances regarding his personal safety, Cassander engineered his assassination by relatives of Cratevas; a sad end to a distinguished Macedonian.

By opening the gates of Pydna, Olympias sentenced herself to death. She would have been just as brutal if the positions had been reversed. For Cassander it was no easy task to eliminate the wife and mother of the greatest kings of Macedonia without bringing the wrath of the people upon his head. The act was given a cloak of legality by having her condemned, in her absence, by a rigged army assembly. Unsurprisingly, no one spoke in defence of the accused but if the required sentence could be easily arranged, finding an executioner was much more taxing. A stratagem was attempted in which she was to be killed while trying to make an escape but the stubborn woman would have none of it. Cassander next sent soldiers to execute her but they baulked at the task when they had to confront the famous and still-potent queen. The act was finally done when relatives of those she had murdered consummated their revenge by stoning her to death.[9]

In this fashion the most formidable of Macedonian queens met her end. It was not an inappropriate death, for Olympias had shown herself to be viciously cruel and vindictive when she held the reins of power. Yet she undoubtedly possessed energy, talent and a certain mystique which inspired loyalty in men as diverse as Eumenes and Aristonous. Antipater, however, had predicted disaster if she ever came to power in Pella, and he was proved totally correct. Perhaps, her character is best illustrated by her beloved Alexander's ambivalent attitude towards his mother. He wished divine honours to be paid to her after his death but he also, in a celebrated comment, complained that she had charged him a high rent for nine months lodging in her womb. In an age when not a few women made their presence felt on the world stage, this Epirote princess was the first to show that the distaff side could wield power with equal brutality and competence as their men.

Chapter 4

The Rise of Antigonus

Indeed, Antigonus, though it was his habit to make fun of himself about his one eye and once, when he received a petition written in big letters, he said 'This is clear even to a blind man', - the same Antigonus later put to death Theocritus of Chios when someone said, 'Stand before the eyes of the king and you will be saved', Theocritus replied 'the salvation you recommend is impossible.[1]

In 320 BC, the simultaneous demise of the two greatest leaders of the post-Alexandrian world meant a total collapse of what seemed to be settled at Babylon. Craterus and Perdiccas had both met bloody ends; their careers, begun so auspiciously, ended in fiasco. The hollowness of the intention to sustain a unified Macedonian empire under the Argeads had been exposed and it was another dynasty that would provide a political design for the generation to come. The founder of this line was Antigonus, the ageing satrap of Greater Phrygia. He emerged from virtually nowhere to dominate the next two decades. Nothing of any great substance is known of him until he had reached nearly sixty years of age, but from then to his death he showed the energy, talent and ambition to outdo rivals often more than twenty years his junior.

Antigonus' father was a Philip, of whom we know nothing except that he sired at least two other sons. Antigonus married the widow of his brother, Demetrius, naming his first son after him. The other brother, Ptolemaeus, saw distinguished service with Alexander and survived until 313 BC.[2] As well as these two there was a half-brother, on his mother's side, called Marsyas, who was a generation younger. An interesting character in his own right, he was educated with Alexander the Great and later produced three books, one on the history of Macedonia, another on Attica and the third on the education of Alexander. Unfortunately, they are lost but his proximity to the future king proves how close Antigonus' family were to the centres of power.[3] Antigonus himself was almost an exact contemporary of Philip II, probably born in 382 BC, and he played a full part in the eventful years of that king's reign. He was a serving officer in many of the campaigns of that era and in one of these he lost an eye. A wound that earned him the epithet 'Monophthalmus' (One-eyed), by which he was known for the rest of his life, but it was not a scar he carried easily. He had one man executed for calling him 'Cyclops' and always insisted that his image was shown in profile so the handicap was hidden.

He was a tall, hugely-built man and this bulk would turn to obesity later in life. Possessed of extraordinary vitality and stamina, on occasion he could be both generous and brave – qualities that made him a leader that Macedonians could respond to. Antigonus marched with Alexander into Asia, commanding the allied contingents, Greek soldiers who followed Alexander as hegemon of the league of Corinth. They came from the very cities that Macedonian might had brought low and, in the early part of the war, their loyalty was not-unnaturally suspect. Not intended as front-line troops, particularly as they might well find themselves facing compatriots serving as mercenaries in Darius' army, they did not play a distinguished role at Granicus and commanding them held no promise of advancement.

Some time after the battle, Antigonus was left behind by Alexander as the satrap of Greater Phrygia. Whilst this meant he was not to reach the Indus and the Oxus with the young king's all-conquering army, it was still a position of real importance, guarding their lines of communication. The province comprised the western section of the Anatolian plateau.

Alexander showed good judgement in detaching Antigonus for this task; the veteran warrior had just the qualities of tenacity required. But there may have been another reason for leaving him behind. He was of a different generation to the king, a hang-over from Philip's army, who may not have sat easily in the councils of a new age.

The garrison duty he had been assigned was to be no sinecure, for Alexander had far from secured Anatolia. More than just establishing himself, the subsequent campaigns that Antigonus and the other Macedonian satraps fought in Asia Minor, although largely unrecorded by contemporary historians, were of vital importance for the maintenance of Alexander's empire.

Antigonus had few first-class troops but nevertheless acted decisively in conjunction with the Lydian satrap, Asander (an adversary in the years to come), taking on the Persians and crushing them in three land battles and a naval battle somewhere near the Hellespont. This campaign of 332 BC changed the balance of power and now the Macedonians were able to take the offensive themselves.[4]

Antigonus decided on a joint campaign with Calas, the satrap of Hellespontine Phrygia, to expand their territories. Calas invaded northeast into Paphlagonia whilst Antigonus marched southeast into Lycaonia. They were entirely successful, bringing both regions under Macedonian control, which now bit deep into the heartlands of central Anatolia. Elsewhere, a Macedonian fleet gradually brought the whole of the Ionian coast to heel whilst the satrap of Cilicia, Balacrus, recaptured Miletus. Even if the eyes of contemporaries, and later historians, were always focused on Alexander, the victories of Antigonus and his colleagues were vital to the king's ultimate success.

By 332 BC, he was fifty years of age and had two sons, Demetrius and Philip, by his wife Stratonice. He must have thought that the most eventful years of his life were over and any remaining family ambitions would have to be fulfilled by his progeny. No word of his activities for the next ten years exists. The government and defence of his province were administered from his capital at Apamea Celaenae, on the headwaters of the river Maeander, in a region of lakes and mountains, ironically, not far from the battlefield where his extraordinary career would end in 301 BC.

In the reordering after Alexander's death, Antigonus was not directly affected. He was reconfirmed in command of Greater Phrygia by Perdiccas, but found himself with a new neighbour to the east. The province of Cappadocia had been allocated to Eumenes of Cardia and Antigonus, along with Leonnatus, was instructed by the regent to support the Cardian in pacifying his new satrapy. 'Antigonus paid no heed to the edict of Perdiccas', explains Plutarch, 'being already lifted up in his own ambition and scorning all his associates'.[5] This inclination to remain uninvolved was made impractical when Perdiccas himself came to impose Macedonian rule on Cappadocia. With the royal army ensconced close by his eastern frontier, for the first time in a decade Antigonus felt his vulnerability. He was arraigned for having failed to help Eumenes but placid acceptance of fate was not a characteristic of any of the Antigonids and he refused the summons to Perdiccas' headquarters. He lulled his prosecutors into a false sense of security by making a great noise of organising his legal defence, while simultaneously preparing his escape. Agents procured passage on some fast Athenian ships and during the winter of 321/320 BC Antigonus and his family fled to Europe. His arrival at Pella could not help but sour relations between Antipater and Perdiccas. But the impact of the exile's presence became decisive when he reported to his hosts that Menander, the satrap of Lydia, had given him information that Perdiccas intended to reject Nicaea, marry Cleopatra and intervene with his army in Europe.

In the ensuing civil war Antigonus played a peripheral, if important role. He invaded Caria with help from an Athenian fleet, then proceeded to Cyprus to oppose Aristonous, the Perdiccan commander there.[6] Little is known of these campaigns but at Triparadeisus he was on hand to rescue Antipater from the unruly soldiery and, when the officers of the armies assembled, the dispossessed satrap of Greater Phrygia found a number of factors working to his advantage. Many of the front-rank Macedonian leaders were dead or discredited; Craterus and Neoptolemus were no more; Pithon and Arrhidaeus had failed miserably in their role as guardians and Ptolemy, Peucestas and Lysimachus were far away. Antigonus was in prime position to reap his reward for recent services to Antipater.

He was to be given command of part of the royal army, together with the court and kings, for the express purpose of eliminating the remaining Perdiccans. These, chiefly Eumenes, Alcetas and Attalus, had been condemned to death by the army assembly in Egypt. Antigonus' power was not to be untrammelled; Antipater did not wish to see him become too mighty and able to threaten him in Europe. To this end, he attached his son, Cassander, as his deputy and Antigonus' authority was only to be for the duration of the war with the rebels; he was given no further lands, merely being reconfirmed in his old satrapy. By now Antipater was almost eighty and wished to return as soon as possible to the west. He and Antigonus divided the army and marched separately out of Syria, over the Taurus, and into Anatolia.

Neither force had a comfortable journey of it. Antipater found his soldiers still disgruntled over lack of wages; a matter that only neat footwork would prevent turning into mutiny on the crossing over to Europe. As his forces approached the western edge of the Anatolian plateau news arrived that this unreliable army was faced by a number of active adversaries. Eumenes, with the triumph on the Hellespont so recently behind him, was concentrated on the plains of Sardis. On the southern flank, meanwhile, Alcetas had established a centre for impenitent Perdiccans in Pisidia, desperate foes who could hope for little mercy and would be bound to fight to the bitter end.

Cleopatra, Alexander the Great's sister, had been established in Sardis for some time and her local significance for those campaigning in western Asia Minor was amplified for Eumenes by the legitimacy her name might give to his cause. Though a friend in the past, on this occasion Cleopatra could not bring herself to support him against the Macedonian royal army. Without this succour, even though his numerous cavalry could have given a good account of themselves on the Lydian plains, the Cardian dared not risk an open battle. He withdrew east and left Antipater with a clear road to Europe. One opponent had melted away but to deal with the other Antipater called on Asander, now the satrap of Caria. He was ordered to lead his own army out to crush Alcetas, who was established in the province to the east of his own. The upshot of this campaign was a hard-fought battle in which Asander met defeat. This victory gave Alcetas and his comrades increasing confidence; men who since the death of Perdiccas had been fugitives now felt themselves again a power in the world, a factor that would affect their attitude to cooperating with Eumenes in the future.

Antigonus, meanwhile, following on with the caravan of the two kings, took a route probably intended to allow an attack on Eumenes' strongholds in Cappadocia. Cassander proved a mutinous subordinate and by the time they reunited with Antipater in Phrygia the rift between them was unbridgeable. The two old generals finally parted somewhere between Phrygia and the Hellespont and the court of the two kings and Cassander returned with Antipater to Europe. The army detached by Antipater to his commander in Asia was not especially large, consisting of nearly 9,000 Macedonian foot, most of them the new levy who had come to Asia the year before, while most of the veterans of Alexander's wars went home for a well-earned demobilisation. Also left with Antigonus were several thousand good cavalry, including a high proportion of Companions, and something over thirty elephants.

Eumenes, in an effort to counter the expected Antigonid offensive, attempted to forge a united front with Alcetas, Polemon and Docimus, who had now recruited quite an army in Pisidia, but they were unable to agree on who should have precedence in command. Eumenes, dispirited, plundered the country to ensure his soldiers' pay then withdrew to winter quarters in his old satrapy of Cappadocia.

The volatile nature of the early successor armies is clearly demonstrated by events of the winter. Both Eumenes and Antigonus faced revolts from within their own ranks. Over 3,000 infantry and 500 cavalry mutinied and deserted the Cardian. But he soon had the situation under control. Sending his trusted comrade, Phoenix of Tenedos, with a larger force, they surprised the mutineers and brought them back to camp. The ringleaders were put to death and the remainder reintegrated into his army. Antigonus' local difficulty was altogether more serious. Three thousand Macedonians deserted and started plundering Lycaonia and parts of Phrygia. He managed to retrieve the situation but only at the cost of allowing the recalcitrant soldiers to return home to Macedonia under escort.

Despite this setback, in the spring of 319 BC Antigonus moved against the Perdiccans. He opened the campaign by attacking Eumenes. The Cardian was found encamped in the plain of Orcynii in Cappadocia with an army of 20,000 foot and 5,000 cavalry. Antigonus had fewer men but his infantry were of better quality and he had also suborned one of Eumenes' generals, Apollonides, who deserted with his cavalry in the middle of battle. This forced Eumenes to admit defeat and withdraw. He suffered 8,000 casualties and others deserted after the defeat, to the extent that he had few infantry left to him as Antigonus took up the pursuit. At least this allowed him greater mobility (even at one point threatening Antigonus' baggage train) as he occupied his opponent in this chase over the uplands of central Anatolia.

Eumenes headed further east, towards Armenia, but even this refuge proved to be beyond him as desertions mounted and Antigonus closed. Eumenes discharged all but 600 loyal retainers, suddenly changed direction and fled south to the Taurus Mountains, on the borders of Cappadocia, and took refuge in Nora for the winter of 319/318 BC.

When Antigonus reached Nora, Eumenes was well ensconced and the walls and cliffs were so sheer that he had no hope of storming them. Disappointed, he settled down to besiege the stronghold. Nora has never been identified but it was a small cramped place off the beaten track and neither Antigonus nor Eumenes would have been inclined to stay there longer than was absolutely necessary.[7] Negotiations were opened and a truce was concocted, while the issue of what to do with Eumenes was referred back to Antipater at Pella. The advantage in this for Antigonus was that he could leave a small force to keep an eye on his enemy's bolthole while the bulk of his army was available for use elsewhere.

While Eumenes had been occupying Antigonus, the other elements of the Perdiccans had been coalescing and growing in strength. The leader of this faction was Alcetas but it included Docimus, who had been satrap of Babylon for the short period between the death of Alexander and the reshuffling of the provinces at Triparadeisus. Commitment to the Perdiccan cause had meant his disinheritance but he had not waited to be displaced by Seleucus and made his way west to join in resisting the new regime. Another significant addition was Attalus, the brother-in-law of Alcetas and Perdiccas. After Triparadeisus he had left Tyre and tried to establish himself in Rhodes with the Perdiccan fleet. The independent islanders defied him and he retreated to join his brother-in-law in Pisidia.

When he heard of these developments, Antigonus determined on immediate action. His objective was Pisidia, a country of narrow valleys and precipitous tree covered ridges, and here he took a force beefed up by deserters from Eumenes' defeated army. A staggering forced march bought him in seven days to Cretopolis on the edge of the Perdiccans' country. Alcetas and Attalus were overconfident and attacked him straight away. But the rebels were outnumbered, 16,000 foot and 900 horse against Antigonus' 40,000 infantry and 7,000 cavalry, and soon found they could not stand against him. Attalus, Docimus and Polemon were captured in the battle while Alcetas was forced to flee to the city of Termessus.[8]

Alcetas was popular here, he had favoured local people equally with his Macedonians and Greeks and it had been appreciated. When Antigonus came up it looked like extracting Alcetas from his protectors would be a protracted business. However, though the younger men were committed to Alcetas some of their elders were more concerned with ingratiating themselves with Antigonus. Under the guise of an embassy, Antigonus worked up a plot with the older leaders and, withdrawing his army so the young men would come out to harass him, he allowed the older citizens space to organise the arrest of Alcetas. In fact, Perdiccas' brother anticipated them and took his own life when he realised his erstwhile hosts now intended to hand him over to Antigonus. When the old marshal brought his army back to the town, Alcetas' corpse was handed over to him and he perversely chose to mutilate it.

The young men of Termessus recovered the corpse, embalmed it, and gave a splendid funeral as testament to the regard they had for him. There is still a tomb in Termessus, decorated with armour of the period, which tradition tells is that of Alcetas. If so, it is a fine tribute to the loyalty of the city's youth.

Antigonus was thankful to be free of this difficult country and relieved that at least one of his enemies would trouble him no more. He had re-established his camp at Cretopolis, in Phrygia, when Aristodemus of Miletus brought him news that would once more throw the Hellenic world into turmoil: Antipater was dead. It was now late on in 319 BC, four years since the death of Alexander and no solution engendered by his generals seemed to hold out the hope of a lasting settlement.

To exploit the opportunities of this new world, the one-eyed veteran had a concentration of military might such as had not been seen since the last campaigns of Alexander. He could field 60,000 foot, 10,000 cavalry and thirty elephants. No other successor could rival such numbers, not even Polyperchon, the new ruler in the fertile recruiting grounds of Greece and Macedonia.

Antigonus first moved in overwhelming force against Arrhidaeus in his province of Hellespontine Phrygia. While he was campaigning by the Sea of Marmara, a boat from Europe arrived, carrying a fugitive of some importance. The passenger was Cassander, who was canvassing aid to retrieve what he regarded as his rightful inheritance from Polyperchon. Though on bad terms in the past, now their interests coincided. Antigonus wished to have a free hand to extend his rule in Asia, and a strong power controlling Macedonia and Greece could only be a threat to these ambitions. Cassander could entangle Polyperchon in domestic trouble and, with civil war erupting in the West, Antigonus could pursue his conquests elsewhere.

Antigonus still kept his official ties with the court at Pella, even while he provided succour for their opponents, though a complete rift could not be long delayed. He next turned his attentions to Cleitus, the satrap of Lydia, a province centred on Sardis and including the Greek cities of Ionia. Like Arrhidaeus, Cleitus could only leave garrisons in the more important cities and flee to Polyperchon with reports outlining the extent of Antigonus' plans. Ephesus resisted but fell at the first assault with assistance from turncoats within its formidable walls. In the harbour, four ships were discovered carrying 600 talents of silver on their way to Pella from the treasury in Cilicia. Antigonus confiscated this windfall, an act of daylight robbery which registered his final break with Polyperchon.

From now on, the forces arrayed against Antigonus would not only include Eumenes and the other dispossessed satraps but the whole array of the legitimist faction. Allied with Cassander, the first encounters of this open state of war took place on the Hellespont and although Antigonus involved himself with his normal energy and enterprise (destroying Cleitus in the process) they were only a prelude to the mighty struggles that would take him thousands of miles east from the Sea of Marmara.

The indefatigable Eumenes was to be the cause of Antigonus' travails and the struggle between these two became one of the epic contests of the ancient world. As the events of 318 BC unfolded, it looked very much as if Antigonus was going to inherit the whole of Alexander's eastern empire with scarcely any resistance. Eumenes seemed to all intents and purposes finished; confined to Nora, for what seemed like an age since the summer of 319 BC, he was not only unable to influence the climactic events outside but feared for his very life. The winter months had been both dreary and uncomfortable for him in his mountain eyrie.

The advent of spring brought little relief, for if the weather was better, the news from the outside world seemed to consist entirely of Antigonid triumphs. Desultory negotiations to bring about his release had been going on for some time with no real results, but with the death of Antipater political allegiances could be redefined. Free from the distant restraint of the dead viceroy's authority, Antigonus could see Eumenes as a talented officer who, with no other party to attach himself to since the demise of the Perdiccans, might be a valuable servant for his own ambition. He sent Hieronymus, the historian, who had earlier acted as Eumenes' envoy, into Nora with an offer that Eumenes and his followers would be released and his satrapy of Cappadocia returned if he came over to the one-eyed general's side. Eumenes gave pledges to Antigonus' officers who had held him caged for so long and he was allowed to retire unmolested to Cappadocia with his small band of followers.[9] There he found many of his old supporters amongst the local nobility still in power and prepared to recoup his strength. Old comrades, dispersed after his earlier defeats, returned and new units were recruited from people who had previously provided some of his finest cavalry. In no time at all his army had swelled to over 1,000 horsemen.

Whether there ever was a real commitment to Antigonus on Eumenes' part is open to question, but when dispatches arrived from Olympias and Polyperchon this link, occasioned by short-term convenience, was soon broken. The queen had written to ask his advice on what action she should take in the developing tussle between Polyperchon and Cassander, but it was the guardian's correspondence that was of far greater moment. Polyperchon was desperate for allies against the combined forces of Antigonus and Cassander and, knowing Eumenes' long-term loyalty to the Argead line, he hoped for his aid. A choice was offered of returning to Europe to become joint royal guardian or of taking up the fight against Antigonus in Asia. As part of the inducements to take on the latter role there were material incentives that were sufficient to overcome any qualms Eumenes might have over breaking his newly-made alliance with the Antigonids. Declining the risks of returning to Europe, he agreed to take over the resources on offer so much nearer to hand. He was given access to the great royal treasury at Cyinda in Cilicia to finance his war effort and offered 500 talents as a personal gift. Cyinda was one of the storehouses of the booty Alexander had accumulated in his campaigns in Persia and with the ready cash it contained Eumenes could hire the soldiers needed to open a new front. As important as the money were the credentials to command the grizzled veterans who had been left to guard this fortune. The infamous Silver Shields, the very cream of the Macedonian phalanx, whose actions would do much to determine the dramatic history of the following years.

When these portentous negotiations were concluded, Eumenes took his small army over the Taurus to assume the office of commander of the royal armies in Asia. Any inclination to dally in the safety of his own province of Cappadocia was quickly overcome by the news that Antigonus had sent an army to deal with him. Commanded by Menander, the ex-satrap of Lydia, this force was closing in quickly.

Once through the Cilician Gates, Menander did not follow and Eumenes and his retinue could move at their own pace as they journeyed to the camp of Antigenes and Teutamus, the commanders of the Silver Shields. These veterans had taken part in all the Macedonian conquests, stretching back to Philip's earliest campaigns, defeating all comers whether Illyrian, Thracian, Greek or Persian. They had fought in all of Alexander's great battles, provided the storming parties in his many sieges and been forced-marched over the greatest mountains and deserts of the known world. Many of them would have been over sixty but the next two years were to show that when deployed in the position of honour on the right of the phalanx, shoulder to shoulder and with sarrissas levelled, they could still defeat any opposition. At the forefront of the mutiny against Antipater at Triparadeisus, they had been sent east to Susa on punishment duty when Antigenes was given Susiane as his satrapy. Neither, he nor they, had remained long in that ancient capital but instead were ordered to bring the treasure stored in the city to Cynda.

Eumenes knew all too well that, while his generalship and sagacity was respected by all, he had never been sure of the loyalty of Macedonian troops. Alcetas had refused twice to serve under him and he had seen the desertion of many of his men to Macedonian rivals. As a Greek, and moreover the Greek who had killed Craterus, he was an alien to many Macedonian soldiers.

This matter of credibility in command is never more starkly in evidence than on Eumenes' arrival amongst the Silver Shields. These ageing men had experienced much in their long lives. Coming east to kill and plunder Persians, they had gradually been turned into a professional army rather than a national levy. But alienation from their homeland had only served to increase their xenophobic inclinations. They hated to see Alexander sullied by his adoption of the ways of the people they had defeated. The tiara, *proskynesis* and the introduction of Iranian companions had shaken to the core their world view. While Alexander lived he had seemed intent on shelving these old veterans but they were still a powerful force; agents from both Antigonus and Ptolemy were at that moment vying for their favours and it was little wonder that Eumenes received a lukewarm reception when he rode into their camp.

Any chance of success depended on Antigenes and Teutamus.[10] They had received Polyperchon's instructions to cooperate but it apparently needed a ploy from Eumenes to get them onboard. The Cardian, on the strength of a dream, persuaded them that if they held their military councils in the royal tent of Alexander then the dead king's shade would assist in their joint enterprise. This, for the moment, established Eumenes' position and donating his 500 talents from Polyperchon to the common treasury also did him no harm.

Antigonus' irritation at Eumenes' flagrant breach of the agreement that released him from Nora turned to anger and alarm when news of his revival in Cilicia reached him. With unlimited credit, the Cardian had sent his recruiting agents to wherever soldiers could be hired. The prospect of Eumenes gathering a large army at the vital strategic crossroads of Anatolia and the Levant was not one Antigonus could bear lightly. First securing his western flank, he turned once more to face his foe.

Antigonus hoped to surprise Eumenes before he had time to properly organise his newly-gathered army. He allowed no notice of his plans to be circulated and took with him only those troops that were immediately available and lightly armed. The resulting force consisted of 20,000 infantry and 4,000 cavalry; the elephants and heavy Macedonian foot being left behind. To forced-march these numbers across half of Asia Minor was an ambitious undertaking and Eumenes had many friends in Cappadocia who were quick to warn him. Eumenes had plenty of time to decamp in good order and march south into Syria.

Eumenes' initial intention was to recover Phoenicia for the kings but he was forestalled. Ptolemy had been steadily gaining control of the region and many of the strong fortified towns and rich ports were in his hands. Eumenes was quick to realise that any attempt to drive out his forces was bound to take more time than he could spare, or that Antigonus would allow him.

Antigonus followed him relentlessly and, now that the element of surprise had been lost, he brought up the elephants and heavy troops. He marched down the coast road past the battlefield of Issus. From here he traversed the Syrian Gates, the pass leading from the Cilician plain through the Amanus Mountains, into Syria. But, once again, Eumenes had slipped out of his grasp, heading for the heartlands of the old Persian empire, where he hoped to enlist the support of the eastern satraps. Antigonus' men, after another hard season's campaigning, settled down to winter in the pleasant surroundings of Northern Mesopotamia.[11] Whilst there, news arrived by letter from Seleucus that Eumenes was set to take control of the whole of Babylonia and he begged Antigonus to come and prevent him.

The risks of continuing to track the Cardian general were clear enough in an age where the only highway where speedy and efficient communication could be maintained was the sea. Antigonus might claim authority over inland satrapies of Asia Minor but his power was based on control of the coastal cities. It was this necklace of populous communities on or near the sea, in the Hellespont, Troad, Aeolia, Ionia, Caria, Lycia, Pamphylia and Cilicia, with their populations of hardy warriors or seamen, rich commerce and navies, that provided the sinews of Antigonid might. To march against Eumenes was to cut himself loose of the east Mediterranean littoral; not a strategy to be undertaken lightly.

Eumenes had enjoyed considerable success, winning through to the eastern satrapies. His army had taken the northern route when they left Syria to escape Antigonus. Recruiting the Mesopotamian satrap *en route*, they skirted south of the Armenian highlands, probably crossing the Euphrates and Tigris at the same points as Alexander had on his march east to Gaugamela. Eumenes had some trouble at the Tigris when some of his officers were careless in their work and unfriendly locals attacked his column, causing casualties and escaping with considerable booty. Further down the river he met resistance from Seleucus, satrap of Babylonia but, with his superior strength and ingenuity, Eumenes outwitted him and overran most of Babylonia almost as swiftly as his old commander had done over a decade before.

Eumenes, Antigenes, the Silver Shields and the rest of the army, now numbering 15,000 foot and 3,000 horse, wintered in several well-provisioned villages north of Babylon. Here Eumenes made diplomatic contact with the powerful men in the Iranian satrapies, whose support was vital if he was ever to have any chance of defeating Antigonus in battle. Recent developments in these lands were to make Eumenes' task a lot easier. Many of the provincial governors had already been working in conjunction against the intrigues of Pithon, the satrap of Media.

The assassin of Perdiccas had retained Media at Triparadeisus but it did not satisfy him. Soon he began to style himself General of the Upper Satrapies and set about making the boast a reality. He invaded Parthia and replaced the incumbent satrap with his brother. The rest of the rulers in the region reacted with exemplary speed, forgetting trivial differences in the face of this greater danger. The man they turned to as leader was Peucestas, satrap of Persia. This man's finest moment had been in Alexander's assault on Multan in India. He had defended his king's prostate, wounded body when a hoard of Mallian warriors looked set to end the king's career of conquest. His reward had been to be made the eighth of Alexander's bodyguards, a position held by only the closest friends and advisors. After that he received the satrapy of Persia, where he had remained ever since. He had had endeared himself to his subjects by his respect for their culture, sporting Median trousers and learning the Persian language. Now this talented Persophile, on hearing of Pithon's activities, raised as large an army as he could and marched with the other satraps to bring the turbulent intriguer to book. He was brought to battle in Parthia and superior numbers ensured the allied satraps' victory. Pithon, undone again by his rashness, made his way back to Media to regroup but Peucestas and the others followed and drove him into exile.

This was the situation that Eumenes' agents reported to him as he prepared to move from winter quarters. The news convinced him that here was the army he needed to defeat Antigonus. Peucestas and the other satraps had pursued Pithon as far as Susiane and he determined to rendezvous with them there. The Cardian's army, split into three columns, trailed through the hills of Elam towards Susa. To smooth his way, Eumenes took the precaution of forwarding letters from Polyperchon and the kings instructing the satraps to co-operate with him.

The combined forces of the satrapal armies consisted of 18,700 foot and 4,600 horse. Quite apart from Peucestas, there were a number of other formidable leaders present. The satraps of Carmania, Arachosia, Aria and

Drangiana had all contributed troops and Eudamus had come from India with the priceless asset of 120 elephants. The danger inherent in the approach of Antigonus kept this disparate collection of men together. Divided, they would be picked off separately by the new power from the west, as the satraps of Asia Minor had been. Eumenes could never be such a direct threat; he needed their support and the armies at their disposal.

The atmosphere in the satraps' camp, near Susa, can be imagined, with this group of strong, ambitious warlords used to virtual independence and with no history of loyalty to their new general. Peucestas would not have relished the loss of first place and, no doubt, others compared their own careers and lineages flatteringly against Eumenes. To counter centrifugal tensions and reinforce his claim to authority, the Cardian general extended the scheme he had used on the Silver Shields to include his new allies. They, too, were invited to the meetings in Alexander's tent, so strategy could be determined jointly, in the spectral presence of the man they still held at the centre of their articulated loyalty. Eumenes also had the advantage of legitimate access to the treasury at Susa that allowed him to secure the goodwill of the rank and file, by paying their wages up to six months in advance. Furthermore, he bound the great men to himself by borrowing, personally, large sums from each of them.

Antigonus was approaching with awesome power. Kept well informed of Eumenes' movements by Seleucus, when the campaigning season of 317 BC opened, he followed his rival's trail across Mesopotamia. Arriving in Babylonia, he was joined by Seleucus and Pithon who, if they could not offer much in terms of military support, at least had local knowledge of the terrain and conditions. A pontoon bridge was thrown over the Tigris and his army crossed the last great natural barrier between Antigonus and Susa.

Eumenes and the satraps knew that they were still outnumbered and decided to decamp when they heard of Antigonus' approach. Searching for terrain which would offset their numerical inferiority, they headed south. They reached the Pasitigris river, which flows down from the mountains into the Persian Gulf, bisecting the Persepolis-Susa road. Broad, deep and fast-flowing, it provided an ideal natural moat to impede Antigonus. Pickets were posted along the bank from the source of the river to the sea, to ensure the enemy could not slip by unnoticed. To cover this vast front was no small matter and, to this end, Peucestas summoned an additional 10,000 Persian bowmen from his adjacent satrapy.

Antigonus was not far behind, he had joined the Royal Road to Susa and, after crossing the Tigris, left a small force under Seleucus to capture that city and pressed on. By now it was late June and the heat was tremendous, hampering his progress as he was forced to march only at night. Even with this precaution, many soldiers, animals and camp followers dropped out through exhaustion and dehydration. Before reaching the Pasitigris he had to cross its tributary, the Coprates River. Eumenes had anticipated this and placed scouts in forward positions to report on the enemy movements. At the Coprates, Antigonus found himself in some difficulties, as his men could not find sufficient boats to transport the army across. On hearing this, Eumenes pounced. An attack with a picked force caught those Antigonids who had already crossed the river while dispersed, earning the Cardian a neat victory that cost Antigonus well over 4,000 men.

Antigonus was frustrated. He had wished to bring on one final combat, yet he could not even reach the enemy. The setback on the Coprates convinced him that it was futile to try and winkle Eumenes out of his position by force and another strategy must be tried. Accordingly, he withdrew the army to the city of Badace and took council with his advisers to determine his next move. Even this took its toll as the soldiers again suffered terribly from the scorching heat. He realised something must be done quickly to revitalise the army's sagging spirits. The lands of the upper satrapies were relatively unprotected with their masters away. Potentially a rich source of plunder, Antigonus decided to ravage them, both to encourage his followers and in the hope that the satraps with Eumenes would insist he leave his position to protect their provinces. The Antigonids set off north to Ecbatana, formerly the Persian king's summer capital in the hills of Media, where they could escape the roasting climate of Susiane.

Impatience almost cost Antigonus dear. He determined to march directly north over the mountains and here the Cossaeans, hardy and aggressive mountain men, demanded tribute so he could pass in peace. Against Pithon's advice, he refused, resulting in fierce fighting and some loss. Eventually Media was reached and in Pithon's old satrapy at least the battered army could recuperate.

As he attempted to repair his own situation, Antigonus was pleased to hear that his strategic withdrawal to the upper satrapies had not been in vain. Their rulers were anxious to return and repel Antigonus' invasion. Eumenes, reluctantly, had to acquiesce and leave his Pasitigris stronghold in order to keep the army together. They marched inland for twenty-four days before reaching Persepolis, the capital of Peucestas' Persia. They had no intention of repeating Antigonus' folly and went via pleasant country where supplies were plentiful and local bowmen and slingers could be recruited.

The enemy, though, was now near at hand, for Antigonus had broken camp in Media and set out for Persia. Eumenes at once moved his army after entertaining them to a lavish banquet. Unfortunately, he emulated that common Macedonian fault and drank too much. This so incapacitated him that he was reduced to following the army in a litter, while temporary command was taken over jointly by Antigenes and Peucestas.

After so many months chasing each other, the two sides finally came face to face. The ravine and river running between them made battle impossible and now, with both armies running low on supplies, they each manoeuvred to be first to arrive on the rich, unplundered plains of Gabene. Eumenes almost made it but his rearguard was caught by Antigonus' vanguard and he was forced to turn and draw up his forces in battle array. The Battle of Paraetacene lasted from afternoon to midnight and, after the initial clash of elephants, seemed to have been decided by the phalanxes where the Silver Shields, battle-winners still, prevailed. However, Antigonus, ever resourceful, sent his heavy cavalry behind Eumenes' victorious phalanx, forcing them to disengage.

By this time it was almost midnight and both sides were too exhausted to fight on. Although Antigonus camped on the battlefield and claimed victory, in reality he had lost far more men than Eumenes (4,000 as compared with a few hundred) and the next day had to withdraw to Media rather than pursue Eumenes, who was now free to enjoy the fruits of the Gabene region.

Eumenes, on the other hand, had much to be satisfied with. His own soldiers had fought remarkably well and his confederates had stayed loyal, despite the lack of a clear-cut victory and the withdrawal from the battlefield. It had been all hard campaigning since his men left Babylonia and, with the end of the year approaching, he led the army to the lush land of Gabene to enjoy the winter in comfort. It had been in competing for control of this region that the battle of Paraetacene had come about, leaving no doubt who had been the real victor.

At Gadamala, in Media, Antigonus had food for thought during the hiatus brought on by the end of the campaigning season. He was far from home, in the very birthplace of Iranian imperialism, without news of recent events in the west.[12] In terms of numbers, the Antigonids still had the edge but this would not long remain the case if they sustained more of the kind of casualties suffered at Paraetacene. Though their overall resources were far greater, much of these were tied up in the riches and manpower of the Levant and Asia Minor and this was not an age when the sinews of political and military might could be transported from Sardis to Persepolis with ease or speed. Laborious Iranian campaigns held no attraction for a man whose ambitions, by now, had certainly grown to include dominion over the Macedonian empire in all Asia, if not in Europe.

Whatever the mechanism of Antigonus' introspection, what was typical was his decision to break the deadlock with swift and decisive action. Winter had just arrived in the mountains of Media when he marched out again. Surprise was of the essence; it was twenty-five days' march to Gabene by good roads, but only nine if the army cut across the Dasht-e-Kavir Desert and Antigonus could hope his march would be undetected in such an inhospitable region. Ten days' rations were distributed and orders given not to light fires on the march. The problem was that after five days the men became casual, and the bitter cold meant fires were inevitably started. Locals saw them and alerted Eumenes to the approaching threat. The Cardian's qualities shine here; he did not panic but made the force that was with him light thousands of campfires to fool Antigonus that he had his whole army in hand. The ruse succeeded and the Antigonids moved off to where they could regroup to face what they thought was the whole legitimist array.

Having won some time, Eumenes called in his dispersed forces as quick as possible. Only the elephants nearly did not make it as Antigonus, aware of how he had been duped, attacked the animals as they returned to the main army. His raid on their caravan failed as a nimble and well-informed Eumenes dispatched a rescue mission to their assistance.

Frustrated and angry Antigonus may have been, but he had set his course to bring the enemy to battle and he intended to see it through. Daylight was short at this time of year and the weather changeable but all had to be risked rather than have the war drag on. He had measured his opponent's mood and realised that the Greek general would accept battle. Indecision and procrastination no more suited him as the Antigonids would only grow in strength with the passage of time. Eumenes could have avoided battle and retreated deep into Iran but his authority might not have stood the test of a policy that left the satrapies of his allies open to the depredations of the enemy. The two armies approached within four and a half miles of each other after several days of manoeuvre and there both sides encamped.

On a vast, uncultivated salt plain they met in the Battle of Gabene. As at Paraetacene, the Silver Shields, waiting with pikes levelled, would be a difficult nut to crack and the Antigonids feared that their own Macedonian veterans might not stand against the furious charge of these violent old warriors. Again, they took up their usual positions: Antigonus and Demetrius with the companions and heavy cavalry on the right wing; Pithon on the other side with his Medes and Parthians; and the infantry with the elephants in front of them in the centre. Both sides had about 40,000 men, with Eumenes short of cavalry, though he had sixty elephants to Antigonus' thirty. After the elephants had jousted to open the fight, the Silver Shields cut like a knife through the opposition phalanx. The cavalry mêlées also held high drama but, decisively, a party of Pithon's troopers captured the baggage train of the legitimist infantry. Eumenes wanted to fight on but Peucestas, and the Iranian cavaliers he led, would not support him. Another great battle seemed to be ending in indecision. But, with the salty soil in everyone's throat, one thing became clear, both sides had decided to talk rather than fight on.

The elephants had fought hard, the cavalry had been important, but these parties would not decide the future. It was the infantry who had shed their blood and triumphed; they were the steel in the army and the Silver Shields, Hypaspists and other Macedonians would deal the casting vote in the fate of the campaign. These men turned from their bitter accusations against Peucestas and discussed amongst themselves how to retrieve the baggage train, which included not just their treasure but their women and children as well. The Silver Shields felt the loss more than most, as the camp represented for them both a form of home and the profit of years of peregrination over Asia. They discounted any ties to Eumenes and their other comrades and 'secretly entered into negotiations with Antigonus'.[13] They began from a position of weakness and, realising this, the one-eyed general demanded nothing less than the surrender of Eumenes' person. The two officers in command of the crack phalangites, according to one source, had even before the battle been so close to betraying Eumenes that the Cardian had taken the precaution of writing his will; an indication that there would have been little determination existing at command level to refuse the terms.[14]

The Greek general was disarmed and restrained and word sent to Antigonus that he had been taken. Officers came to take over the captive, but not before Eumenes was able to make a last appeal to his army: 'Is it not a dreadful thing, then, that in the hour of your victory ye should acknowledge yourselves defeated for the sake of your baggage...?'[15] Trying to shame the soldiers to revert to their old allegiance, or at least allow him an honourable death by his own sword, Eumenes addressed as many of the men as could hear. But they were disinterested or lacked the mettle to outface the Silver Shields. Even before the battle began, the allied camp had been rife with discord; not an environment where, in defeat, he was likely to find sufficient supporters who would fight to rescue him. 'Some wept', says Plutarch, 'but the Silver Shields shouted to lead him along and pay no attention to his babbling.'[16]

The man who had baulked Antigonus at every turn now stood before him in chains. Anger was not his uppermost emotion but relief that he need not chase him through the outermost reaches of Iran. Eumenes could not be another Spitamenes, who must be fought across the Oxus or Indus, and without his leadership the opposing army's high command was hopelessly fractured. They must flee or come to an accommodation with Antigonus. Kept captive 'as you would an elephant or lion', Eumenes' gaoler did not immediately decide how to dispose of him.[17] They had known each other at Philip's court and, if those attachments of sentiment meant little, there were voices in council that pressed for mercy. Nearchus and Demetrius argued he should be kept alive and made an ally as his value as an officer could hardly be gainsaid. But, against them was raised a chorus of Eumenes' old officers and allies who, having changed sides, would have been embarrassed if he had lived. Alive, he might gain power enough to revenge himself on those who had failed him in adversity.

In truth, it is difficult to believe Antigonus had any intention except to eliminate his prisoner. The Cardian's talents were plain enough but he had tried to recruit him once before and paid the price in two years' hard campaigning. Untrustworthy as a potential subordinate, he was far too dangerous to be left at liberty. Death was the only solution and, though the versions of Eumenes' going are numerous, Antigonus was not vindictive and sent his remains in a silver urn to his wife and children.

This was not the end of the executions. Antigenes was cruelly burnt alive in a pit and Eudamus, the satrap from India, eliminated.[18] Most of the rest of Eumenes' followers immediately enrolled in the victor's forces. From the jaws of defeat Antigonus had been handed victory and he did not intend to let slip the benefits of his good fortune. Uncontested ruler of most of Asia, he allowed his army to renew its winter rest in the comfortable villages around Ecbatana, the capital of Media.

In 323 BC, Antigonus had been only one of many satraps and senior officers, now his tenure at the pinnacle of power in the Macedonian world had begun in earnest. Yet, though Gabene marked the beginning of his imperial years, nothing he would achieve in the future had quite the drama of his duel with Eumenes amongst the mountains and deserts of Iran. It had been one of the great military contests of ancient times, comparable with Scipio and Hannibal or Caesar and Pompey; an epic contest that brought out each of Antigonus' qualities. Determination, invention, energy and bravery; he had shown them all but only succeeded by the skin of his teeth against an opponent who seemed to match him at every turn. Eumenes was always able to counter each stratagem and bring to nothing his opponent's remarkable forced marches and surprise attacks. Not that this is any slight against Antigonus, as the Cardian had no superior and few peers as general and warrior amongst the ranks of those who survived Alexander's wars. And he'd had the Silver Shields, a double-edged weapon, who had shown that while none could stand against them in battle, their capacity for disloyalty and treachery was in every way equal to their ferocity.

Chapter 5

Stalemate

The wickedest of the kings . . . was Cassander in my judgement; it was through Antigonus he re-covered the kingdom of Macedonia, yet he went to war against the man who had been generous to him.[1]

There is a story that Cassander had such hatred and fear of Alexander the Great that, long after the conqueror's death, he could not look at a statue of the man without trembling uncontrollably. At Babylon, shortly before Alexander's death, he had been publicly disgraced by the king. On an honourable mission to advocate his father's case against replacement he had been bemused by the whole business of *proskynesis*. Cassander, observing the practice for the first time, was perhaps unaware that Polyperchon and others had incurred the king's anger over the matter; he burst into laughter when some Persians prostrated themselves in their traditional way. While Cassander's response may have found a sympathetic echo in the hearts of some die-hard Macedonian traditionalists, Alexander was far from amused. Furious with rage, he seized him and rammed his head against the wall. This regrettable induction to the court was compounded later when the king, reacting to complaints from certain Greek communities, indicated the whole past administration of Antipater in Europe could well be exposed to censure if their charges were substantiated.

It seems almost predestined that the son of Philip and son of Antipater were bound to incompatibility. While Alexander's life followed a Homeric model in battle or the chase, Cassander never courted danger during his years of campaigning and at the age of thirty-five, according to one improbable story, he still had to sit, not recline, at his father's table because he had not achieved the ritual feat of spearing a wild boar without the aid of a hunting net.[2] The conqueror, one suspects, would have preferred death to such continuing public humiliation. The most extravagant fruit of the tradition that makes so much of the antagonism between the two men is the supposed plot that ended Alexander's life. Cassander is accused of carrying poison to Babylon, which his brother, Iollas, the king's cupbearer, administered at the party that saw the beginning of Alexander's fatal illness. There is no shred of real evidence for this allegation and it almost certainly originates from the vitriolic pen of Olympias years later. That Cassander left Babylon unmolested under no cloud of suspicion proves no contemporary considered the possibility of foul play emanating from the family of Antipater.

Whatever the truth of these centuries-distilled scraps of gossip and propaganda, what does seem unequivocal is that Cassander was a man particularly marked by his early setbacks. The experiences at Babylon and the final refusal of Antipater to entrust him with the reins of power had their effect on his psychological make-up. The scars of rejection and the shadow of Alexander that loomed over him formed a mature man who could be accused of paranoia at most, and at least a tendency to be suspicious of the success of his subordinates.

Such was the man whose fortunes were now at the crest; the kingdom his father had refused to entrust to him was securely in his hands. Olympias was dead and Polyperchon a discredited refugee in Perrhaebia. The only cloud to darken his horizon was the presence of Alexander, Polyperchon's son, in the Peloponnese. Pella had been won and lost by a bewildering number of contenders in the two-and-a-half years since Antipater's death, but now it seemed as if the Macedonians were happy to rest from war and intrigue under the son of the man who had governed them so well for so long.

Everything inclined Cassander to eliminate Alexander IV and his mother Roxanne but the dynasty's hold on popular imagination was still very powerful and the risks were too high, especially following his disposal of Olympias. He was mindful of the opprobrium that she had brought down on her head by the callous treatment of Arrhidaeus and Eurydice. Alive, the young king could be of use to him, a totem that allowed him to aspire to represent the rule of traditional legitimacy. The seven-year-old king and his mother were taken from Pydna and kept under house arrest at the citadel of Amphipolis. The young prince's court was cut to a minimum and he was denied the attendance of royal pages.

The true extent of their condition was probably not known in Pella and the fact they were alive was sufficient to quell comment in the political circles there. To further the image of a loyal royalist, Cassander retrieved the corpses of Philip Arrhidaeus and Eurydice and ceremonially laid them to rest in lavish and regal style. He also took the opportunity of the presence of some other royal remains to crown the spectacle. These were of Cynane, Eurydice's mother, who had been brutally cut down by Alcetas five years earlier. Now, in death, she unwittingly joined her daughter in helping Cassander to show himself a pious Macedonian, honouring the royal family that had presided over the country's rise to greatness.

But Cassander, not content with honouring the royal line, also wanted to attach himself to it. Here he was fortunate, for amongst the royal court that had fallen into his hands at Pydna was Thessalonice, a woman of the highest status. She was the daughter of Philip and half-sister of Alexander. Her mother had been one of the less distinguished of the much-married Philip's wives and she had been brought up comparatively unnoticed at the court of her father. Unlike Cleopatra, she had neither attracted nor sought attention from any of Alexander's generals. But, for Cassander, she presented much too good an opportunity to miss; she was an ideal partner. By marrying her, this scion of Philip's greatest servant connected himself to the Argead line itself. There is no doubt he was already contemplating removing Alexander IV and substituting his own lineage on the throne of Macedonia. Thessalonice would allow him to claim a crucial legitimacy when it came to putting his ambitions to the test of popular tolerance. Primogeniture was far from the rule with respect to Macedonian succession, but to aspire to the throne some link to the royal line was needed. His new wife would give him this by marriage, while the sons of such a union would have it through her blood.

With the confidence of this royal connection, the ruler of Macedonia now usurped a prerogative which must have been a strong indication to contemporaries of his ultimate intention. The establishment of new cities had been an exclusively royal activity; both Philip and Alexander had exercised it to an extraordinary extent. These were not communities founded, like the colonies of many Greek cities, as an outlet for excess population and to service trade routes, but specific tools of dynastic dominance. The population became clients of the founder, receiving lands to sustain their families and owing him military support and sympathy in return. They were reservoirs of strength, whether in the alien lands of Asia, or Macedon itself, where they had been crucial in breaking local allegiance to princes who might have rivalled the Argead line. In 316 BC, Cassander founded the town of Cassandreia on the southwest of the peninsula of Chalcidice. Cassander had great hopes for the city, intending that it should develop as his particular stronghold in what was still an unsettled land. Of more long-term significance, it was probably about this time that Therma (on the Thermaic Gulf) was re-founded as Thessalonica, in honour of his wife, and remains to this day the second city of modern Greece.

Like his father, Cassander preferred domestic administration and politics to risky adventures on the battlefield. He was unusual in that he never strove for military reputation like the rest of the Successors. He spent many years of his life fighting but always from necessity rather than inclination, and in the great campaigns at the end of the century he was happy to leave the military responsibility to others. Nevertheless, in the first year of his rule he was forced to take the field against Alexander, Polyperchon's son, who still had a powerful force in the Peloponnese.

Polyperchon himself had a miserable winter of 317/316 BC in the hills of Perrhaebia. The old guardian had entertained high hopes of Olympias retrieving her position and only on hearing of her death was he stirred into action. He slipped away with his few remaining followers and fled to Aetolia, on the way reuniting with Aeacides, the exiled king of Epirus.

These two discredited soldiers had some luck with the Aetolians. Their consistent distaste for whoever ruled in Macedonia made them willing allies against Cassander. On hearing the Macedonian army was marching south, they took up their customary position defending the pass at Thermopylae. The previous year when Cassander was hurrying north he had simply sailed round them, but now his aim was different; he could not afford to leave such an obstacle in his rear. His supply and communication lines had to be cleared. Painstakingly, Cassander forced his way through and debouched into central Greece. Advancing through Locris, the army reached Boeotia, where Cassander made a singular decision for a ruler of Macedon. He ordered the collection of the population of Thebes, razed to the ground by Alexander nearly twenty years earlier, and re-founded the city. Alexander's ferocious disposal of the Theban problem had horrified Greek sensibilities at the time but had the full support of his own people. They had seen the Thebans as doubly treacherous for deserting Philip to fight with the Athenians at the Battle of Chaeronea, and later for revolting when they thought that the newly-crowned Alexander had been defeated in the northern Balkans. While feelings may have abated over the intervening years, Cassander was still risking a backlash by this controversial action. But it was a highly popular move amongst many of the Greeks which was borne out when places as far away as Sicily contributed to the rebuilding programme and this could only do his cause good in the forthcoming struggle. Furthermore, new Thebes, like Cassandreia in the north, would act as a personal stronghold in central Greece.

With Athens already secured under the trusted guidance of Demetrius of Phalerum, Cassander could be well satisfied. But there remained the problem of Polyperchon's son, who was dug in at the Isthmus of Corinth. Like Thermopylae, this had always been a natural defensive position and Alexander would be hard to overthrow. Cassander, though, was nothing if not flexible and while he had dislodged the Aetolians at Thermopylae, he knew he could discomfit Alexander by bypassing him. From Megara he shipped his army the short sail across the Saronic Gulf to Epidaurus. From there Cassander marched to Argos, intimidated the city fathers into line and, having outflanked

Alexander, marched southwest across the peninsula, pressuring most of the places into submission through bribery, force or negotiation.

Cassander wanted a victory to enshrine his triumph in the south but Alexander would not be drawn out of his lair. He did not have the numbers to fight a battle and had to swallow his frustration at the sight of the coalition he had built up crumbling before his eyes as he remained ensconced in his isthmus fortifications. As the campaigning season closed, Cassander set off home leaving 2,000 soldiers in the Gerania hills, on the Attic side of the isthmus, to block up Alexander in the Peloponnese. He remained a nuisance, but hardly a threat as few communities in Greece were likely to take his part when Cassander's success seemed so complete.

In the East, Antigonus, a man already well advanced into old age, was, after the defeat of Eumenes in 316 BC, incontestably the greatest power in the Asian empire Alexander had left to his followers. No single rival could even contemplate pitting their strength against the one-eyed warrior and the army he now led into winter quarters in the Median hills around Ecbatana.

To secure and organise his newly-won eastern provinces was the most immediate task facing Antigonus and this complex undertaking was already being made more difficult by the incurable trouble-making of Pithon. After his failure to secure sovereignty of the Iranian satrapies, he had just begun to experience the richly-deserved discomfort of exile when Antigonus' arrival on the scene allowed a resurgence in his fortunes. No sooner had the army dispersed to its winter billets than he reverted to his old ways. Travelling amongst the off duty soldiers, he gave out gifts and promises of preferment in preparation for a coup to overthrow and replace Antigonus. But Antigonus, well informed, ordered Pithon to report to him on the pretext of discussing plans for the next campaign. Pithon had hardly reached the gates of the camp when he was summarily arrested, quickly convicted by a council of officers and executed, ending a career memorable for its restless and incompetent conspiracy.

Having settled Median affairs, and after rifling 5,000 talents of silver from the treasury at Ecbatana, Antigonus moved in the new year to Persepolis, the heart of the old Achaemenid empire. On his entry into the city the populace hailed him as a king, a not-unreasonable precaution for a people who had provided considerable support to Eumenes.

Many old foes were allowed to retain their offices, notably the rulers of Carmania and Bactria, as well as Oxyartes, the father of Roxanne and grandfather of Alexander IV, in Parapamisadae. Long campaigns in difficult country would have been needed to dispose of them. But in the province of Persia the situation was different. The satrap, Peucestas, posed a particular problem; not only was he a great Macedonian warrior and former bodyguard of Alexander but he had made himself extremely popular with his subjects. He had gained their respect and had shown himself capable of creating a coalition of the disparate individuals who governed the upper satrapies; a combination that made him too dangerous to leave in power. Yet, it had been his alleged desertion at the battle of Gabene that had substantially contributed to Antigonus' victory. His reward was to keep his life, but not his satrapy. Added to the entourage of Antigonus, he was still alive twenty years later. But in all that time he seems to have played no discernible part in events until after Antigonus' death, when he regained favour with Demetrius.[3] It was unfortunate that the most genuine Macedonian admirer of Iranian culture should end his days so far from Persepolis.

If Peucestas engages our sympathies, the same cannot be said for the victims of Antigonus' final disposal, those grandfathers of treachery, the Silver Shields. These veterans had sold out the commander who had led them so gallantly from Tarsus to Persia and the point was not lost on their new paymaster. His fear of them was further exacerbated when he heard rumours that they had been involved with Pithon in his last dangerous intrigue. He designated the most unruly of the old soldiers to the command of Sibyrtius, the reinstated satrap of Arachosia. His satrapy was a land of high mountains and upland valleys situated between the Iranian plateau and the Indus valley, a province including what became the Northwest Frontier of British Imperial fame. From antiquity, it had been the home of warlike tribes who accepted central control with the greatest reluctance. Antigonus ordered Sibyrtius to use the Silver Shields against them, but with one important caveat. They were not to be sent out as one unit but split into small groups and despatched on separate missions with the specific intention that few should return.

The journey from Persepolis down from the Persian hills, north across the plain of Susiane to Babylon, took twenty days of comfortable marching. From Susa, much of the route was along the great Royal Road, where if the army could travel quickly so could the news of their approach. If Antigonus' arrival was not itself an unexpected event for Seleucus, the Babylonian satrap, the old man's attitude was. A demand for a detailed accounting of satrapal revenues persuaded the incumbent that a similar fate to that of Pithon or Peucestas awaited him. This eventuality he forestalled by fleeing his capital to seek refuge with Ptolemy in Egypt.

It was November 316 BC and Antigonus had been away in the East for almost two years. The other *Diadochi* were justifiably alarmed at his success and obvious ambition. While he had been in Northern Syria, envoys had arrived from Ptolemy, Lysimachus and Cassander. Prompted by the exiled

Seleucus, they came with a long list of demands, claiming with some exaggeration that they had been instrumental in aiding Antigonus in his recent campaigns by keeping Eumenes' allies busy and should share in the rewards. It is stated that Lysimachus demanded the Hellespontine provinces; Ptolemy, Syria; Cassander most of the rest of Anatolia and Seleucus to have Babylonia returned to him, claiming Antigonus had no authority to depose satraps at will. While these demands were so exorbitant that the authors could have had no expectation of them being granted, they wished to place the onus of blame for the coming conflict at the door of the returning general. He did not disappoint his rivals, giving the envoys short shrift and telling them to inform their masters that he would continue negotiations on the battlefield.

According to Diodorus, Cassander had asked for Lycia and Cappadocia. This has raised much discussion as to whether Asander, the satrap of Caria, was meant instead. Why Cassander should want territories so far from Europe is difficult to understand, but the alternative suggestion of Asander is usually dismissed on the grounds that he was not a leading member of the coalition against Antigonus and would be in no position to make such demands. But this is to ignore the evidence. Asander was probably a brother of Parmenion (both are designated as sons of Philotas) and also distantly related to Antigonus. He had long been a senior figure in the Macedonian army. As far back as 334 BC he had been made governor of Lydia by Alexander and in 333 BC he was active against Orontobates in Caria. The following year he combined with Antigonus to defeat the Persians in Anatolia. His last notice under Alexander had him bringing Lydian reinforcements to the king in 329 BC. He is recorded as satrap of Caria under Perdiccas. In status and power he was a comparable figure to Antigonus at the time of Alexander's death. After the settlement at Triparadeisus, Antipater made him responsible for leading the first assault on Alcetas. Logic suggests that Asander would make claims to both Cappadocia and Lycia which lay so close to his own province, a conclusion of much greater sense than one that sees Cassander making demands for lands so distant from Macedonia.[4] Antigonus' very success had created this coalition against him, like Perdiccas five years earlier. Then, as now, the battle lines were drawn between the centre and the periphery. Antigonus, the greatest commander of the day, with incomparably the best and largest army and an almost bottomless treasury, faced the other powerful despots who had emerged from and survived the conflicts following Alexander's death. These enemies had not been inactive during the past two years; nor had they waited for a formal rejection of their proposals before making incursions into Antigonus' territories. Asander had sent an army into Cappadocia and it was investing Amisus when Antigonus arrived in Cilicia, while Ptolemy had been strengthening his position in both Phoenicia and Coele-Syria.

The one-eyed veteran prepared for this new war with undiminished vigour. The huge treasure brought from the east was supplemented by 10,000 talents from Cyinda, while the lands that the Antigonids controlled produced annual revenues of 11,000 talents, a reservoir of wealth that was soon circulating to good effect. City defences were refurbished from the Hellespont to Syria and mercenaries hired. His agents, liberally supplied with coin and gifts, were despatched to ensure the allegiance of friends and to make allies out of enemies where possible. The petty kings of Cyprus were contacted and canvassed for support while other envoys made sure of the important maritime republic of Rhodes.

Antigonus looked to the issue of sea power where he considered himself vulnerable. He desired hegemony over the sea that would complement his awesome power on land. To start on this massive enterprise he needed to win control of the great ports of Phoenicia. At the start of the campaigning season of 315 BC, Antigonus left his winter quarters in Cilicia and marched his whole army south to Tyre. Despite the awful treatment they had received from Alexander seventeen years earlier, once more the pride of the Tyrians caused them to refuse submission to this new conqueror.

While Antigonus settled down to a siege, preparations were put in hand to construct a war fleet virtually from scratch. He had few, if any, ships at that time and if he wished to face Ptolemy he would need to build hundreds of first rate war-galleys and man them with premium crews.[5] The cedars and cypresses of Lebanon were ideal for ancient ships but such was the extent of Antigonus' ambition that this local timber had to be supplemented with wood brought from the Taurus Mountains. Shipwrights and carpenters were commissioned from all the ports under Antigonus' control and the minor rulers of Phoenicia and Syria were dragooned into providing the labour and supplies that the huge enterprise demanded. Three great shipyards at Tripolis, Byblus and Sidon were the main centres of construction, towns with a tradition of shipbuilding and seafaring that reached back to a time when the Macedonians had hardly emerged from prehistory.

Neither the investment of Tyre nor the fleet construction programme was sufficient employment for Antigonus. A small force of 3,000 soldiers was all that was needed to contain the Tyrians and the army was of little use in ship building. Some were engaged to cut timber and transport it but by and large the fine army he had built up was letting its talents waste. Seleucus, now in the pay of Ptolemy, was harrying Antigonid encampments on the Phoenician coast and news arrived that other Ptolemaic agents were trying to subvert his new-found allies in Cyprus. No more incentive was needed for the general to act. Andronicus was left to command at Tyre, while Antigonus stormed south into Palestine. There Ptolemy had held sway since the death of Antipater, though his position had never been entirely secure. Many of the cities opened their gates to the invader when they saw his military might. Two stayed loyal, Joppa and Gaza, where the garrisons were prepared to fight for their pay. Joppa, now a suburb of Tel Aviv, was an important coastal town and would remain so until the Crusades. Gaza, famous to this day, was two miles inland and was one of those fortress cities from which the Philistines had commanded the coastal plain of Palestine when Saul and David roamed the hills. Alexander had experienced problems in his siege of the town because of the size of the mound it was built upon and had vented his frustration after a successful but protracted two month siege by dragging the corpse of the garrison commander round the walls of the city behind his chariot. Antigonus was not in the mood for such delays and his veterans assaulted both Gaza and Joppa and took them without fuss, incorporating survivors from the garrisons into his own army. The ease with which he took Gaza seems quite extraordinary, bearing in mind Alexander's experience. The likeliest explanation is that the mound Alexander built to overtop the city mound was still in existence and was successfully reused.

Antigonus, content with these successes and after reorganising his conquests and garrisoning them, returned north to the main camp at Tyre. The siege was to last for fifteen months, a measure both of the town's strength and Antigonus' determination. Its fall in 314 BC proved to be one of the first fruits of his fleet-building programme. Like Alexander, before him, the old marshal was unable to really affect the city until his ships were capable of sustaining a blockade. Ptolemy had been able to supply the city with impunity and it was not till the first vessels of the great Antigonid fleet were launched that this lifeline was cut. New Tyre had virtually no space uncovered by buildings, no free land to grow food or keep cattle, and when ship-borne supplies were no longer available famine was not long in coming. The citizens did not, in this instance, fight on to the end and, in consequence, Antigonus was less brutal than previous conquerors. He installed a strong garrison, however, to ensure he would not have to go through such a siege again.

Soon a fleet of 240 fully-manned ships was available, whilst more were still under construction. Half had been finished in Phoenicia, the remainder coming from allies. The Hellespontine cities contributed some while others came from Rhodes. The result was a technologically up-to-date force consisting of ten *dekeres* or 'tens', three 'nines', ten *penteres* or 'fives', and ninety *tetreres* or 'fours', the balance being made up of *trieres* (triremes) and smaller undecked vessels. This force was ensconced in the harbours along the Levantine coast from Joppa to Cilicia. Each port bustled with warships, while oarsmen and warriors queued up for the prime wages Antigonus could afford to pay. Naval supremacy had always been a matter of hard cash; to get the most skilful and experienced rowers the highest wages had to be offered.

Finally, with a force to challenge Ptolemy's control of the Aegean, Antigonus put his nephew, Dioscurides, in charge and instructed him both to support his allies and agents in the Peloponnese and to attempt to secure the Aegean islands that were such crucial bases for the enemy's fleets in the region. But the old man's first venture into naval affairs was not without its setbacks and this first year in a new element saw one of his squadrons destroyed by Ptolemy's admiral, Polycleitus.

The resources at Antigonus' disposal meant he could shrug off this reverse and 314 BC saw the fleets under Dioscurides still flying his flag in the Aegean. Large numbers of the island cities came over to his nephew or were captured by his marines. The Cyclades in the south of the Aegean were of particular strategic significance as they straggled southeast from central Greece across to southwest Anatolia. The power that controlled them both possessed a secure, well-protected sea route from the great Greek colonial cities of Asia Minor to the Peloponnese, Attica and Euboea and were well placed to block penetration into the Aegean itself by an enemy from the south. If Antigonus' fleet was strongly established here, it could frustrate communications between Ptolemy in Egypt and Cassander and Lysimachus in Macedonia and Thrace.

Nor was it just in the southern Aegean that his fleet took pains to establish itself. Lemnos in the north was an equally important base; a former Athenian colony, it was from there the routes to the Hellespont could be monitored and the crucial Pontic grain trade controlled. That this intrusion of Antigonid naval might was considered a major danger by his enemies was made clear, soon enough, when the Egyptian fleet combined with the Athenians in an attempt to drive them out of Lemnos. All this expedition actually accomplished was to indicate how dominant Antigonus' navy had become in the short time they had been at sea. The Athenian fleet was captured by Dioscurides and the Egyptian contingent under Seleucus forced to leave for the safer waters of Caria and Cyprus.

Dioscurides was not the only member of the Antigonid family who had accomplished great things. Ptolemaeus, another of the old man's nephews, also proved a capable lieutenant. Appointed as one of Philip Arrhidaeus' bodyguards at Triparadeisus, his only other previous distinction had been that he was a hostage of Eumenes at the siege of Nora, but in 315 BC he showed his mettle as a general. Sent to clear out Asander's invading warriors from around Amisus, he not only drove them out but also had the energy and enterprise to march to Bithynia, where the local people were fomenting trouble. Zipoites, the king of Bithynia, was attacking the Greek cities of Astacus and Chalcedon at the eastern end of the Sea of Marmara. His lightly-armed raiders were no match for Ptolemaeus' professional fighters and the cities were swiftly relieved. He made alliances with the grateful citizens of the area and took hostages from Zibytes to ensure against further trouble. On the way to Bithynia he had also found time to make a diplomatic marriage to the daughter of Dionysius, the tyrant of Heraclea, a vital Black Sea port. Antigonus soon required his nephew's presence elsewhere and he was directed to march to Ionia to protect the coast from an attack by Seleucus. This, too, he accomplished with great panache, forcing the ex-satrap of Babylon to raise the siege of Erythrae, an Ionian town across from the island of Chios, and sail away. With Ionia safe, it was only a short march south to his next objective, Caria.

In Greece and Macedonia, Antigonus' support had been the vital factor in Cassander's success, for it was with the one-eyed satrap's ships and soldiers that he had got his initial impetus. But in the two and half years that had passed, everything had changed. Antigonus had by now defeated Eumenes and dispossessed Pithon, Seleucus and Peucestas of their lands. After the abortive negotiations in Syria, it was all too transparent that Antigonus had designs on reconstituting the whole of Alexander's empire. Whilst Cassander had been a useful tool in defeating Polyperchon, he was now superfluous to Antigonus' plans. When envoys from Seleucus and Ptolemy arrived with an invitation to form a coalition against Antigonus, he needed little persuasion to join them.

Antigonus, typically, responded swiftly. He sent Aristodemus of Miletus to the Peloponnese, the soft underbelly of Cassander's realm, there to make common cause with Polyperchon and Alexander. Aristodemus was a life-long agent of Antigonus, his loyalty and acumen were qualities that marked him out and, though no military man, he had a breadth of imagination and quickness of thought that made him an invaluable diplomat and counsellor. His knowledge of the Aegean and Greece was extensive and with a sure hand he picked his way amongst local rivalries to construct a powerful coalition. Initially landing in Laconia in the south of the peninsula, with his purse full of eastern gold, he recruited 8,000 mercenaries. He needed the permission of Sparta to recruit but that fading power was only too happy to encourage any enemy of Macedonia.

This new development bestirred Polyperchon to leave Aetolia, cross the Gulf of Corinth and join Aristodemus in the Peloponnese. An alliance was consummated without delay and the deposed guardian was restored to something of his former glory as the Antigonid commander-in-chief in the Peloponnese. To cement this united front, his son, Alexander, sailed east to meet Antigonus and thrash out the finer points of their cooperation.

Alexander met Antigonus at the veteran's camp at old Tyre where he was treated with great ceremony. To bolster the campaign in Greece, Antigonus had arranged a Macedonian army assembly and proceeded to condemn Cassander and his actions. Amongst other things, they denounced Antipater's son for killing Olympias, marrying Thessalonice by force, ill treatment of Alexander IV and his mother Roxanne, and generally trying to set himself up as king. He was condemned for resettling the Olynthians, bitter enemies of the Macedonians, in Cassandreia and for the re-establishment of Thebes. He was ordered to destroy these cities, release the king and his mother and, most importantly, to yield authority to Antigonus who now styled himself as the guardian of the king. In part a fatuous propaganda exercise, the assembly also passed a decree which was potentially much more of a threat to Cassander.

This was a declaration of freedom for all Greeks, stating they were to be free of garrisons and foreign interference, a ploy familiar to Alexander, whose father had issued an almost identical decree four years earlier. For Antigonus to pose as a liberator cost him nothing and helped sow dissension between the oligarchic and democratic factions in the Greek cities.[6]

Polyperchon and his son were largely isolated, with little local support, as the towns of the Peloponnese were reluctant to risk the wrath of the powerful ruler in Pella. They had seen more battles and sieges in the last two decades than the previous eight and the desire for peace and tranquillity was growing even amongst these intransigent and bellicose citizens. But the very presence of this Antigonid intrusion was danger enough to bring Cassander down to defend his hard-won gains.

Cassander's main concern was the arrival of Aristodemus. He knew the problems a man with gold and a fleet could cause in Greece, having been in that very position himself, not so long ago. Determined to extirpate this incipient ulcer, he came south. Unlike the previous year, he found the Isthmus of Corinth insufficiently defended to stop him. He evicted Alexander's garrisons from a couple of fortresses in the area and managed to capture the port of Corinth, a notable coup, before pressing on southwest into Arcadia to attack Orchomenus. A faction in the city betrayed it to him and their reward was permission to slaughter their opponents, a vengeance carried out despite them having sought sanctuary in the temple of Artemis. By now the Macedonian army's progress was taking on the proportions of a triumphal march and the only consolation for the Antigonids was when Cassander reached Ithome in the southwest, he was unable to force its surrender and turned back. Still, it had been a fine campaign and in the high summer of 315 BC any opposition to the Macedonian ruler looked a spent force.

Not content with this solid achievement, the season was rounded off with an extraordinary coup. Alexander was approached about an alliance and, surprisingly, turned out to be very open to offers. He agreed to dump his allies to become Cassander's commander in all the Peloponnese; and this only a matter of months since he had returned from his meeting with Antigonus. That Alexander should be the subject of such attention is not in itself strange. He was now a man of much more potent reputation than his father. Since 318 BC he had been sustaining the fortunes of the family in the Peloponnese. He had found mixed success but never lost the support of his small but veteran army, and his personal contacts with powerful elements in many of the southern cities were second to none. His garrisons were strong around the Isthmus of Corinth, while his father's power centred on Messene, a far less strategically significant region.

For Polyperchon, who in four years had slumped from royal guardian to virtual impotence, finding that he could not even depend on his son was a setback that needed all his resilience to endure. He still had the support of Aristodemus and his 8,000 mercenaries but this was scant consolation. In the event, this fascinating situation, where father and son held the same commission but for bitterly opposed factions, did not last long. At the beginning of 314 BC, Alexander controlled most of the northern coastline of the Peloponnese. Cyllene in Elis was, however, refusing to kow-tow to Cassander's new Peloponnesian viceroy, so he attacked the place. He would have certainly taken it except for the arrival of Aristodemus who, having just arranged an alliance with the Aetolians, led his mercenaries back across the gulf and marched directly to Cyllene. Alexander was either ill prepared or taken by surprise, as Aristodemus not only raised the siege but drove him completely out of Elis. Flushed by his initial success he pushed east and drove Cassander's garrison from Patrae. Next, Aristodemus took Aegium with the aid of a faction in the town, but victory was soured when his mercenaries sacked the place wholesale, behaviour not best designed to ensure cooperation from other towns.

Alexander now fought back. At Dyme, another north coast port, the inhabitants had tried to wall up Cassander's men in their citadel. This place now became the storm centre of the whole Peloponnesian campaign. Alexander first re-established control but then Aristodemus' mercenaries stationed at Aegium recaptured it and watched impassively as the inhabitants, tainted with Cassandran sympathies, were massacred out of hand by local rivals. Alexander aimed to respond but any chance of a final confrontation proved academic as he was assassinated after marching out of Sicyon with his army. In his brief career he had shown himself a leader of some military talent and it was his misfortune not to have a wider stage to parade his worth. The assassins were Sicyonian patriots, but their hopes of independence were to be dashed from an unexpected quarter. Another remarkable Macedonian woman now showed her mettle as Alexander's wife took command of his army. Her first actions were decisive. This female warlord crushed the Sicyonian militia and proceeded to a ruthless purge, crucifying her opponents and strongly reinforcing the garrison of Sicyon, activity that earned her the name Cratesipolis, 'conqueror of the city', a singular honour for a woman.

The next year Antigonus' officer, Telesphorus, arrived with a fleet and army to add his weight to the opposition to Cassander.[7]A squadron of fifty ships and numerous infantry, released from the war in Asia, made straight for the Peloponnese. But, since the assassination of Alexander, the situation in the peninsula had changed. Cratesipolis had formed an alliance with her erstwhile father-in-law, Polyperchon. He had cut his Antigonid connection when Aristodemus had departed, taking his gold and what was left of his men. Telesphorus had hopes that the decree of autonomy issued two years earlier by Antigonus would still ensure some support when he landed. In this, he was not wholly disappointed. Recent convulsions ensured that in every community disaffected factions existed with good reasons to wish revenge on their rivals and willing to welcome any potential champion. Several towns went over to Telesphorus, but when his envoys read out Antigonus' decree outside the walls of Sicyon and Corinth the gates did not open for them. Cratesipolis' isthmus heartland was well held and without her cooperation the Antigonids could only hunker down in the Argolid.

Cassander's attention was now drawn to Caria, where he had heard of Ptolemaeus' activities with concern. He sent a force to aid Asander, a considerable army under the command of his trusted general Prepelaus. But he achieved little, losing a detachment of 8,000 under Eupolemus, who were scooped up wholesale in a surprise night attack by a well-informed and active Ptolemaeus. The success of his nephews on land and sea inspired Antigonus to lead the main army on a major campaign. He decided the time was ripe for a concerted effort to crush Asander, Lysimachus and Cassander once and for all. But his impatience almost led to disaster. Hoping to cross the Taurus Mountains in the winter of 314 BC, when the snow was still deep, he was forced to turn back after suffering great losses. The next expedition was properly scouted and the men equipped for the terrain. It was arduous but successful and Antigonus reached his old capital Celaenae, in Phrygia, with little loss and the army settled into winter quarters.

Spring of 313 BC allowed Antigonus to concentrate his forces for the year ahead and good weather saw the remainder of the fleet built in Phoenicia sail west. Medius, the admiral entrusted with this task, not only brought them safely through but captured thirty-six Ptolemaic ships on the way. The main army prepared to complete the conquest of Caria that Ptolemaeus had begun.[8] The old general's strategy was to establish firm control of the Maeander valley. This river not only watered some of the broadest and most fertile acres in southwest Asia Minor but was also the major route from the coast to the interior.

The great Greek cities of Ionia were already allies, with the exception of Miletus. Antigonus sent the ex-Perdiccan, Docimus, with a detachment to attack it whilst Medius blockaded the town from the sea. Miletus was held by Asander's men and whilst promises of freedom persuaded the townsfolk to let the Antigonids inside the city walls, a siege was required to take the citadel. While his officers were securing the mouth of the Maeander, Antigonus had taken the main army down the valley from the river's headwaters to Tralles. Its importance was that it sat at the point where a usable road to the south met the east-west route along the river valley. The town was taken by siege and Antigonus could feel he now held the key lines of communication for in and out of Caria.

South of Miletus the coast consisted of rocky headlands pushing into the Aegean. Ptolemaeus was sent to reduce resistance there while Antigonus himself had moved on from Tralles, continuing down the inland route to the city of Caunus. He wanted it as a major naval base and when Medius was sighted off the coast the citizens quickly submitted. Again, the citadel resisted but Antigonus, impatient, brought up his siege engines and sent in assault after assault; it soon fell, rounding off his invasion of Caria.

Asander's lands had been cut completely away from him. Now this satrap, who had been a great man in the Aegean and Anatolian world for almost twenty years, disappears from history without a word. Like Mausolus, he had tried to create a Carian empire that might compete on equal terms with the great powers of his day but, unlike his predecessor, left no monument to mark his passing.

Antigonus' strategy had been completely vindicated and his authority was virtually unopposed along the whole of the Aegean and Mediterranean shoreline of Asia Minor. Cassander could not fail to recognise the danger. His allies in Caria and Ionia had fallen before the military might and persuasive diplomacy of an enemy who threatened to establish control of the whole Aegean seaboard of Asia. Only the sea barred Antigonus' way and this Cassander could never hope to hold against his opponent's ever-increasing navy. In these circumstances, whether the isthmus held against Telesphorus or not would be irrelevant as the whole coast, from Thrace to Salamis bay, was open to an invasion armada.

This war to the finish would be a far different thing from skirmishing amongst the hills of Arcadia, the Argolid and Messene. The risk would only be accepted by Cassander if there was no other option. There were reasons for peace on both sides; Antigonus seeking to divide the coalition against him and Cassander wishing to be safe from intervention in what he regarded as his rightful domain. They met in person near the Hellespont. Antigonus was at the very height of his power and this, together with a natural arrogance, made him pitch his demands too high. Cassander would have done much to avoid war but not at the cost of his independence. Unprepared to even consider a position as vassal or client, the peace talks soon aborted.

When it became clear war was inevitable, Cassander prepared his defences as best he could. The peninsula, south of the isthmus, was left to its own devices as he secured his Aegean shore. If the Peloponnese was the barbican that defended the southern doorway into Greece then the island of Euboea fulfilled the same purpose to the east and would be the target for any Antigonid armada sailing from the ports of Asia Minor.

Cassander set out with thirty ships and sailed down to the northern tip of Euboea. The target was Oreus, a port commanding the channel between the island and the mainland. He put the town under siege but, as he was thus engaged, an Antigonid fleet hove into sight. Telesphorus, on hearing of the war in Euboea, had brought up twenty ships and rendezvoused *en route* with Medius and 100 vessels sent from the eastern Aegean. The Antigonids outnumbered Cassander four to one and early in the resulting engagement four of Cassander's ships were destroyed and many others near to being caught up in an awful conflagration. Forced to admit defeat, the siege of Oreus was raised. But maritime combat in this age was an unpredictable matter. The Antigonids on this occasion relaxed their guard and beached their warships almost unprotected. Cassander called up reinforcements from Athens and surprised the enemy sailors. Before they could react, his captains had sunk one ship and towed off three others as prizes.[9]

Antigonus heard this news with impatience. Another large fleet was despatched, 150 warships with 5,500 troops under the command of his nephew, Ptolemaeus. Ptolemaeus joined Medius and they established themselves at Bathys-the deep, near Aulis on the coast of Boeotia. The capture of Chalcis was decided on first, as it commanded the shortest crossing point from the mainland to Euboea. Ptolemaeus was intriguing with the local democratic faction to let him in the walls when Cassander, who was reinvesting

Oreus, was alerted to what was happening and forced-marched fifty miles to rescue the town. He sent out for the rest of his forces on the island to join him and a decisive confrontation appeared in prospect. But the crisis never broke as Antigonus again changed his strategy. Ever the disciple of the direct approach, he decided on an overland strike at Macedonia itself. For this he needed his fleet to ferry the army over the Bosporus. Medius was recalled and almost the whole of Ptolemaeus' navy vanished over the horizon on the orders of his uncle. When Cassander realised what this portended he knew the danger he faced was of a magnitude that he had not experienced since coming to power at Pella. The prospect of the main Antigonid army and its formidable leader marching on Macedonia through the forests of Thrace was a nightmare of altogether different dimensions.

Cassander, slipping out from Euboea to face his main antagonist, tried as best he could to shore up his position in Greece. He landed on the mainland at Oropus, in Attica, stormed the town and installed a garrison. Then he garrisoned Thebes and appointed Eupolemus in charge on the mainland while at Chalcis his brother, Pleistarchus, was left in command.

Ptolemaeus was directed by Antigonus to press the attack on Chalcis. Pleistarchus with few troops left and a hostile citizenry was compelled to sue for terms. Ptolemaeus, with Euboea now secure, was well set to intervene on the mainland. He did not garrison Chalcis, knowing the value of appearing as the sponsor of Greek freedoms. Then he drove out the garrison of Oropus and again left the citizens free of foreign control. Now the benefits of this policy showed clear dividends. Places from as far afield as Eretria in Thessaly and Carystus in southern Euboea sent pledges of allegiance.

Although assured of a friendly reception if he moved north, Ptolemaeus' turned towards Athens. Demetrius of Phalerum had been in charge for six years and had brought domestic stability even if the cost had been to exasperate nationalist sentiment. But with Cassander's garrison in Piraeus and Ptolemaeus on the border, it looked as if they would suffer between these two powers. The Phalerian managed, in fact, to negotiate a non-aggression pact with the Antigonid general. With his southern flank secured, Ptolemaeus marched on Thebes, threw out the garrison and again declined to put in his own troops. This victory march continued unabated and Phocis was next on his itinerary. He expelled Macedonian garrisons where he found them, and made sure friendly regimes were installed. With the whole of central Greece under his control, he marched on Locris, south of Thermopylae. He needed suzerainty there to isolate Cassander in Thessaly and Macedonia. The Locrians were, for the most part, happy to accept nominal Antigonid hegemony and only Opus had to be won over by force.

Cassander could only helplessly watch these events from Pella. In fact the main threat from Antigonus never materialised; Byzantine truculence had stopped him at the Bosporus. But, for the first time since the Lamian War, the ruler of Macedonia was no longer the predominant power in southern and central Greece. Outside of Macedonia, his influence was largely confined to Thessaly.

Fortunately for Cassander, in 312 BC Antigonus was forced by the defeat at Gaza to turn his attention to Ptolemy. For two years his son, Demetrius, had been left as viceroy in the Levant. At twenty-two years of age he was taking up his first truly independent command of a career that would dramatically affect all the successors of Alexander for the next three decades. Of all the generals mentioned in these years, only Demetrius and Pyrrhus of Epirus, with whom his life was so entwined, would be considered by contemporaries to be touched by the genius of Alexander the Great, though neither had been directly involved in that monarch's career.

If Demetrius' great qualities were apparent as a young man, Antigonus also had some inkling of his faults, as he was made to serve an apprenticeship in arms before being given his head. He had led a cavalry wing in both battles against Eumenes but under his father's overall command, and even now, in the Levant, he was not left without restraint. A council of veteran advisers were with him to guide his steps in the task of defending the Antigonid frontiers east of the Taurus. These notables included Nearchus, the admiral of Alexander; Pithon, recently arrived from his satrapy of Babylon; Andronicus, who had commanded at the siege of Tyre; and Philip, another veteran officer. All had served with Alexander and had the credibility and competence meant to ensure the headstrong young man would listen to their advice.

The forces left to Demetrius were considerable: 2,000 Macedonian infantry, 10,000 mercenary foot, 1,000 light infantry from Anatolia and Persia, 5,000 cavalry and forty-three elephants. This was no garrison but a large field army which, Antigonus expected, would be needed to counter Ptolemy's plans to invade the region once he had left. As it transpired, it was only in the campaigning season of 312 BC that Demetrius' position was threatened, when the Egyptian satrap took the opportunity of successes in Cyprus to test his mettle. Ptolemy raided some cities near the mouth of the Orontes in northern Syria and then moved on against Cilicia, where he took the city of Malus. He did not linger long nor occupy the place, a caution justified when Demetrius showed he had inherited much of his father's capacity for swift and decisive action. Taking only the cavalry and light-armed troops, he hurried north in a gruelling march intended to catch the enemy while they were still plundering Cilicia. This marathon lasted six days but the general found his quarry had gone when he arrived, so he returned at a more leisurely pace to his base in the south. This had just been a start for the young Antigonid, the months that followed would be extremely full, there would be extraordinary reverses in fortune, chivalric exchanges, an intensity of action and a geographic breadth of activity that would be a microcosm of his life.

The recuperation that the coming of winter normally presaged was to be rudely shattered both for Demetrius and his relaxing soldiers. Ptolemy had returned from Cyprus to Egypt but with no intention of conforming to the dictates of the season.[10] In a short time he organised an army to continue his assault on Demetrius while Antigonus was far away. This time he was determined on conquest, not plunder. Demetrius prepared to defend the frontier of his father's empire and concentrated the troops at Gaza straight from winter quarters. When he appeared before them prior to the battle, Demetrius was reportedly given a rapturous reception; he was the rising star, young and unknown enough to not have made many enemies or tarnished his reputation. But youthful enthusiasm and facile popularity were not sufficient to overcome the guile and experience of Ptolemy and Seleucus; Demetrius was defeated. He found himself not at the head of a mighty army but a fugitive who kept running for thirty miles through the night before reaching the safety of Azores. This had been a catastrophic episode, with Pithon and many close followers killed.

Demetrius had tasted disaster, the army his father had left him was almost totally destroyed, yet he now showed that energy and resilience, when his fortunes were at rock bottom, that would be so characteristic of his career. He sent to his father asking for reinforcements before turning to attempt to salvage something from the wreck of his first exercise in independent command. He gathered what troops were available, at Tripolis and from the garrisons in Cilicia and Syria, to create a field army around the stragglers who had made their way back from the rout at Gaza. More mercenaries were hired and military colonists called to the colours to bolster his capacity to stem the tide of Ptolemy's success, which had already reached Tyre and Sidon. When the situation looked at its bleakest, the Egyptian satrap failed to press home his advantage, leaving Cilles, one of his Macedonian generals, to reduce the remaining Antigonid strongholds in Syria.

Cilles still had a sizeable army to conquer Syria from his base in Phoenicia. But he underestimated Demetrius, discipline became lax and the soldiers marched as if on a triumphal parade. Demetrius learnt that part of the Egyptian force had camped near Myus, unprepared for danger. He forced-marched his scratch army and attacked before dawn. Almost without a fight, 7,000 men and a vast amount of treasure and baggage were captured. Despite this success, there were still large numbers of Egyptian troops around and Demetrius chose to withdraw into a strong position guarded by marshes and swamps to await the arrival of his father.

Although Antigonus had not hastened back to his rescue, he could not delay too long. The last few years had been productive enough, Caria was subdued and the coast of Asia Minor largely under his control. His fleet more than held its own in the Aegean, with federate allies of the Delian League providing the bases his navy needed to sustain its presence. His own armies and those of his allies were causing Cassander plenty of problems in mainland Greece and his recent agreements with the Aetolians and Boeotians offered further opportunities. What he had not been able to achieve was to crush either Cassander or Lysimachus and it had become clear that to accomplish this aim would mean several more years of hard campaigning. Against this had to be balanced the threat from Ptolemy and now Seleucus, who, since Gaza, was re-establishing himself east of the Euphrates. What havoc these two might wreak in the years to come, if he did not return with the main army, was the stuff of nightmares. Demetrius could only realistically be expected to conduct a desperate defence that in the long run could not be sustained without help. Antigonus could not risk the Levant with its rich trading cities that were the heart of his naval strength. Confident that, at least, Cassander and Lysimachus had plenty to occupy themselves with, he led his army out of Celaenae and onto the road to the East. He crossed the hills and plains of Phrygia and Cappadocia that he seemed to have been crossing and re-crossing all his life. It was spring 311 BC at the Cilician Gates and no snow or mud slowed the rate of the progress of the thousands of men and animals. From Cilicia, it was only a matter of days before his army travelled the easy road to the Orontes valley and a reunion with his son and heir.

His immediate objective was to recover what had been lost and the arrival of his veteran army soon accomplished this. Ptolemy's forces withdrew back to Egypt, razing to the ground many of the cities they had captured. With the enemy refusing to face him in Phoenicia or Coele-Syria, Antigonus prepared to follow into Egypt.[11] However, for this to be a success, some preliminary work needed to be done. The debacle of Perdiccas was all too recent a memory to point up the difficulties of invading Ptolemy's domain. One danger Antigonus wished to eliminate before attempting the enterprise was located where Palestine merged into the deserts of northern Arabia. The inhabitants of this region were nomadic Arabs, a people Alexander had marked down for conquest in his last days at Babylon. The petty kingdoms of these tribal peoples had failed to send ambassadors to the conqueror and he had not intended their temerity to go unpunished.

The Nabataeans lived on the desert flank of the route to Egypt and the Antigonids, father and son, wasted most of the rest of the campaigning season on a botched campaign against them. But, if this foolishness in the sands of what is now the state of Jordan did not completely scupper the project of Egypt for that year, then news from the east certainly did. Seleucus had taken Babylon and defeated the Antigonid army of Iran. For the first time since the demise of Eumenes there arose the spectre of a hostile power in control of the wealth and manpower of Mesopotamia and the Iranian plateau.

To knock down this menace every other task had to be shelved. Demetrius concentrated a force sufficient to crush the resurgent Seleucus, in the valley of the Baroda, at Damascus. Antigonus remained behind but he left his son with very specific instructions to get back in double quick time. Fifteen thousand phalangites and mercenary infantry supported by 4,000 cavalry marched from the oasis of Damascus, across the arid country to the Euphrates before turning to follow the river valley south; a week or so's journey down the route taken by Cyrus the younger and his ten thousand Greek mercenaries.

Seleucus' commander at Babylon had not tried to hold the city itself and when Demetrius arrived at the massive triple defences he found little immediate evidence of resistance. The town was semi-evacuated and only two citadels were held against him. Both were besieged and one was taken quickly but the other proved stubborn and it looked like a lengthy investiture would be needed to ensure its capture. This was exactly what had not been allowed for in Antigonid plans, a long-term commitment in the east had never been contemplated when so many enemies of the family ranged elsewhere. Demetrius had seemed to have made a good start to the war but, with no swift conclusion possible, he knew he had to go back. So the main army retraced its steps back up the Euphrates while 6,000 men were left to occupy Babylon under an officer named Archelaus.

The difficulties inherent in conquering his enemies in Europe were now understood. Nearly seventy, Antigonus was eager to create something permanent and each season showed military might alone was unable to secure it. No war or peace party, as such, existed in his council, only the two contradictory drives of an ageing man; desire to enshrine his achievements and the arrogance of a personality that so often cancelled out the other.

Arrogance and over-confidence had ruined the chance of a compromise before, but in 311 BC, a new understanding pushed for change. Failure to deal with the likes of Cassander and Lysimachus had been lesson enough and now the success of Seleucus meant a threat in the east existed that had to be dealt with. Gaza, alone, had not changed his policy, the Antigonids had known defeat in battle before; it was the experience of frustration learned against the multi-tentacled coalition that their own success had brought into being. Recognising he could not battle against all his foes at once, Antigonus now determined to split his enemies in the west from those in the east. He needed peace in Europe if he was to win in Asia.

In 311 BC, envoys, including Aristodemus, left for Macedonia and Thrace with word of the one-eyed ruler's intentions and they found a cordial reception. This time no face-to-face summit was convened. Prepelaus acted for Cassander on this occasion, and perhaps this made things easier, but both Cassander and Lysimachus welcomed the proposal for a cessation in fighting that would allow them peace to secure their domestic circumstances. Few secrets could be kept for long in the world of the Macedonian Mediterranean and Ptolemy's court at Alexandria was soon buzzing with rumours regarding this communication between enemies and erstwhile friends. Eager to ensure he would not be left to face the Antigonids alone, the ruler of Egypt hurried agents to achieve his incorporation into the treaty.

In a new environment, even Ptolemy's advances were accepted. A peace treaty was made although no serious attempts appear to have been made to resolve outstanding issues; Coele-Syria, the position in Greece and round the Propontis, all was left on hold. Cassander was enshrined as ruler of Macedonia and protector of Alexander IV, Lysimachus retained Thrace and Ptolemy was confirmed in possession of Egypt and Cyrene. An unconvincing declaration of the guarantees for the liberties of Greek cities meant little, but left each party with ammunition for the future. And the final fudge at the heart of the arrangement shone a light into the recess where Antigonid motivation was hidden. The details of the treaty found at Scepsis show the disposition of the East was left open.[12] Diodorus reports Antigonus was to have 'first place in all Asia'; woolly enough terminology in itself and Seleucus was not mentioned at all.[13] Learned debate has surrounded the fact of this exclusion but the reality must be that any attempt to reconcile the irreconcilable would have threatened the whole process. This Asian dilemma was not of key interest to Cassander and Lysimachus but, to Ptolemy it involved a man who was at least his protégé, if not his agent. The art of *realpolitik* gave both Antigonus and Ptolemy enough for the time being. The former could take breath to prepare to recover his territories in the East, while the latter remained free to support Seleucus in the coming war, if he felt it was in his interests and within his capability.

Chapter 6

Ptolemy

*For indeed, that prince was exceptionally gentle and forgiving and inclined
towards deeds of kindness. It was this very thing that most increased his
power and made many men desire to share his friendship.*[1]

Best known of Alexander the Great's successors, Ptolemy made himself first in
a line of Macedonian Pharaohs. An exotic and ancient glamour derived from the
traditions of Egypt, combined with the more accessible intelligence of the
Hellenistic mind, has made the dynasty he founded most attractive to the non-
specialist.[2] The Cleopatra image of sultry princesses stalking the pyramids gives
their story an impact on the Western European consciousness denied to the
other Hellenistic kingdoms. Equally, a concentration of scholarship on ancient
Egypt – at least since Napoleon's invasion of the Nile delta brought so many
extraordinary artefacts to the attention of Europe – has meant much more is
known about this state than the others. A wealth of papyri give insights into the
day-to-day existence of the river kingdom; the country estates, the labyrinthine
structures of local administration and even the mores of family life.

The founder of the dynasty's own reputation has been coloured by both his
unique role as very partial historian of Alexander's reign and from the
tendency of analysts to see him as the man who discovered the fundamentals
of the Hellenistic age; who first danced to the new tune that the sweep of
history played when the conquering king's early death ensured the dissolution
of the unitary Macedonian empire. He (it is supposed) understood that the
glorious but forlorn attempts of Perdiccas and Antigonus to hold together an
empire that stretched from Epirus to the Oxus were ill-fated, seeing that to be
successful and secure required that he should carve out a cohesive, rich and
defensible state based on the river that had seen the growth of one of
humanity's most ancient civilisations. If his intelligence and talents cannot be
denied, there is more than a suspicion that many of these conclusions on his
qualities and success have come down to us from his own writings. Like any
memoirist, ancient or modern, his output is inevitably suspect; the very act of
writing up one's own place in history should ring warning bells. Only the
defence, not the prosecution, is heard.

Ptolemy was not a balanced chronicler from the beginning. Not only do we know that the histories that depend on him exaggerate his contribution to Alexander's success, the problem is exacerbated because little remains to put up against them. In the pages of Arrian (based largely on Ptolemy's writings) he is mentioned on twenty-three occasions, far more than any other officer, save Craterus. Yet the evidence is unequivocal that he was never of the highest rank in Alexander's army. Curtius and Plutarch, who use other sources and dip more widely than Arrian, highlight him far less often.[3]

Mystery surrounds Ptolemy throughout his life and it is appropriate that controversy begins even from his conception. He was reputedly the illegitimate son of Philip II by a concubine named Arsinoe who, on being found to be pregnant by the king, was promptly married off to a Macedonian named Lagus. An extravagant tradition even claims that as an infant he was exposed by his step-father in a wood but was nurtured by an eagle, which persuaded Lagus to rescue the child, who was clearly destined for great things. A more probable account has it that Arsinoe was royally born herself and Lagus was happy to take on the child as an integral part of such an advantageous marriage. The mystery is compounded by the fact that Ptolemy made no attempt to advertise a connection with Philip that was bound to benefit him. Indeed, on the contrary, he specifically acknowledged Lagus as his father. The line of kings he founded were known as the Lagids and he even used this family name for a military order established in Alexandria in his later years. Only Curtius and Pausanias mention the connection with Philip but it has a certain credibility as the explanation for young Ptolemy's closeness to Alexander, the heir to the throne. Lagus is nowhere described as an aristocrat and is occasionally specifically designated as of low birth, not a father who could under normal circumstances have expected his son to be raised as one of Alexander's companions. That he was the prince's friend is indisputable; he enjoyed the benefit of Aristotle's tutelage and suffered from the association when exiled after the collapse of the Carian marriage intrigue.

In 334 BC, this close friend of the new king did not hold high office in the invasion army. No evidence exists of his having any military responsibility for some years after the Hellespont was crossed. His actions receive no mention in the great battles against Darius.[4] The first definite appearance is when he is enrolled in the king's bodyguard on the death of a Demetrius, one of many who lost their lives in the aftermath of the Philotas affair. From then on incidents recur from his own history, channelled through Arrian, that emphasise his particular closeness to Alexander, most of which are not corroborated by other sources. In the apprehension of the pretender Bessus, in the attempt to save the life of Cleitus the Black, in the revelation of the pages' plot, triumphing in single combat with an Indian chieftain, leading the storming party at the Aornus Rock and, most trivially, in the discovery of petroleum by the Oxus river in 328 BC, he alone is mentioned while other traditions mention the likes of Perdiccas and Leonnatus and sometimes don't support Ptolemy's involvement at all.

This is something more than normal self-aggrandisement. The pages of Arrian shout out that an attempt to rewrite history is being perpetrated. Ptolemy clearly intended to suppress anything detrimental to Alexander's reputation, to claim a special place for himself in the king's affections and to downgrade the importance of those who subsequently became his rivals. Certainly though, by the time of the Sogdian campaigns, he had become an officer of some importance, rising like so many of the new men of the king's generation.

Interestingly, it is soon after this that the pattern of exaggeration in Arrian is broken over an incident where Ptolemy was seriously wounded in India. Some weeks after the brutal combat at Multan, operations were begun against Brahmin-led resistance at the city of Harmatelia and, in this campaign, the rising general was badly hurt. Alexander, deeply concerned about his friend, made up his bed beside Ptolemy to attend him in the night. During the vigil, the king fell asleep and dreamed of a snake carrying in its mouth a plant that was an antidote to the poison affecting the wounded man's left shoulder. When he awoke, Alexander instigated a search to find the plant that when eventually discovered indeed saved Ptolemy's life. The story, almost certainly, is a fabrication but significantly it is not mentioned at all in Arrian but appears in Curtius. Perhaps the Greek historian's more sober approach drew the line at these credulous legends while his Latin counterpart was only too prone to indulge in such whimsy. Ptolemy, himself, may never have mentioned the story and most likely it came from one of the more colourful of the contemporary chroniclers, like Cleitarchus.

A debilitating wound would explain Ptolemy's frequent absence from the action during the rest of the Indian wars and the harrowing march back to Carmania. Arrian says nothing of him, possibly because he used Nearchus as his prime source for this period, while Curtius is satisfied with a cursory mention of Ptolemy receiving command of one quarter of the army that reduced the Oreitae, in present-day Pakistan, to prepare for Alexander's march into the Makran. However, the years in Sogdia and India had been good for Ptolemy's career; not, perhaps, to the extent that he wished posterity to believe, but he had certainly become an officer of importance in the greatest conquering army the world had known. At Susa his substance was recognised by marriage to Artacama, whose father, Artabazus, had been Alexander's governor of Bactria from 329 BC.

In Arrian's account of Alexander's last year, the partiality of Ptolemy's history becomes grossly apparent. Without doubt, he recorded events in the light of the need to legitimise his own status as the ruler of Egypt and to denigrate those generals who, in the years after the Babylonian settlement, became his deadly foes. The most noticeable case is Perdiccas who, in receiving Alexander's ring, embodied the idea of a unified empire (which Ptolemy's own actions first ruptured) and who invaded Egypt in the initial campaign of the Macedonian civil war. We look in vain for him in the pages of Arrian; for his involvement in transporting the body of Hephaistion to Babylon, for his accession to the post of chiliarch and for the deathbed transfer of power. All we hear of is Ptolemy's involvement in the winter war against the Cossaeans, but nothing of those far more significant arrangements that Alexander was forced to make to plug the holes left by the absence of Hephaistion and Craterus. We know from other sources that they were made, but for Ptolemy to acknowledge them would have granted legitimacy to his rival. He described the world left by Alexander as peopled by followers of the king who were all of equal status, but with himself differentiated as the closest in affection to the dead man. Patently not an accurate reflection of a reality in which the reputation and authority of Craterus, Antipater and Perdiccas far outweighed those second-rank men like Antigonus, Leonnatus, Seleucus, Lysimachus and Ptolemy himself.

This rewriting of history took place long after the events of that steaming Babylonian summer. Nonetheless, it is not unreasonable to extrapolate a coolness developing between Ptolemy and Perdiccas, even at that time, and it was with some mutual relief that the new governor of Egypt left Babylon in 323 BC. Travelling westwards with a caravan of friends and followers and a small force of Macedonian and allied troops for his escort, he would not have received much of an army, as his satrapy was well pacified and possessed its own garrison. It was not upon what he brought with him that Ptolemy would build his fortune, but on what he found on his arrival.

Egypt was a plum prize, steeped in an ancient past, and with a potential wealth only matched by Babylonia. Alexander's short stay there in 330 BC suggests more of the tourist than the ferocious invader. The journey to the oracle of Zeus Ammon at Siwah in the Libyan desert provides the drama during the months in Egypt, not great sieges or battles. It is not intended here to unravel the significance of this episode for Alexander but it is pertinent to note that the main details of the adventure come down to us from Ptolemy. It was he who described the king's caravan being guided by hissing serpents and his desire to advertise the connection between Alexander and Egypt would be served by exaggerating the mystery and significance of the desert pilgrimage.

Shortly after his arrival in Egypt, Ptolemy had Cleomenes, the previous satrap (and now appointed by Perdiccas as Ptolemy's deputy), murdered and his treasure of 8,000 talents confiscated. Now firmly established, Ptolemy showed he was not averse to expanding his frontiers. The direction of his new interest was towards Cyrene, 500 miles west of the delta.

The Greek communities there had remained independent before Ptolemy came to Egypt but had been particularly riven with internal strife. Thibron, a Spartan mercenary, aggravated the situation by his arrival after he had killed his paymaster, Harpalus, and taken his bodyguard of 5,000 veteran mercenaries from Crete. Landing near Cyrene city in 324/323 BC, he defeated the citizen army as the start of a tour of extortion round the communities of the region. But the freebooters fell out over the spoils and one of Thibron's officers returned to Cyrene city and stirred up the citizens against his old commander. A considerable war developed and Thibron recruited more men from the Peloponnese. A battle was fought with 30,000 claimed on the Cyrenean side, but Thibron's men still cut through them, dispersed all resistance and set about besieging the city itself. Up to this point, the Cyrenean war had been a local affair, but that soon changed. A democratic coup in the beleaguered city meant exile for many wealthy citizens. Some found refuge in Egypt where they implored their powerful neighbour for help, an opportunity far too good for Ptolemy to ignore. An intervention force was sent under Ophellas, a talented, ruthless and ambitious Macedonian.

Ophellas crushed Thibron and the Cyrenians who had made common cause to oppose him. The Spartan adventurer was captured and crucified while Cyrene and its neighbours came to terms. Now Ptolemy came in person and disposed of Cyrenean affairs with considerable sensitivity to Greek opinion. The cities were given a new constitution, of which we have an extant copy.[5] Citizen assemblies, councils of elders and some elections by lot were enshrined but, crucially, the real power in the place was made transparent as Ophellas stayed put with a considerable garrison.

This activity in the Libyan wastes had undoubtedly contributed to the stew of frictions that was bubbling to the boil in the first Macedonian civil war. But it was when Ptolemy feloniously dragged the embalmed body of Alexander to Memphis that the battle lines were finally drawn. He made what diplomatic arrangements he could to shore up against an uncertain future as the giants of

Alexander's old court sparred across the Hellespont. And it was as Antipater's ally and husband of one of the old man's daughters that Ptolemy entered a war in which his own domain would be the crucial cockpit. When Perdiccas was assassinated he made no attempt to take command of the royal army. Egypt had been made secure and Ptolemy was led by the logic of that country's interests in domestic security and sea power rather than the ephemeral dreams of universal empire. With Antipater at the head of imperial affairs, there seemed to be no particular points of friction that need lead to immediate conflict. The old regent showed no qualms about the Egyptian satrap's established sphere of influence extending to Cyprus and Cyrene and their marriage alliance had reinforced a concordat forged in the face of a powerful enemy.

The false dawn of the Triparadeisus settlement faded soon enough, but while it lasted Ptolemy was content to concentrate on domestic matters. In 319 BC, however, the death of Antipater and the advent of civil strife from Epirus to Cilicia offered him new opportunities. He stoked the embers by allying himself to Cassander against Polyperchon, whilst ordering his army out of Pelusium and across the frontier to Palestine in the first of many attempts to occupy this region. Ptolemy at first offered Laomedon, the incumbent satrap, a large sum of money to purchase the province, but when this was rejected he sent his general, Nicanor, who overran the country and captured Laomedon. The resourceful ex-satrap managed to successfully bribe his guards, however, and escaped to join the Perdiccan enclave in Pisidia. Coele-Syria and Phoenicia were easily occupied and it was probably on this occasion that (according to the Jewish historian, Josephus) Ptolemy's armies captured Jerusalem on the Sabbath, when the defenders supposedly refused to offer resistance on the holy day.

These Levantine acquisitions, though desirable, unfortunately took Ptolemy closer to the front line of the war. Eumenes, in Cilicia with the Silver Shields, posed the threat of an enemy with a considerable army encamped only a few days hard march from his frontiers. Ptolemy launched his fleet, not to go to the Hellespont (as Cassander had requested, to support him there) but to the coast near Eumenes' headquarters, in an attempt to subvert the Silver Shields. This importuning was unsuccessful and Ptolemy withdrew.

A two year period of silence on Ptolemy's career and events in his expanded dominions characterises all our sources from 318 BC. In this time, the Hellenistic Levant alone knew some kind of tranquillity while in Europe, Asia Minor and the upper satrapies the other Successors were at each other's throats.

The end of this hiatus was ominously advertised by the downfall of men well known to Ptolemy from his years with Alexander. Pithon had been eliminated, Peucestas removed from his satrapy and Seleucus sent fleeing from Babylon for fear of Antigonus' power. Seleucus arrived in Egypt with dire warnings that Ptolemy would be next to suffer. Whatever the analysis of Antigonus' long-term intentions, Ptolemy knew that he would soon enough be returning from inner Asia with an army of awesome power and the route he would take was bound to threaten Ptolemy's holdings in Coele-Syria and Phoenicia.

Antigonus' rejection of the settlement proposed by Ptolemy, Lysimachus and Cassander made war inevitable. It was a conflict that soon saw the loss of Egypt's Levantine barbican and the imbalance of military might meant Ptolemy, his armies driven back over the frontiers of Egypt, could only contemplate a counter strike at sea.

As soon as the weather permitted, Seleucus had been dispatched with a battle fleet to burn and harry the coast from Tyre to the Aegean, wherever the Antigonids or their allies were in power. Asander, in Caria, was sent an army of 10,000 men to help against Antigonid penetration into western Anatolia.

It was becoming a grinding conflict and though, as the inheritor of the fleets of Phoenicia and Egypt, Ptolemy had been ascendant at first, as each year passed the pendulum swung towards the man who had invested so much in shipyards from Sidon to the Hellespont. One episode suggested an end might be possible when an officer, named Polycleitus, went with fifty warships to help Cassander against Polyperchon. In fact, this clever sailor found he was not needed and instead ambushed an Antigonid squadron of newly-built ships on the coast of Pamphylia. These Rhodian-built vessels were escorted by an army that marched along the coast. Ptolemy's man bagged both army and fleet, making prisoner large numbers of sailors and soldiers. A summit was convened at Ecregma to talk about exchanging these prisoners and for a moment it looked like a real peace might be an option, but soon enough negotiations foundered with still no end in sight.

In 313 BC, Ptolemy decided on a personal intervention and that it was directed to Cyprus was no surprise. From 321 BC, he had been in alliance with some of the local rulers and had left a garrison of 3,000 men to support them. Then, in 315 BC, he had sent his brother, Menelaus, with 100 warships and 10,000 soldiers to turn Cyprus into an unassailable bulwark of Ptolemaic power. But, Cyprus was a difficult place to secure and a campaign was required to completely batten control on the island.

Some local potentates had been dealing with Antigonus so he decided the settlement of Cyprus needed to be secured in the most radical fashion. Heading the invasion force, he ruthlessly eliminated a number of princes and the city of Marion was obliterated. Ptolemy now decided to abandon his policy of loose alliances and he determined to raise Nicocreon, the king of Salamis, the greatest city on the island, as his commander-in-chief.

A meeting between Ptolemy and Seleucus occurred during this campaign. The latter was a persuasive man and his words may have played a part as Ptolemy dramatically changed the direction of his strategy for a war of conquest in the Levant and with it an attempt to reintroduce Seleucus back into his old satrapy of Babylonia. The new policy would not have been made on the hoof, much needed to be prepared, but it could be contemplated now Palestine and Coele-Syria was defended by the young, untried Demetrius, whose father was far off in western Anatolia. Troops and officers were withdrawn from the other fronts to swell an army of invasion and Seleucus himself brought veterans who had fought with him in the Aegean and Cyprus.

Ptolemy returned to Egypt before striking at the onset of winter to steal a march on his young enemy. The initiative showed great imagination for so usually-cautious a tactician.

The army Ptolemy inherited on his arrival in Egypt had not been large but subsequent efforts allowed him to field an invasion force of 18,000 infantry and 4,000 horse. Much of it was made up of Hellenic mercenaries, the best money could buy, though some men were apparently recruited from the subject population, probably as servants or skirmishers rather than front line phalangites or cavalry.

At the head of this band of mercenaries, exiles and place-seekers were Ptolemy and Seleucus, each being one of Alexander's few surviving senior commanders. Pelusium was the advance headquarters of the campaign and from there the direction of the invasion was already decided. Geography allowed no sophisticated strategy of manoeuvre, the awful desert to the south and the sea to the north dictated that the army follow the coast road. The plan was to take Gaza, the gateway to Palestine, and from there on to Coele-Syria and Phoenicia. It was only a few days march but in that time Demetrius' soldiers had been brought from winter billets to contest the intrusion at Gaza. Demetrius had to overrule the council of veterans left by his father to advise him. They worried over the size of the invading army and the qualities of its leaders but the young general still determined to fight. A decision that was, as we have seen, a disaster for Demetrius, with his war elephants falling foul of Ptolemy's anti-elephant traps and 8,000 of his soldiers surrendering to Ptolemy.

Antigonid military power in the Levant had been destroyed in a few hours and Demetrius was a fugitive with a handful of loyal followers to his name. But

Ptolemy was not fool enough to believe that in trouncing the son he had finished off the father, so he was not overbearing in victory. He not only returned the bodies of his enemies who fell at Gaza but he sent back Demetrius' personal baggage without ransom. The captured soldiers were sent back to Egypt to be settled as military colonists, while the invaders overran Coele-Syria and entered Phoenicia, where Sidon and Tyre were captured.

Ptolemy, of all his peers was, however, the most susceptible to cold feet. Though Demetrius' fortunes were in tatters, Antigonus far away in western Anatolia and the most important towns of Phoenicia, Palestine and Coele-Syria taken, still his policy was half-hearted. He did not stay at the cutting edge of the campaign but left an undistinguished and, it transpired, incompetent general called Cilles. Ptolemy and the main army withdrew to southern Phoenicia and when Antigonus appeared over the Taurus Mountains in the spring of 311 BC, they decamped altogether. A clever victory had not changed the fundamental balance and, at the start of the summer, Antigonus was settled with a huge army near the Egyptian border, more of a threat than ever; a circumstance that made it unsurprising that Ptolemy acquiesced in a Macedonian peace.

It was over Cilicia that Ptolemy first fell out with Antigonus, barely a year after the fragile truce had been agreed. Being so close to the vital island of Cyprus, it was always of strategic importance and to ensure his control, Antigonus had been putting garrisons into certain cities in flagrant breach of the agreement to respect the autonomy of Greek communities. Ptolemy's response was forthright; strongly-worded complaints were delivered to the Antigonid court while ambassadors were despatched to the other *Diadochi* to resuscitate the alliance against their old enemy. A military effort to redress the situation by sending an army to Cilician Trachea proved abortive; Ptolemy's generals managed to capture a few towns, but were swiftly evicted when Demetrius arrived with a larger force.

If the Cilician intervention had been something of a token gesture, elsewhere enterprises were pursued with greater seriousness. Ptolemaic hegemony in Cyprus had been enforced with some success in past years but, since the peace, Antigonid agents had again been distributing eastern treasure and advertising the benefits of their master's growing naval might to considerable effect. Nicocreon, the king of Salamis, had been the main plank of Ptolemy's power but he had died and Nicocles, the king of Paphos, was eager to take over as Cyprus' ruler with the aid of Antigonus.[6]

The response to such a dangerous defection was ruthless and decisive.

Menelaus, Ptolemy's brother, had returned to command the armies on the island and the Egyptian ruler sent agents who, after consultation with Menelaus, surrounded the king of Paphos' palace and ordered him to take his own life. When Nicocles realised pleas for clemency would be fruitless, he obeyed and in doing so began a train of domestic tragedy rare even in these bloody times. The king's wife killed her daughter and then herself to avoid dishonour at the hands of her enemies. Moreover, before she breathed her last, she enjoined the king's brothers to share her fate. These fraternal exemplars promptly locked the doors of the palace and set it on fire, perishing in the flames. As Ptolemy had guaranteed the woman's safety this orgy of self-destruction seems excessive, unless his given word was less of a golden bond than is often suggested.

Since the Perdiccan war, Ptolemy had frequently played the part of the spider king. From his lair in the Nile delta he had sent out agents, generals and envoys to plot with his friends and sow dissension amongst his enemies. Now, in 309 BC, he emerged to lead his fleet and army in an effort to build on the brutal but effective action of the previous year. The focus of his attention moved from Cyprus and Cilicia to the southwest of Asia Minor. He first directed his armada against the coast of Lycia, where he captured the towns of Phaselis and Xanthus. Exploiting the shock effect of his descent on this rocky coastline, where communication overland was then and still is today very difficult, he pressed on westwards. Caunus was occupied and it seemed he was set to overrun Caria as well. It is almost certainly in this campaign that he besieged the city of Halicarnassus.[7] It had become an Antigonid stronghold and crucial naval base that, together with Caunus, commanded the sea-lanes along the southwest coast of Asia Minor. Its importance was such that its loss could not be contemplated and Demetrius was sent to its relief with a large army. Ptolemy, forced to raise the siege, withdrew to the nearby island of Cos.

The Coans had been in Ptolemy's camp since the previous decade when Seleucus had used their island as a base for the Egyptian fleet. We do not know whether Cos was garrisoned, or if they were willing allies, but it was clearly a Ptolemaic strongpoint for controlling Aegean waters. While his warships were refitting and revictualling, Ptolemy received a communication of the greatest interest. Antigonus' nephew, Ptolemaeus, who had defected from his uncle's cause to Cassander, sent word that he was sailing to rendezvous with him at Cos. Whether he was acting as the Macedonian ruler's lieutenant or in his own right is unclear, but his adherence meant a powerful reinforcement for Ptolemy's campaign. Ptolemaeus was received graciously and his host, no doubt, learnt much to his advantage about the situation in mainland Greece and Antigonus' intentions in general. Cordial relations were, however, short-lived and whilst still on the island Ptolemy had his guest arrested and forced him to drink hemlock.

This was something of a damp squib of an exit for an individual who had been a great man in both the Greek and Asiatic Aegean for over five years. Ptolomaeus' career bore a stamp of high quality; in war he was swift, energetic and had never been defeated since he first emerged to drive Asander's encroaching army away from Amisus. His administrative and diplomatic skills shine out, from setting up a league of cities in the east Marmara to the welding of an anti-Cassandran alliance in all of central Greece. In this, and the shortness of his career, he brings to mind Alexander, son of Polyperchon, and the parallel holds true in their demise. Both turned against their own side on the instigation of Cassander and neither lived long after to enjoy the power and independence they so craved.

The justification for the execution was that Ptolemaeus was treacherously trying to suborn Ptolemy's troops by offering them bribes. Yet the neatness of the outcome for Ptolemy is in itself suspicious and there exists another explanation for both this and a number of other events that occurred at this time.

Evidence points to a rapprochement with the Antigonids. If this volte-face seems at first incredible, it would go far to explain a new direction that Ptolemy took in the years 309 and 308 BC. A sensitive nerve had been touched when Ophellas, the governor of Cyrene, had revolted in 309 BC. The rebel had made contact with the Sicilian condottiere, Agathocles of Syracuse, who was attempting to batten his rule on the empire of Carthage in North Africa. Ophellas was married to an Athenian noblewoman, a descendant of Miltiades, the hero of Marathon, and would in time end up married to Demetrius Poliorcetes. Ophellas had sought a formal alliance with the Attic city but, while nothing was ratified, many Athenians joined and fought for the rebel governor of Cyrene. Demetrius of Phalerum, Cassander's nominee, quite clearly failed to stop these adventurers being transported to Africa, which inevitably soured relations between Alexandria and Pella.

As for Ophellas, he met a predictably sticky end. Agathocles had promised him the kingdom of Libya if he helped him destroy the Carthaginians. Thus tempted, Ophellas set off for Carthage with a powerful army of over 10,000 men and the same number of non-combatants. After a perilous journey of over two months, Agathocles ambushed the adventurer and he was killed in a vain attempt to defend himself. His army was swiftly incorporated into the Sicilian's. Ptolemy, determined not to repeat his mistakes, installed Magas, his own step-son, as the new governor of Cyrene.

If these events turned Ptolemy away from Cassander and into the arms of

Antigonus then what more probable guarantee of good faith would the old marshal expect than the head of Ptolemaeus, whose defection had so weakened the Antigonid war effort in Greece. In 308 BC Ptolemy for the first time intervened directly on the Greek mainland. He sailed first to the large Cycladic island of Andros where he drove out the garrison before landing near the Isthmus of Corinth.[8] He set foot on the European mainland for the first time in over twenty years.

The key cities on the isthmus were Corinth itself and Sicyon, communities ruled by Cratesipolis, the widow of Alexander, son of Polyperchon, who had been governing this part of the world since the death of her husband six years before. It is a moot point whether she invited Ptolemy to the Peloponnese in the first place. That Ptolemy chose these two highly-defensible towns to establish a bridgehead suggests he was sure of a welcome. He 'took Sicyon and Corinth from Cratesipolis'[9], according to Diodorus, but we hear of no siege or escalade.

All this was a promising start to the Greek adventure and his next move showed it was Ptolemy's intention to remake the league of Corinth. Control of Corinth gave him both a physical and spiritual centre to mobilise the Greeks against Macedonia. He sent his envoys to the other Peloponnesian powers proposing a joint assault on Cassander's garrisons in Greece, and reaffirmed his commitment to the freedom and autonomy of the Greeks at the assembly of the Isthmian games. But, when it came time to stump up the money, provisions and presumably soldiers to prosecute the war, the Greeks completely let him down.[10]

Another setback also occurred elsewhere. Whilst supposedly allied to Antigonus, Ptolemy had been intriguing behind his back. The object of his attentions was Cleopatra, the sister of Alexander, who had been languishing in Sardis since the days of Perdiccas, when she was the matrimonial prize that tempted so many now-dead successors. Ptolemy's role in these events is obscure and whether he (or for that matter Cleopatra) really contemplated a serious bid for Macedonia is debatable. Whatever the real motives, the exiled queen would have served as a formidable talisman in securing Macedonian support for his adventures. But an attempted coup to spirit her away from under Antigonus' nose failed disastrously as the old man, discovering what was going on, had her killed in short order.

The upshot of all this was that Ptolemy offered to treat with Cassander who had been observing with alarm his old ally's antics on the mainland and was happy to accept terms whereby each retained what they held. The ruler of Macedonia could afford to accept Ptolemy's control of a few Greek towns as the price of the renewal of the alliance against Antigonus.

The government at Alexandria was aware that Sicyon and Corinth were luxuries, irrelevant to the real heart of Ptolemaic power. So, when Demetrius arrived in Athens in 307 BC, Ptolemy made no attempt to intervene to protect these holdings. But when Antigonus ordered his son to abort his Greek campaign and invade Cyprus the response was very different. This was an attack aimed at the jugular of Egypt's naval might.

Antigonus had been trying to undermine the allegiance of the petty rulers of the island for years, but now determined to directly confront Ptolemy. Demetrius re-embarked at Piraeus and sailed to Caria. He paused briefly to attempt, unsuccessfully, to recruit the Rhodian fleet to the cause, but reinforcements were duly picked up in Cilicia as the fleet coasted east along Asia Minor before making the short crossing to descend on the northern shore of Cyprus. He landed 15,000 infantry and 400 horsemen near Carpasia, beached his armada of warships and transports and set up a defended camp. Two local towns were quickly captured to make secure a base in the northeast of the island. Then Demetrius struck at the heart of Ptolemaic power in Cyprus by marching on Salamis. There Menelaus had his headquarters. The garrison consisted of 12,000 foot and 800 cavalry and with these Menelaus marched out to face the invader, just over four miles from the walls of the city. This army was not of the quality fielded by Demetrius and was overrun with the loss of almost a third of its number and driven back into Salamis.

Word was sent from Menelaus to Alexandria that the Cypriot army had been defeated in battle and that the whole island looked set to fall. Every arsenal and port was scoured to mobilise a navy and army that might take on Demetrius with a chance of success. Ptolemy personally commanded this, the largest fleet he had ever mobilised, and sailed as soon as the warships were fitted out. They made landfall at Paphos, a port on the west end of the island, far from the enemy concentrated outside Salamis. Sailing east, close to the coast, Ptolemy called on the allied cities he passed to provide warships for his forces. The fleet totalled 140 vessels when he reviewed it at the advanced base of Citium.

From Citium, it was only twenty-three miles overland to Salamis and Ptolemy slipped a messenger through the siege lines to Menelaus. The news was relayed that the Egyptian fleet would attack the following day and that his brother expected him to send out the sixty warships he had in Salamis harbour to join in the battle. These reinforcements would give Ptolemy numerical superiority and the priceless advantage of attacking the enemy from both front and rear. Demetrius, far from blind to this threat, assigned ten vessels to block up the narrow exit from the port to the sea, a precaution of considerable importance in the day ahead. He also took advantage of his control of the countryside to deploy cavalry along the coast, to rescue or capture men and craft that would be washed up on land after the battle.

Though one tradition suggests Ptolemy hoped to enter Salamis without a fight, there is no doubt he expected and prepared for a full-scale sea battle.[11] The resulting combat was a disaster for Ptolemy. Outmanoeuvred by Demetrius, his fleet was already in flight by the time a flotilla from Salamis managed to break through the Antigonid lines. The Ptolemaic position in Cyprus was now impossible. What allies he had left on the island were bound to transfer allegiance to Demetrius and, deprived of supplies from outside, he could neither pay nor feed the considerable army that was trapped in the city. The sources, again, differ but well over 10,000 foot and horse were incorporated into the Antigonid army when Salamis surrendered, and Menelaus withdrew to Alexandria with what small part of his army he could pile onto the remaining boats.

It had been the worst day of the ruler of Egypt's career; having committed all his military resources to this confrontation the result had gone disastrously against him. Diodorus is the most generous in accounting what was left of Ptolemy's defeated navy when he claims forty ships captured, eighty disabled or sunk, and twenty remaining to flee with their commander. To compound the discomfort the vessels carrying his treasure, personal furniture and mistress had also been captured. Nor was it just a battle lost when Salamis surrendered; it was the end of the contest for Cyprus, the island he had fought so long to dominate. He had not previously been a man to gamble everything on one throw, but now he had and little remained of his empire outside of Egypt when it came to count the cost. The Antigonids wasted little time in sweeping any residual Ptolemaic influence from the Aegean and it was to be years before Lagid vessels confidently travelled the sea-lanes between the Cyclades and the Levant again. Ptolemy worried, as he limped back to Alexandria, whether his rule would survive this setback.

It had been almost fifteen years since an invasion of Egypt had been tried and that had ended disastrously for the man who had instigated it. Antigonus had been planning to deal finally with Ptolemy for some years and only unexpected problems with the Nabataeans and Seleucus had prevented an expedition against Egypt in 311 BC. Now, the success of his son offered an opportunity that would allow him to attack with important advantages that Perdiccas had not possessed. After Salamis, his fleet would face no effective opposition and he fully expected this to be the key to the eventual outcome of the invasion.

The enterprise would be led by two kings and the army that gathered in the

Orontes valley in the autumn of 306 BC was the greatest military force that Antigonus had ever led. No less than 80,000 infantry, 8,000 horse and eighty-three elephants were mobilised to make an end of Ptolemy. Demetrius was to command the fleet, to give support on the long and arduous march to the south. He had 150 warships and 100 transports to carry the heavy baggage, siege engines and ordnance.

The task of overcoming the natural defences of Ptolemy's realm made it imperative that they chose a moment that offered the best possible coincidence of events to maximise chances of success.

To strike at Ptolemy before he had recovered from the blow of Salamis was one reason for beginning this campaign so late in the year but it was not the only one. Equally important was that the Nile flooded from mid-June to mid-September and it was then and just after that large boats would be best able to use the river's tributaries and the canals. Also, in autumn a prevailing wind blew south and this might blow a great armada up to Memphis, the centre of power at the apex of the delta.[12]

Ptolemy's enemies intended to have two strings to their bow. If they could not fight their way across the difficult delta terrain then the fleet could transport the army inland down the waterways. Ptolemy heard of the massive force as it moved through Coele-Syria and arrived at Gaza in late October. To reach the edge of the Nile delta the invaders would have to march for several days through waterless desert and cross the Sirbonian Bog. Crossing this terrain was difficult enough if left alone, but Antigonus feared that the Nabataeans might attack his communications. He cut loose, dumped his paraphernalia and marched fast and light to surprise Ptolemy. They took just ten days' provisions; it was risky but Antigonus intended that Demetrius' fleet could provision him by sea if necessary.

Early in the forced march the army lost men and animals at the Barathra Pits, an area of quicksand, and the fleet hit trouble. Near Raphia, autumnal storms struck the ships, transports were lost and others driven back to Gaza where a number of warships were damaged in the shoals. Nonetheless, the bulk of the fleet reached Casium, though here the lighter galleys suffered when anchored in heavy surf. Drinkable water was also scarce and disaster was only averted when Antigonus arrived with the army bringing water to slake their thirst.

The dusty and weary soldiers finally arrived at the easternmost tributary of the Nile. The sight of lush vegetation refreshed their spirits but less welcome were the well-prepared pickets of Ptolemy's army on the far side of the river. The attempt at surprise had failed and time was running out. Ptolemy was already well dug in behind this, the first arm of the Nile, and even if it was successfully negotiated Antigonus would find even greater resistance beyond. Antigonus now decided to turn Ptolemy's seaward flank with Demetrius' battered but still-powerful fleet. Most of the stragglers from the storm had returned and crack troops from the main army were embarked to attempt a landing in force further west along the coast. The first place they tried was Pseudostomon (probably an outlet of Lake Menzalah) but even here the beach was defended by catapults and a strong force of infantry, who held off Demetrius' assaults till darkness fell. Thwarted, the young Antigonid sailed at night and tried to land once more at Phatniticum, the later site of Damietta, where a break in the swamps and marshes made landing a possibility. But once more Ptolemy's men were there to defy him; they had followed Demetrius' progress through the night. With no more prospect of success, the decision was taken to return to Antigonus at Casium.

As if this was not sufficient humiliation, the weather turned against them and a storm from the north struck the fleet, forcing three 'fours' and some transports onto the shore, where Ptolemy's soldiers snapped them up. Demetrius got the bulk of his ships back to his father's camp but it was a defeated force which brought little to gladden the heart of Antigonus. An impasse had been reached, 'Since', Diodorus explains, 'Ptolemy, however, had already occupied every landing-place along the river with strong guards'.[13] Ptolemy's people clearly had been working night and day. With both their terrestrial and naval endeavours come to naught, the invader took counsel, not usual for a man renowned for his autocracy. Antigonus knew he had to retreat but was reluctant to be seen making this decision by himself, preferring the outcome to look like it had been forced on him.

This retreat from the Nile did not have the drama of Alexander the Great's withdrawal from the Beas river on the edge of the Gangetic plain, but for both kings these reverses ended an age of triumphs. Antigonus would never have conceded this himself and, indeed, there were still victories to come, yet the great days were over and the tide of success inexorably began to ebb away. Certainly, he had failed in the strategic purpose of destroying Ptolemy but, superficially, he had been little reduced in power when he ordered his men to pack up and return north from Egypt.

In the end, the unique defensibility of Egypt, combined with energetic and skilful generalship, allowed Ptolemy's survival against the odds. With the blow to his reputation from the Cypriot debacle it would have been easy for Ptolemy's government to lose its nerve in the face of the Antigonid host, but it didn't. The satrap and his officers had scraped together a defence just in

The Ishtar Gate of Babylon, near which the traumatic assembly after Alexander the Great's death took place. It is seen here as reconstructed out of excavated material and now in the Pergamum Museum Berlin. (*Author's photograph*)

An Egyptian relief of Alexander IV, Alexander the Great's posthumous son by Roxanne. He was proclaimed as co-king with his uncle, Alexander the Great's mentally-impaired half-brother, Philip III Arrhidaeus, but both were mere puppets. He was imprisoned by Cassander in 317 BC and murdered in 311 BC at the age of twelve. (*Courtesy of Jona Lendering/Livius.org*)

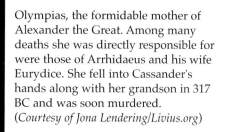

Olympias, the formidable mother of Alexander the Great. Among many deaths she was directly responsible for were those of Arrhidaeus and his wife Eurydice. She fell into Cassander's hands along with her grandson in 317 BC and was soon murdered. (*Courtesy of Jona Lendering/Livius.org*)

The most famous view of the so-called 'Alexander Sarcophagus' from Sidon, now in the Istanbul Archaeological Museum, which shows Alexander and some of his Companions battling Persians, possibly at Issus. (*Courtesy of Jona Lendering/ Livius.org*)

A detail from the sarcophagus. This figure is thought by many to represent Perdiccas, who became regent for Philip III and the unborn Alexander IV on Alexander the Great's death. Others have suggested it is Antigonus Monopthalmus, but he was a generation older than Alexander and the features appear to be of a younger man. (*Courtesy of Michael Greenhalgh, Australian National Univers*

A less well-known scene from the pediment of the sarcophagus, thought by some to represent the murder of Perdiccas by his own officers while campaigning against Ptolemy in 320 BC. (*Courtesy of Michael Greenhalgh, Australian National University*)

k cut tomb from Termessus in Pisidia, modern Turkey, believed to be that of Alcetas, Perdiccas' ther. Alcetas killed himself to avoid being handed over to Antigonus by the elders in Termessus. young men of the city, disgusted by this, recovered the corpse and gave it a magnificent funeral, ting this fine monument which can still be seen today. (*Courtesy of www.Cambridge2000.com*)

Bust of Ptolemy son of Lagus, later Ptolemy I Soter (Saviour) of Egypt. His hijacking of Alexander's corpse challenged Perdiccas' authority and sparked the first open conflict between the conqueror's former companions. Ptolemy founded the most enduring of the Successor dynasties, which ended with the famous Cleopatra, and he achieved the rare feat of dying peacefully in 282 BC, aged eighty-four.

Scene from end panel of the Alexander Sarcophagus, thought by some to represent the Battle of Gaza in 312 BC, where Ptolemy and Seleucus defeated Demetrius Poliorcetes and where Abdalonymos, the most likely occupant of the Sarcophagus, was killed. *(Courtesy of Dick Osseman)*

Bust of Lysimachus. Noted for his great physical strength, he was one of Alexander's personal bodyguards. Following the king's death he was appointed to govern Thrace where he later styled himself as king. A key player in the alliance that defeated Antigonus Monopthalmus at Ipsus, he gained much of Asia Minor and in 285 BC he defeated Pyrrhus of Epirus to become king of Macedon too. He died in battle against his former ally Seleucus in his eightieth year. (*Archaeological Museum, Selçuk. Courtesy of Jona Lendering/Livius.org*)

Bust of Seleucus I Nicator (Victor). Seleucus was the last man standing of the original Diadochi once he defeated Lysimachus at Corupedium in 281 BC, but a few months later he was murdered by Ptolemy Keraunos (Thunderbolt), son of Ptolemy I. The Seleucid dynasty, however, continued to dominate the eastern provinces for a further century and more. (*Louvre, Paris. Courtesy of Jona Lendering/Livius.org*)

Bust of Demetrius, now in the Naples Archaeological Museum. The son of Antigonus Monopthalmus, he earned the sobriquet Poliorcetes (The Besieger) through his penchant assaulting cities with massive si engines. Though king of Maced from 294 to 287 BC, he ended a chequered career as a prisoner of Seleucus and drank himself into early grave in 283 BC.
(*Author's photograph*)

Bust of Pyrrhus of Epirus, now in the Naples Archaeological Museum. A relative of Alexander the Great himself, he was rated as one of the best generals of the age but was too easily distracted by adventurous opportunities. At various times he was king of Epirus (twice), Syracuse, Macedon (twice) and much of southern Italy. He was slain in 272 BC while storming the city of Argos, after being ignominiously felled by a roof tile hurled by a woman.
(*Author's photograph*)

The remains of a temple, dominated by the impressive fortress of the Acrocorinth in the Peloponnese, Greece, scene of many clashes involving Demetrius, Polyperchon and Cassander. These formidable natural defences failed to resist The Besieger in 302 BC. (*Author's photograph*)

The rather melancholy site of ancient Megalopolis, scene of an epic siege in 318 BC. The city's heroic defiance of Polyperchon began his downfall and enabled the rise of Cassander. (*Author's photograph*)

Babylonian Chronicle 10 (reverse), British Museum. Fragmentary as it is, without such evidence we would have no knowledge of the war between 310 and 308 BC in which Babylon was sacked by Antigonus and retaken by Seleucus. (*Courtesy of Jona Lendering/Livius.org*)

The impressive walls of Heraclea-under-Latmus (Pleistarcheia) in Turkey, built by Lysimachus as he secured his grip on Anato after Ipsus. (*Author's photograph*)

Remains of the famous temple of Apollo at Didyma, Turkey, built either by Seleucus or Demetrius circa 300 BC. Passing through with Alexander's army, Seleucus had famously consulted the oracle here and was told his future lay in Asia. (*Author's photograph*)

time. Garrisons had been stripped from Cyrene in the west to the first cataract in the south, and every available man brought in from the military colonies. Ptolemy was everywhere to forestall the invaders, using the advantage of interior lines to decisive effect. The delta with its multiple riverine defences, flanks covered by impenetrable desert and few good anchorages along its northern coast, had proved impossible to conquer.

An eventful period had left Ptolemy with his power pared down to little greater than when he arrived in his new satrapy in 323 BC. If the achievements of the intervening years had been largely lost, events had illustrated that the first of the Ptolemaic line had not chosen badly when he took Egypt as his reward at Babylon. Whatever the travails of the wider world, entrenched behind the Nile, he could recoup and wait for better days.

Ptolemy's first act after surviving the Antigonid assault was to trumpet the triumph to Lysimachus, Cassander and Seleucus. But the belligerent tone of these reports could not hide how close-run a thing his survival had been. At such times of trauma it is not unusual for an opportunity of dynastic aggrandisement to be milked to full effect and Ptolemy had never been a man to make light of public relations. Antigonus and Demetrius had assumed the diadem after Salamis, and the other *Diadochi* had followed suit soon after. Now Ptolemy had himself proclaimed king of Egypt. He had been recognised as pharaoh by his Egyptian subjects almost since his arrival but now, to ensure a parity of status with rivals and friends alike, he required his Hellenic subjects to honour him as king.

This was a big step for Ptolemy, for of all the Successors he paid most lip service to the feeble vestiges of the Argead line. The great temple at Karnak includes a shrine to Philip Arrhidaeus and the nearby temple at Luxor was restored in the name of Alexander IV. Here was found a giant 9-foot statue of the hapless boy king. In his decrees Ptolemy was scrupulously careful to proclaim 'In the absence of King ...'. Most astonishing of all, though, was that he chose to keep this formula going for several years after Alexander IV had died, maintaining a fiction that he was still alive. The repelling of Antigonus was a convenient point to end this curious episode and start his own reign proper.[14]

Wearing the diadem ostentatiously round his Macedonian hat did nothing to conceal that the influence of the dynasty had been substantially eclipsed on the world stage. War with the Antigonids continued but the new king of Egypt could have little impact on events. The small navy that had been saved after the Cypriot campaign needed conservation and nurture, not to be risked in any more confrontations with a now-far-stronger maritime enemy. And the army that had successfully defended the delta was too valuable to be dissipated in risky adventures.

If the direct approach of violent confrontation was largely closed, Egypt still possessed enormous wealth and an expert diplomatic network that might play its part in embarrassing the enemy that had brought him to the edge of ruin in 306 BC. The economic aggression practised by the Antigonids only encouraged these activities and it was in support of one of Egypt's major trading partners that Ptolemy became re-involved.

The Rhodian connection with Alexandria had been strong since the founding of Ptolemy's capital. It was only a few days' sail between the two cities and Rhodian captains and their crews were a familiar sight in the quayside taverns of Alexandria. When their community became the prime object of Demetrius' aggression there was no doubt about Ptolemy's attitude. In the first year of the epic siege his main contribution was the despatch of 500 mercenaries, many themselves Rhodians, to reinforce the garrison.

The scent of an important reverse for the Antigonids encouraged Ptolemy to further risk ships and men in running Demetrius' blockade of Rhodes, this time to bring in essential foodstuffs for a population nearing starvation. The supply vessels that docked at the port of Rhodes (after avoiding the enemy fleet and their pirate allies) contained 300,000 measures of grain and legumes, six times the amount sent by the other kings. A further reinforcement of 1,500 soldiers and more supplies were sent after fifteen months of the siege and these injections were crucial in keeping the defenders of Rhodes at the task of resisting Demetrius. When the siege ended, Rhodian appreciation was shown when they raised a statue, alongside those of their other royal Macedonian benefactors, to honour the Egyptian king as a god at a new square temple precinct known as the Ptolemaeum. Probably these events won for Ptolemy the sobriquet of 'Soter' (Saviour), for his efforts in this crisis of communal survival.

Again, frustratingly little is known about the activities of Ptolemy or his subordinates in the years between the siege of Rhodes and the Ipsus campaign.

When, in 302 BC, the grand alliance took the field against Antigonus it certainly included Ptolemy. Yet his soldiers were not present at the decisive battle in Phrygia and his whole participation in the campaign was less committed and more limited than that of the other kings. Certainly, with Antigonid control of the sea and the road through Phoenicia and Syria, it would have been difficult for Ptolemy to have brought his forces to join the crucial campaign. But, if Seleucus could come from India, it was surely not impossible.

With the main enemy army far off in Anatolia, Ptolemy once again contemplated his appetite for Coele-Syria. In the summer of 302 BC, for the third time, he led a large army up past Raphia along the coast road. It is possible that an attack on this front was what had been agreed by the coalition kings as Ptolemy's role, but they probably expected more than he was prepared to risk. At the least they must have hoped for him to press the attack nearer to the Anatolian heart of the war, thus forcing Antigonus to divert his efforts to the defence of Cilicia, Antigonia and the Orontes valley, rather than snapping up nearby provinces to attach to his own kingdom. The key towns of Coele-Syria were easily captured and garrisoned. When the invaders moved on to Phoenicia they found the defenders at Sidon more prepared to offer resistance and Ptolemy settled down to besiege the city.

Word now reached Ptolemy's camp that Lysimachus and Seleucus had been crushed in battle and Antigonus was on his way back to Syria with a victorious army. There was no reason for precipitate action, yet the king of Egypt acted as though Antigonus himself was almost upon him: it was the ultimate display of pusillanimity. He concluded a truce with the defenders of Sidon, reinforced his recently-established garrisons in Coele-Syria and led his army back on the road they had so recently travelled to safety beyond the Nile.

On his return to Alexandria firm news made Ptolemy and his generals aware that they had fled from a chimera. Nothing is known of any communications between the allies in the winter of 302/1 BC before the cataclysmic campaign of Ipsus, but it is difficult to believe that his confederates did not make some attempt to encourage Ptolemy to shoulder his share of the wartime burden. Certainly their attitude to him when it came to sharing out the spoils of victory suggests they considered his contribution to the war effort at least inadequate, if not downright treacherous.[15]

Chapter 7

Seleucus

Seleucus, they used to tell us, constantly repeated that if people in general knew what a task it was merely to read and write so many letters, they would not even pick up a crown that had been thrown away.[1]

The remnants of those two recognised wonders of the ancient world that still exist in Turkey, are far from visually impressive. Neither the temple of Artemis at Ephesus nor the Mausoleum at Halicarnassus retains enough of their original structure to give an impression of how they may have looked in their heyday. But another site in that country has kept a great deal of its main fabric and, though not accredited one of the seven wonders, it most certainly deserves inclusion on that list for its architectural magnificence. This is the temple of Apollo at Didyma and what can be seen today is stunning, even in a region where treasures of antiquity are to be seen on every side. It is situated forty-odd miles south of Ephesus, down the road that passes first Priene and then Miletus on the way to the modern beach resort of Altinkum. These ruined cities, now landlocked because of the silting up of the Maeander river, were great ports in the fourth century BC and Alexander stopped at all of them as he passed on his way to the East. Didyma, however, is associated with a different man.

Seleucus, *en route* through Asia Minor in Alexander's army, stopped at this oracle and received the advice 'do not hurry back to Europe; Asia will be much better for you'.[2] Time would bear out the validity of the prophecy, but the celestial source already possessed a pedigree that went back to the seventh century BC. Then, the voice of Apollo is recorded as having sanctioned the profession of piracy as long as it had been the family business of the perpetrator for some time. The building Seleucus entered on his way to fame and fortune in the East, was not the one that can be seen today. The huge colonnade and vast temple platform, the remains of which can be viewed from the roadside fish restaurants in the small town of Didyma, were begun around 300 BC, when the area was controlled by Demetrius. Later involvement by Seleucus is almost certain as the shrine was a particular favourite and there is a tradition that he consulted there before invading Europe at the very end of his life.

The founder of the Seleucid dynasty had a life of extraordinary adventure. He first came to prominence during the campaign against King Porus in India, a contest that included Alexander's most gruelling battle. When the conqueror led his picked assault force up the banks of the Hydaspes River in the monsoon rain to find a crossing point, Seleucus was with him. He held a command in the guard infantry and accompanied the king in the boat he took across the river together with Perdiccas, Ptolemy and Lysimachus; men who all would play such a resonant part in his future. When the Macedonians had disembarked and reorganised on the muddy bank opposite they found themselves under attack from Porus' son. Seleucus was little involved in this initial encounter but in the confrontation with the main Indian army he had the opportunity to impress his king, leading his veteran infantry in the centre of the battle line against the novel terror of charging elephants. The enemy was eventually overcome, but not before they had exacted terrible casualties. It was Seleucus' first known involvement with elephants, beasts that would play a central part in his life.

If this was the first mention of the future ruler of Hellenistic Asia, it was not his first taste of action. An aristocrat of high, if not princely, rank, an apprenticeship in war would have been a normal part of his early life. Born about 358 BC, his father was named Antiochus and had been an officer of some distinction in Philip of Macedon's army.

Seleucus had been with Alexander's army of invasion from the beginning and his performance during the Persian wars must have promised enough of courage and skill for him to receive a command in the elite regiment of foot guards (*Hypaspsists*). A large, powerful man, one story has him restraining a sacrificial bull which was set to run wild and cause embarrassment for the king presiding over the offering. Seleucus recalled this incident with such pride as to have it commemorated it in several horn-decorated statues set up of him in later years. His strength and courage brought him through the hard-fought Indian campaigns where his guardsmen are mentioned frequently in fighting across the Punjab and along the Indus river.

At Susa his increasing status is reflected in a marriage to Apama, the daughter of Spitamenes of Bactria, a very high-born Iranian aristocrat who had been one of Alexander's most competent opponents and boasted a pedigree that included a blood relationship with Zoroaster, the prophet of Persia's royal religion. Seleucus was a coming man, an important officer by the final year of Alexander's life and, evidence suggests, part of the king's inner circle of closest friends.

There is a tradition that while Alexander was boating in a lagoon near Babylon, just before his death, the royal diadem fell from his head into the water and Seleucus swam out and retrieved it for the king.[3] The point of this is undoubtedly allegorical, to foretell his eventual accession to the kingdom of Asia. A second tale sustains the impression that, though he had risen late, he had risen high in the inner circle of genuine companions. When the king was near death, some of his closest friends visited a local shrine to ask for advice on treating him. Seleucus accompanied them in this effort to halt the unthinkable demise of their leader. Much is questionable here, as is inevitable when the earliest extant sources date from hundreds of years later.[4] Still, a framework of accuracy in the matter of those who were involved can be assumed and puts Seleucus in company with some of the highest Macedonian officers at this time.

Elevated by the patronage of the dead king, Seleucus still had not achieved a following or reputation that could have put him in the front rank of those who disputed for power in the assembly at Babylon. As a second-string player, he supported Perdiccas against Meleager and his long-standing contacts in the foot guards probably helped in the eventual subversion of the Macedonian infantry away from the phalanx commander. Part of the victorious party, he gained considerable advantage out of the eventual settlement, a reward not measured in the wide lands of a fertile province but through promotion to the most senior command in the royal army. Kept at the new regent's side, this capable and loyal officer was made general of the Companion cavalry, an office once filled by Hephaistion and Perdiccas himself.

These horsemen had been Perdiccas' greatest support against Meleager and were the strike force of the army. Commanding them was a responsibility only given to a soldier whose loyalty was undoubted. Seleucus led these formidable and well-born warriors in the campaigns in Anatolia and on the fateful march to Egypt; he was certainly in the camp when Perdiccas was cut down by Pithon's conspirators. Only one source suggests that he was involved in the assassination and the balance of evidence exonerates him as having stayed loyal, while it was possible, only coming to an accommodation with the murderers once their position had become unassailable.[5] His reputation with the soldiers still stood high during the retreat from Egypt when the royal army seemed to be on the point of disintegration. While Eurydice intrigued and Pithon and Arrhidaeus were forfeiting their authority, he, as the senior officer, was able to maintain a semblance of credibility and control that proved vital in preventing the total collapse of discipline when the royal court reached Triparadeisus.

The army had followed three leaders in as many weeks, insecurity and confusion reigned supreme and the men wanted the pay they were owed.

Antipater, with no funds, was confronted by an angry mob when he crossed over from his camp on the far side of the river from the main army. He found no welcome; indeed, his life looked in danger when some soldiers began to stone him. In the nick of time, Seleucus and Antigonus intervened. Antipater hastened back over the river, considerably discomfited but alive. The temper of the army soon cooled and a few days saw Antipater securely in control. So, at the second great regional settlement since the death of Alexander, Seleucus gained the advancement he had dreamed of. With many of his peers dead or discredited, his own distinguished record and recent service to Antipater guaranteed a plum prize. He was given as his satrapy the ancient lands of Babylonia.

Civilisation had flourished there since a time so antique it was even beyond the ken of people living 2,500 years ago. The confluence of the Tigris and Euphrates and the industrious people who lived there had combined to create some of the richest and most productive agricultural land in the world. Only Egypt compared for potential wealth; no ruler who tenanted the triple-walled bastion of Babylon would ever run short of money. The government had been unstable since Alexander's death; Archon of Pella had been made satrap by Perdiccas but he soon became involved in intrigue and the regent had sent out a close friend, Docimus, to replace him. This substitution had only been achieved after Archon had been defeated and killed in battle, and Docimus was *in situ* when Seleucus was given his new appointment.

Fortunately for the newcomer, Docimus did not emulate his predecessor but on hearing of Perdiccas' assassination fled to Pisidia, where others of the dead regent's supporters were gathering to oppose the new order.[6] Seleucus entered his new capital, in October or November of 320 BC, unopposed; a bonus for any new ruler. He understood, as Alexander had, that to successfully exploit these lands, which had as yet hardly felt the impact of Hellenism, he must enlist the aid of the local ruling classes. Ancient customs and traditional authority patterns would be bound to make the imposition of an alien administration counter-productive, even if there had been a sufficient number of Hellenes to both man the government machine and provide garrisons to impose his rule. Babylonia was a complex economic, religious and political organism that had developed over thousands of years, often enough under the tutelage of foreign rule but never losing its cultural pride and particularism. A network of interlocking elites controlled the real power and the new regime needed to gain their backing, if the riches of Mesopotamia were to be thoroughly exploited.

Details of the first years are lacking but they would have been used to conciliate the ideologically and economically important temple bureaucracies. According to the Babylonian Chronicle, the traditional gesture of removing the dust of Esagila, a donation (in reality, a bribe) for cleaning the temple of Bel Marduk at Babylon, was made shortly after Seleucus' arrival.[7] For his part, the new ruler found no problem in adhering to their unfamiliar gods and rituals. The craft guilds and local landowners were left with most of their traditional status and influence and, in return, they ensured the production of tax revenues that were the cornerstone of Seleucus' power.

State security however depended on other powers and Seleucus kept himself well informed on the behaviour of his neighbours to the west. Merchants and agents picked up much at the courts, cities and camps of Antigonus, Ptolemy or Cassander. Closer than the dangers from that direction were threats from east of the Tigris. The powerful satraps of Persia and Media felt the historical imperative to look with acquisitive eyes on the rich lowlands west of the Zagros Mountains. The main defence of Seleucus' province lay not in soldiers or walls but in the internal rivalries of the rulers to the east who normally contrived to fight each other rather than combine against a rich and vulnerable neighbour.

So, it was no coincidence then that in 317 BC, when Seleucus' activities are again noticed by Hellenic sources, he is involved in the volatile cauldron of Iranian politics. The intriguer Pithon driven out by his neighbours, had arrived at Babylon a defeated exile. Self-interest prompted Seleucus to consider offering support for a return to the fight against Peucestas. While they hatched their plans, however, the imminent arrival of Euemenes from the west with a powerful army threatened to turn the whole Hellenistic East upside down. Furthermore, agents soon brought word that Antigonus was not likely to be far behind.

Eumenes showed an intent to parley, sending ambassadors with the credentials he carried from the infant king, Alexander IV. This approach left the court at Babylon on the horns of a cruel dilemma; aiding Eumenes would bring down the wrath of Antigonus but refusal risked immediate reprisals from the powerful army already in the vicinity of the city. They tried to delay a decision but, not prepared to await the outcome, Eumenes marched east towards Susiane. Seleucus and Pithon, now, committed themselves irrevocably for Antigonus; they had limited forces available but nonetheless intended to hold up Eumenes' movement eastwards to allow time for Antigonus to arrive and crush him. Their attempts to stop him crossing the Tigris failed and a truce was eventually offered which would allow Eumenes to proceed on his way east.

Seleucus' army hardly amounted to more than a few hundred horsemen and as one powerful invader left Babylonia another was just approaching. Antigonus finally arrived in the spring of 317 BC. Both Seleucus and Pithon had little option but to attach themselves to his entourage. Seleucus accompanied the army as it marched towards Susiane, where he was detached to press the siege of Susa. However, only when news of Antigonus' victories in the East was received did the garrison surrender. Seleucus, like Pithon, had played his part in Antigonus' victory and their reward was reinstatement into their satrapies. The return to Babylon was triumphant but he was not long left in peace to enjoy it. The early months of 316 BC brought news from Iran that caused great concern: Pithon had been executed and Peucestas despoiled of his province. So it was with no pleasure that he anticipated the arrival from the upper satrapies of Antigonus. The latter immediately demanded an account of the satrapal revenue, something of a quarrel arose over the issue and Seleucus became convinced an excuse was being manufactured to justify his deposition.

Seleucus stayed at Babylon, hoping to ride out the storm. But once he felt his life was in danger he acted, fleeing his capital and riding into exile. His party travelled west across the Euphrates, over the desert trails that led to Egypt, outrunning the pursuit despatched by Antigonus.[8] Ptolemy's welcome, when he reached Egypt, was warm enough to raise the spirits of a man as naturally resilient as Seleucus.[9]

In the first of the wars against Antigonus, Seleucus played a considerable part as a senior officer in Ptolemy's service. Early in 315 BC, he took charge of a fleet of 100 warships and cruised the Levantine shore, disrupting shipbuilding activities and wooing away the allies and dependants of the Antigonids. Next, he raided westwards along the coast of Asia Minor into Lydia and Ionia. Intending to establish a base, he besieged the port of Erythrae, but fled from news that Ptolemaeus was on his way from northern Anatolia with a force that far outnumbered his own.

Denied a foothold in the Aegean, Seleucus headed for Cyprus where Ptolemy needed him to secure control of that vital island as a number of important seaports had openly come out against Ptolemaic rule. Seleucus attacked first along the north coast. Lapithus and Ceryneia were swiftly captured and the ruler of Marion intimidated into transferring his allegiance to Ptolemy. Then, the prince of Amathus was brought back into the fold. Last on his list was Citium but our sources are ambiguous on the outcome there. A new campaigning season would see him continuing as Ptolemy's admiral but without similar success. Lemnos, Aeolis, Ionia, Caria and Cos saw his fleet but little was achieved before he returned to Cyprus to winter and refit his ships.

The next year he continued to impose a harsh Ptolemaic rule on Cyprus. A number of rulers were executed and one particular place suffered the ultimate fate. Marion had been besieged half into extinction in the first civil war and now Seleucus' fleet sailed into the bay east of the Acamas Peninsula. The place was set ablaze and the dazed population driven south to populate new Paphos on the west coast of the island. Nicocreon, king of Salamis, was left in command of the whole island as Ptolemy recalled his admiral to Egypt.

Years in the western seas had not made Seleucus forget the satrapy he had been evicted from almost half a decade before. He was still ambitious to reacquire the rich lands of Babylonia and Ptolemy's plans were to make what had long seemed an idle dream into a real possibility. The opportunity was clearly very much of his own engineering; he had encouraged for some time the idea of an offensive to the east and, with the main enemy army gone to Anatolia, his suzerain had at last been persuaded. Ptolemy led his invasion force into Coele-Syria in 312 BC and Seleucus accompanied him in a position of high command. He played his part in trouncing Demetrius at Gaza and pushing deep into Phoenicia. There he got the chance to grasp again at the dizzy prize of independent authority.

In the siege lines outside Tyre, a plan was put in motion, almost certainly conceived well before the commencement of the invasion. Seleucus was outfitted to reconquer Babylon, an enterprise that for Ptolemy offered the prospect of the Antigonids being tied up elsewhere for a limited investment of military effort.[10] Even so, this cautious gambler ventured only to send a small force with Seleucus. Something over a thousand men, it was not enough to weaken the main army but a sufficient bodyguard to get through to Mesopotamia, where Seleucus' old connections and reputation with the local people would give him a chance of regaining control. It was a throw that appealed to the natural chancer in Seleucus' psychological make-up; all through his life he showed a restless inclination to risk what he already had for greater gains.

His own sense of optimism did not immediately permeate the spirit of his men. Hardly had they started out northeast from Ptolemy's camp than a number of them wanted to turn back, seeing only folly in challenging Antigonid might with the puny forces at their disposal. But their leader was not just a gambler; he was also an orator and would talk himself out of tight corners on no few occasions in his life. He calmed their fears by recalling that he had followed Alexander in Asia and that he possessed some part of his old commander's skill and good fortune. Not just this, but his success had been forecast by the oracle at Didyma when the voice of the god greeted him as

'King Seleucus'. These arguments had the effect of keeping his party moving forward but more crucial for their morale were events at Carrhae. It was a long journey there, almost 350 miles from Tyre, and only then did the road turn east and make the desert crossing to reach the river Tigris. Carrhae itself would later become forever associated with the demise of Crassus' Roman army, but these travellers had better fortune. The Macedonian garrison, left by Alexander years before, did not oppose them and, indeed, many of the more adventurous joined up. Others who had got used to their new homes had to be conscripted but all were a welcome addition to Seleucus and his followers.

Even so, when they actually entered Mesopotamia their numbers were still hardly sufficient to provide the garrison of an average sized city, never mind conquer a province. Better would follow when the Tigris was reached and they turned south to follow that river to Babylon. It became clear Seleucus was still held in some esteem by the people of the region. Local landowners welcomed him and ensured they were adequately supplied and, most important, Polyarchus, a Hellenic general, brought in a trained force of 1,000 men. This was something more than recruiting a few Macedonian pensioners from a desert garrison; it virtually doubled the size of Seleucus' army and had a profound effect on the rest of the Antigonid officers in Babylonia. The administration in the capital became convinced Babylon itself was indefensible as the locals were likely to side with the invader and they fled, leaving only a small garrison in the citadel.

If he exhibited high confidence at the sight of Babylon's open gates, Seleucus' relief at the turn of events was profound. His wager had paid off; he had put his head in the lion's mouth but it had licked him with affection instead of biting it off. Even the Antigonid garrison commander failed to prepare his defences properly and the citadel fell to an assault after only a brief siege. Several old officers and supporters from his first reign as satrap were found imprisoned in the fortress and he had real pleasure in liberating them and rewarding their fidelity. Control of the capital, however, gave no reason for complacency; his army was still weak and vulnerable to counterstrokes from west or east.

News arrived that the first threat was likely to materialise from Nicanor, Antigonus' commander in Media, who was mobilising an army of invasion in the east. Nicanor was de facto ruler of inner Asia and had no intention of allowing a rival in Babylon to establish himself with impunity. He raised a large army of 10,000 foot and 7,000 horse and marched through the Median Gates and down the Tigris valley, intending to face Seleucus in the flat lands of Mesopotamia where his predominance in cavalry was likely to prove decisive.

Seleucus did not await his arrival, his policy of energetic daring had achieved much so far and a defensive posture risked his enterprise losing its momentum. Leaving the security of the walls of Babylon behind, he marched northeast. The Tigris was already crossed and his men settled on the east bank when word came that Nicanor was only a few days march away to the north. Seleucus with his scratch force of just over 3,000 men could not risk open battle, so he hid his men amongst the marshes that stretched along the banks of the Tigris. Nicanor, coming down the Royal Road from Media, reached the great river and encamped by an Achaemenid way-station, built for officials travelling on the Great King's business.

Seleucus, hiding nearby, decided on a night assault on the enemy position. Nicanor's sentries were lax, surprise was complete and many of Nicanor's men were killed before the rest could even get under arms. The advantage of surprise was compounded by luck when Evagoras, the satrap of Persia and Aria, perished early in the battle and his demoralised troops went over to Seleucus' side. Nicanor, deserted by his allies, gathered what men he could and retreated north into the desert.

Seleucus had snatched victory from the jaws of disaster and, for the moment, he let the enemy withdraw until daylight allowed him to reorganise his considerably-increased but disorganised forces. All opposition in Babylonia had now been crushed or dispersed and, in the few months since he left Tyre, his fortune and status had been radically transformed. No longer a landless exile and condottiere, he controlled the core of the wealthy realm that had been snatched from him four years before. Knowing Antigonus was still the most likely to disturb his peace, Seleucus retained his links with Ptolemy who, alone, could ensure the old marshal was kept occupied in the Levant while Seleucus consolidated his position east of the Euphrates. Detailed despatches on his success were drafted and sent back to Memphis, communications that emphasised his dependent position in relation to the ruler of Egypt who had originally sponsored him.

If Antigonid might in the west was the greatest menace, it was in another direction that possibilities lay. The situation in the upper satrapies had never been particularly stable. Nicanor's defeat on the Tigris showed the depth of regional tension and from this chaos Seleucus could profit. Experience as ruler of Babylon alerted him to the danger of allowing others to dominate the plateau of Iran and with the current political dislocation he had a unique opportunity to forestall that eventuality. He spent the rest of 312 BC in Media or Persia and was not around when Demetrius invaded Babylonia.

An officer called Patrocles had been left in charge at Babylon when the

20,000 or so Antigonid veterans were reported approaching the city. He evacuated what he could; not just most of the soldiers and government official's left but a good proportion of the civilians who were determined to save their movable wealth from the clutches of Demetrius' greedy soldiery.

The non-combatants were herded out to Susiane or down south to the head of the Persian Gulf, as Patrocles constructed a strategy using the topography of Babylonia to delay the invaders and cut their supply lines. Small garrisons were left to hold the two citadels of Babylon while he kept his small army mobile and on the march 'using river courses and canals as defences.'[11] He sent to Seleucus for help but his chief did not return to contest his satrapy; he just could not face Demetrius in the field. Indeed, his nightmare must have been that the invader might cross the Tigris, like Alexander running down Darius, and that, unable to offer his followers any hope of victory, he would share the Persian king's fate. In fact, the Antigonids, frustrated by Patrocles strategy, took one of Babylon's citadels, left a garrison to hold it and returned the way they had come.

Patrocles' resistance had sufficiently held up Demetrius that an impatient Antigonus recalled his son to the west. Seleucus' luck had held and now the freedom from interference allowed Seleucus to put in hand one of the great achievements of his long life, yet one that is virtually ignored by the sources for the period. He had known when Patrocles called for help that he had to refuse. He knew his future hopes rested on building his strength in the upper satrapies in preparation to fight the Antigonids another day.

The conquest of those Iranian provinces, which comprised the largest geographical region in all of Alexander's empire, can hardly have been in Seleucus' mind from the beginning. But he did have the inestimable advantage that there was something of a power vacuum east of the Zagros Mountains. This allowed him to secure control of most of the upper satrapies and the important cities that Alexander had taken long years to subdue. The great government centres of the Achaemenids, royal palaces and treasure houses - Susa, Ecbatana in Media, Persepolis in Persia and Maracanda (Samarkand) in Sogdia - needed to be secured. Yet to reach them would take months of hard marching and the new towns the Macedonians had planted needed to be won over. These military colonists were the bulwark of Hellenistic rule in an Iranian world.

Since the passage of Alexander's army, there had been a great influx of warriors from the West: Macedonians, Greek mercenaries, Thracians, Anatolians; some barbarous tribesmen and others from Hellenised towns. These men had settled over the years in the seventy-odd new Alexandrias or in already-established communities. Thousands were planted by later leaders; Pithon, Eumenes and Antigonus, all had brought soldiers from the West and a good proportion remained. They were the able and fit, required for the imposition of Macedonian rule, and the wounded or veteran soldiers who looked for their reward in a settled life. These planted communities were the bedrock and power-base of Hellenistic hegemony in Iran. They kept the hill tribes in check, policed the royal highways, collected revenues in the hinterland of the Iranian plateau and provided recruits for the royal army. In return for their estates and the servitors to work the land, these warrior families had to produce the future generations of phalangites.

The colonial communities varied widely in type, some were full-blown cities on the Greek model with the appropriate amenities and facilities, whilst others were mere walled villages where the local people slaved to provide for a collection of rough and unlettered mercenaries. Seleucus saw the increase and expansion of these communities as fundamental to the security of his government and many of the hidden years before Ipsus were spent founding cities in Mesopotamia and Iran.

With these places in the hands of his officers and allies, he could be sure of the key strongholds along the roads, the trade routes and in the fertile lowlands. But they were still just Hellenistic islands in an Iranian sea. Only by winning over the local aristocracy, the great land-owning barons, could his rule be surely founded in the upper satrapies. Their local clout was crucial in squeezing revenue out of the rural population. Seleucus knew he had to conciliate these country gentlemen. Alone of the Successors, he held fast to his Bactrian wife and kept Iranian princes about the court or in positions of influence in the provinces. The two great pillars that held up state power in the Iranian lands were the Hellenistic cities and the feudal aristocracy.

The chronology and itinerary of Seleucus' eastern anabasis is not at all clear but after at least two seasons in the upper satrapies he returned to Babylon, where the Antigonids still controlled part of the city after Demetrius' invasion. Left out of the peace of 311 BC, he found himself deserted by those who had previously shared in facing the might of Antigonid power. The old marshal had sponsored the peace of 311 BC to free him to face the resurgent Seleucus in the east. The wide sun-baked regions east of the Euphrates, unvisited for half a decade, demanded his complete attention.

The war of 310 to 308 BC between Seleucus and Antigonus is essentially a twentieth-century discovery. Coming to light with the unearthing of references in a Babylonian chronicle, it has since been given great weight and consideration. Much has been properly reinterpreted in the light of it, ranging

from the reasons for the peace of 311 BC to the final demise of Antigonus
Monophthalmus.

The chronicle, discovered languishing in the vaults of the British Museum
in the 1920s, was part of a series of cuneiform texts on stone tablets relating
the deeds of the Babylonian kings from Sargon in 2,700 BC to Seleucus. The
fragments of two stones that relate to the *Diadochi* when Philip Arrhidaeus,
Alexander IV and Seleucus were 'kings' of Babylon are barely sixty-five lines
long and many contain only five or six words. They add little to our
understanding of the period 323-311 BC, apart from further intensifying the
chronological difficulties, but it is to the chronicle, alone, that we owe our
knowledge of the conflict between Antigonus and Seleucus.[12] That there is no
real hint of it in our other major sources is surprising, even given the fact that
it ended in a major defeat for the Antigonid patrons of Hieronymus of
Cardia.[13]

From such sparse and incomplete evidence it is difficult to draw any firm
conclusions. Antigonus commanded in person, several towns were besieged, at
least one major battle fought and Babylon suffered greatly, being taken and
plundered by Antigonus' troops before Seleucus recovered it. Any study of the
Diadochi by its very nature exercises the ability to extrapolate on a few facts, a
tendency that is easy to allow to get out of hand; drawing far reaching
conclusions from will-o'-the-wisps of uncorroborated information cannot
always be resisted but it should be recognised for what it is. In the Babylonian
conflict we are virtually forced into this but as long as it is clear what a tangled
jungle-track of evidence we are following no harm comes in taking a walk, as
the mere bold statement on the results of the war would satisfy no one.

What area the satrap of Babylon controlled in 310 BC is a matter of
speculation. In 311 his victory over the Antigonid satraps of Media, Persia and
Aria[14] meant that he had 'easily won over Susiane, Media and some of the
adjacent lands'.[15] At the time of Demetrius' attack on Babylon, Seleucus had
been far away campaigning in Iran, somewhere between the Zagros Mountains
and the frontiers of India. His relations with the Macedonian rulers of Bactria,
Sogdia and Arachosia would have been in flux. Undoubtedly his presence in
the East impinged on their spheres of influence but equally a rampant
Antigonus returning from the West would not have been in their interest
either. Seleucus was probably able to depend on neutrality if not friendship
from these neighbours to the east. More than this, our meagre sources attest
to his personal popularity in his recently-reclaimed domain. Even so, real
control would not have run deep in many areas and the favourable sentiments
of the indigenous ruling class offered little to rectify an obvious imbalance in

the field where Seleucid armies could not hope to face the Antigonids in open battle. He had perhaps a few thousand European troops, made up of those Ptolemy had given him, the garrisons he had picked up *en route* to Babylon and those from the armies of Nicanor and the other satraps who he had overcome or recruited to his side. Iranian cavalry from Persia and Media and light infantry could be had in abundance, funded from the treasures of Susa and Ecbatana, but recent history had shown their inadequacy against the heavy pikemen and cavalry of the West.

Seleucus needed all the help he could get and in the chronicle there is a tantalising glimpse of an alliance: 'In the month of Marcheswan an alliance and friendship.... The troops of Gutium and the troops...'.[16] The Gutii are tentatively identified with the Cossaeans, that warlike mountain tribe of Media that had been decimated by Alexander.[17] More recently, in 317 BC, Antigonus had refused to pay tribute to them and had suffered at their hands for his arrogance. A subsequent alliance with Seleucus against their common enemy is more than probable.

Seleucus must have fought a war of manoeuvre, utilising the vast tracts of difficult terrain over which it was waged to avoid a decisive denouement. He had only to survive to win. Most of the fighting took place in the lands watered by the lower Tigris and Euphrates. Babylonia and its capital, in particular, were ravished in a manner so destructive as to deeply imprint it on the minds of the local chroniclers:

> There was weeping and mourning in the land. A storm .... he set out from Babylon, he plundered town and countryside, the goods .... on the 2nd he went to Kuthah and he plundered .... He burnt the people with fire.'[18]

The suffering and famine became so great that Seleucus was forced to supply the people with corn from elsewhere.

If Antigonus' well-equipped conventional forces had great success in the cultivated basins of the Tigris and Euphrates, elsewhere they were deeply frustrated. The marshlands in the lower reaches of the great rivers, as they approach the Persian Gulf, and the mountain strongholds of western Iran would have been much less conducive to an invader trying to impose his rule. Whilst Antigonus would have had the best of the war in open country, Seleucus, by delaying tactics and constant harrying, no doubt expertly abetted by such allies as the Cossaeans, denied him in the more difficult areas. Indeed, Antigonus' very success in the towns brought even more problems. The populations he had subdued, added to the numbers of his own soldiery, would have been hard to supply in a land where famine had taken a strong hold. He was also trying to impose his will on a deeply hostile local population; all his efforts only seemed to have reinforced Seleucus' popularity. Three seasons of this ground down even the redoubtable Antigonus and it must have been a tired army which brought Seleucus to battle in August 308 BC.

If we are to believe an anecdote from Polynaeus, the Seleucids, in comparison, were fresh and willing.[19] After one long day's fighting they overcame their enemies by remaining in full battle armour overnight and catching the Antigonids unawares in the morning. This stunning defeat meant that the following year Antigonus was back in the west, having endured three years of costly and ineffective campaigning. His failure to stamp out Seleucus was to have dreadful consequences for the future.

With his eastern frontier reasonably secure, and having survived an awful threat from Antigonus, Seleucus could settle to governing his vast realm. Like his Achaemenid predecessors, he probably spent some of the winter months of each year in his western capital, whether this was Babylon or later Seleucia on the Tigris, and then, in the summer, climbed up the Royal Road to Ecbatana, where the cool mountain winds of Media made court life bearable. Ancient rulers were always peripatetic, but the size of this eastern realm made this even more necessary. Others of the great capitals like Susa and Persepolis would also have seen him in these middle years of his life, in the last decade of the fourth century. Yet, despite the vast areas he had brought under his rule since returning from exile, Seleucus' ambition had not been sated. All of the Iranian provinces Alexander had conquered were his, but he felt impelled to round off this achievement by incorporating into his domains those parts of Afghanistan and India his former monarch had briefly ruled. Bactria and Arachosia were retaken and Seleucus eventually found himself at the head of a large army poised to take the age-old route of invasion through the Khyber Pass into the exotic lands of the Indus and Ganges. Descending towards the sweltering plains of modern Pakistan and northwest India, his hopes were high.

What is inescapable in any study of Alexander of Macedon is that much of his busy life was spent in the east subduing Bactria and Sogdia and fighting his Indian wars. The heart of the Achaemenid state had been overcome in three years. There good roads had carried administrators, tax collectors and the 'king's eyes' who supervised a well-ordered empire. When Alexander had lopped off the head of this edifice he was largely able to substitute himself in its stead. This was far from the case further east. Bessus, the new Great King, and his supporters were barons from Bactria and Sogdia with personal power bases there. These eastern satrapies had a tradition of autonomy which bred resistance of a more fundamental sort against Macedonian intrusion. If the Sogdian nobles (whose great rock fortresses Alexander had to reduce one by one) had been approached by any ruler demanding more than nominal submission they would have resisted. They fought the reordering of their provincial arrangements with the backing of the local ruling class and when one was defeated it did not mean the rest would submit. Indeed, unlike their more tractable western peers, once pacified they were far more inclined to revolt when the main body of the invading army passed on. As it was in eastern Iran, it was more so in India. Rajas ruled their separate kingdoms, independent confederations of cities flourished and tribal peoples lived lives untrammelled by outside authority. This certainly allowed Alexander to play a divide and rule game and he never faced a united front of regional opposition. But, the corollary was that each political unit had to be defeated in detail. Time consuming and dangerous, Alexander came closest to death whilst assaulting a minor Indian city.

But if it had been a divided India that Alexander found, radical changes had taken place between then and the second Macedonian invasion. Seleucus found himself confronted by a united and powerful empire under a vigorous ruler. When Alexander reached the Beas River, the furthest extent of his conquests, both he and his followers had a distorted vision of the land that lay beyond it. The soldiers had been terrified by tales of an empire on the Ganges that could mobilise 400,000 men and, even more horrifically, 4,000 war elephants. In fact, the Magadha kingdom's incumbent dynasty was in terminal decline, with its Nanda monarchs having forfeited the support of much of the ruling class. Frustratingly for Alexander, his footsore veterans would not allow him to take advantage of this weakness, but there was another who would.

Chandragupta Maurya supplanted the exhausted Nanda line. Though allegedly a commoner (from the self governing tribe of Moriya), he raised sufficient support to lead a rebellion against Dhana Nand in 324 BC, only a short time after Alexander had left. One tradition has it that Chandragupta, while in exile, had joined the Macedonian army on its march through the Punjab and encouraged the king to invade the Magadha kingdom, outlining the weaknesses of that empire in the hope that Alexander would place him on the throne.[20] Whether there is any truth in the story, the final outcome was the same, though Chandragupta made his bid for power with local means, not the backing of Macedonian spears. He did not achieve immediate success but he snapped at the periphery of Nanda power. By 321 BC his patience had paid off and the rebel established himself as ruler at Pataliputra from where his dynasty would create an Indian empire that reached the heights of civilisation, power and renown.

Soon after his accession, Chandragupta was sufficiently secure to expand the Magadha boundaries to the west, into regions Alexander had held. The situation in these provinces had deteriorated considerably since that king had left and when the Mauryan armies crossed the Beas, they experienced little organised opposition. It was a power vacuum he was moving into, largely created by the intrigues and rivalry between those left to govern these rich lands.

Trouble had begun immediately Alexander left. The tribes of the Swat highlands had broken out in revolt, the Macedonian garrison commander was defeated and killed and Macedonian control of this crucial gateway to India ended. Further to the southeast at Taxila, in 325 BC, the Macedonian officer in command was assassinated by his own men. The satrapy itself was divided between King Ambhi of Taxila and Eudamus, the officer in command of the garrison troops.

Another Macedonian, Pithon, had been left to garrison the province that stretched east from the Indus to its tributary the Beas. He had begun to feel the pressure from Chandragupta soon after his accession and was gradually driven back across the Indus. In 316 BC, Chandragupta benefited as Eudamus and Pithon were sucked into the conflict raging in Iran. With them gone, little is heard of further resistance to Chandragupta's armies and the new ruler showed tolerance both to Indian rulers and residual Hellenic communities, undermining any tendency to desperate local resistance.

Chandragupta now ruled a kingdom stretching from the Ganges plain to the Khyber Pass and in a few short years made himself one of the great potentates of the era. The dynasty he founded would produce the amazing Asoka, the Buddhist emperor who experimented with a state not based on repression, a concept with few parallels in any period of history.[21] But in the time of Seleucus the royal house established by Chandragupta was in a youthful phase of militant expansionism. After his triumphs in the north, the king turned south and for several seasons campaigned on the Narbada River in central India. Sometime in 305 BC, while so engaged, news reached him of the approach of Seleucus and he turned back immediately to defend his northwest frontier.

Seleucus marched his army down from the highlands of Afghanistan, taking a route that Sakas, Kushans, Arabs and Mongols would travel in the centuries to come. On his arrival, he found Chandragupta facing him with an army reputed to include 9,000 elephants and certainly containing the same brand of brave warriors that had caused the Macedonians such hard fighting on the Hydaspes and elsewhere. No details of the campaign are known, only its strategic outcome. But a school of scholarship suggests the Macedonians must have been soundly defeated to agree to cede all the provinces that Seleucus eventually did. This treaty surrendered to Chandragupta all the

Indian lands conquered by Alexander as far as Kandahar, giving him control of southern Afghanistan. In return he gave Seleucus 500 war elephants, a marriage alliance and guarantees for Hellenic settlers left in his territories.[22] This, at least, maintained the status quo and, most importantly, secured the frontier with his powerful neighbour. Relations between the two eastern rulers seemed to have remained good through the years. We know Seleucus' ambassador to Chandragupta, Megasthenes, stayed long enough in the subcontinent to get the material for a book and that communications with the Hellenistic world allowed a successor of Chandragupta to ask Antiochus I to send him wine, figs and a sophist.[23]

Seleucus could now turn his attention west, an option that a lengthy war in India would have closed off. As with the other Successors, it was the Hellenic heartland around the Mediterranean that dominated his ambition. It is no coincidence that at the age of nearly eighty years he would be leading armies in a war of conquest in Thrace, not in Bengal or the Deccan, even though the potential riches and fame were surely greater there than in barbarous Balkan forests.

The sojourn in the east had been lengthy and there must have been an element of relief for Seleucus as he was able to turn back from the Indus towards Persia. His prolonged absence was bound to risk the chance of revolt along the long lines of communications to Babylon. He did not know it, but events were to take him not just back to Mesopotamia but all the way to Anatolia and the Hellenic West. Whilst on the return journey, his line of march was intercepted by emissaries from Cassander and Lysimachus offering an alliance against Antigonus, a momentous event culminating in the victory at Ipsus that shaped the rest of his life and that of his dynasty.

Chapter 8

Ebbtide

*When he sent Demetrius, his son, with many ships and forces to make the
Greeks a free people he said that his repute kindled in Greece as on a lofty
height would spread like beacon fires throughout the inhabited world.*[1]

The story of Alexander IV is strangely insignificant for the offspring of such
an extraordinary father. He waited on the periphery of events while others
competed for the domain he was heir to. Nothing is known of his character or
features and, like his uncle Arrhidaeus, his only relevance was as a cipher for
others to claim legitimacy through. With him in this shadow world was his
mother, Roxanne, and if the life of the conqueror's only legitimate male
progeny was short and tragic, it may be he paid for the brutal circumstances in
which his status was assured. Legend has tried to make a romance from
Alexander's relationship with the Sogdian woman who became his first wife,
but the facts indicate a more prosaic truth. It was a normal dynastic
arrangement with the hallowed aim of marrying into a conquered elite and
producing a successor. There is no way of knowing if any emotional interest
was sparked between the two, but for Roxanne it is certain her position as
Alexander's only legal consort was of ultimate importance. All this was
threatened at the Susa weddings when her husband took Darius' daughter,
Stateira, as his second wife. She was bound to take second place to this better-
born spouse but friction was, for the most part, avoided by Stateira remaining
with her mother's household while Roxanne travelled with the main army.

When Alexander died, Roxanne's position was entirely dependent on the
child she was carrying; without it she was but a 'barbarian' widow of no
consequence. When rumours were heard that Stateira was also pregnant she
acted immediately. Her rival was at Ecbatana, hundreds of miles from
Babylon, and this gave her the opportunity. She sent a forged letter,
purporting to be from Alexander, ordering Darius' daughter to come to
Babylon. The messenger travelled at such speed that he outstripped the news
of the king's death and Stateira obeyed the summons, accompanied by her
sister, the widow of Hephaistion. When they reached the court, Roxanne had
them both unceremoniously murdered and their corpses dumped in a well

with orders for her servants to fill it in.[2] A potential for dynastic complication was eliminated.

We have no details of the court of the two kings that emerged after the Babylon settlement. Unlike that of Alexander, it was not the source of any power or patronage and so hardly attracts the attention of our sources. The rituals and ceremony of kingship continued but the real military, judicial and administrative prerogatives lay elsewhere. One of the undistinguished royal pair had fallen away by the time the peace of 311 BC brought a hiatus in the conflict and another act of violence removed Alexander IV that same year.[3] Nearly twelve, the boy had reached an age were he could become a potential focus for domestic opposition to Cassander. To prevent this, the prisoner at Amphipolis was poisoned along with Roxanne. Usually interpreted as another example of Cassander's vicious antipathy to the family of Alexander, this explanation is unsatisfactory as it fails to explain why he kept them alive so long. The timing was not coincidental; the snuffing out of the legitimate line of Macedonian kings was not just on the head of one man, as Diodorus explains:

> Cassander, Lysimachus, and Ptolemy, and Antigonus as well, were relieved of their anticipated danger from the king; for henceforth there being no longer anyone to inherit the realm, each of those who had rule over nations or cities entertained hopes of royal power.[4]

There had been general complicity in the murder. What the timing makes probable seems almost certain given the ample opportunity to arrange the disposal of the inconvenient boy during the peace negotiations and the fact that hardly any complaints were made after the event. His passing did not shake the world. The legitimate line of Alexander the Great was extinguished with hardly a whimper of regret. He had been living under a sentence of death all his short life and the end came as a shock to few. Only in a later era was the propaganda of opprobrium mobilised against the name of his executioner. For contemporaries in the market places and garrisons so much had happened in the twelve years since Alexander's death that he was just another great name come to an untimely end.

There was a bevy of beneficiaries from the demise of Roxanne's son: Cassander saved from an imminent threat; others relieved of the necessity of genuflecting in the direction of a distant dynasty; and Antigonus the One-eyed, as the power who alone was in a position to fill the vacancy at the head of the Macedonian world.

But the parameters of the possible had now visibly cramped in this veteran of nearly seventy years. A drop in gear in the Aegean is noticed but not due to any decline in effort or physical stamina in the head of the Antigonid house. The pause in the West was policy. The old marshal had sponsored the peace of 311 BC to free himself to face dangers from a different direction as the regions east of the Euphrates, unvisited for half a decade, demanded attention. The result was the Babylonian war with Seleucus that occupied him from 310 to 308 BC.

Instructions and exhortations took time to be transmitted in this era and, with the moving spirit of the Antigonid cause thousands of miles from the Aegean, it is no surprise their fortunes had also taken some knocks in that arena. Great damage was done when Ptolemaeus allowed himself to be subverted by Cassander. Antigonus' nephew, having campaigned successfully in Greece since 312 BC, found himself starved of resources by an uncle whose priorities lay elsewhere. His army required the momentum of success, the encouragement to push on, not a static role with no prospect of fame or benefit. In a world of shattered loyalties, the combination of a successful subordinate and a veteran army that had not seen its commander-in-chief for years was volatile. Ability, ambition and the right opportunity were enough of a catalyst for treason.

The new player secured his position with great care, constructing a power base in Euboea by garrisoning cities like Chalcis, which he had previously impressed by leaving independent. He also showed real strategic foresight by establishing forward bases in the Cyclades. His exact relationship with Cassander is unclear, but where Cassander before had a potent enemy on his southern march, this was no longer the case.

Antigonus must have begun to weary of the news his messengers brought when the sailing season of 310 BC opened and Ptolemy took his chance to exploit the absence of the main army in the east. The relentless antipathy of the Lagid ruler was evidenced when he sent an officer called Leonidas against Cilician Trachea, claiming the mantle of liberator from the Antigonids, whom he accused of breaching the peace of 311 BC by putting troops into cities there. Ptolemy had struck in this region before and, with the nearby island of Cyprus as a base, the coastline was always vulnerable.

With resources stretched, the response to these blows in the west was of necessity multi-faceted, complex and subtle. The cutting edge of efforts against Cassander and his other enemies in Greece was forged by an almost forgotten individual who, years before, had been a greater man than Antigonus himself, Polyperchon. Who approached who is unclear, but with advantages to both parties self evident, Polyperchon's status as an Antigonid officer was resuscitated after a lapse of five years. But, in this second period of association, he was to have an extra and fascinating card to play against Cassander: Heracles, the natural son of Alexander the Great by his mistress Barsine. At least one eminent historian has cast doubt on the very existence of this son, who bore the name of the legendary founder of the Macedonian kingdom, but this ignores a number of reliable references to the boy.[5] Most notably, he is mentioned at Babylon after his father's death when Nearchus had briefly proposed him for the throne. Since that summary rejection of his royal claims he had spent most of his seventeen years in comparative obscurity in the city of Pergamum in Asia Minor.

While Alexander IV lived, Heracles' existence was of little import but, subsequently, as the last male of Alexander the Great's bloodline, he had become a potent weapon in the armoury of Cassander's enemies. We know nothing but the name and age of this king over the water. At the same age his father had already won his first campaign but nothing of this precocious talent and personality seemed to have been passed on to his son. He proved to be merely a puppet who gave an aura of legitimacy to Polyperchon's ambition and caused considerable embarrassment to Cassander, who had hoped in killing his half-brother to extinguish the dynasty of Alexander forever.

By the time the hapless youth was shipped across the Aegean, Polyperchon was well advanced in his preparations. Crucially, for his ambitions, he now had access to Antigonus' treasury to fund recruitment to his own army and encourage subversion amongst Cassander's allies. Ptolemaeus' treachery had meant the reversion of much of central Greece to Cassander's side but there were still enough towns and cities that longed for ancient independence. Nor was it just in Greece he looked for friends, he tirelessly canvassed for support in Macedonia through his still-numerous contacts amongst the aristocracy.

The first fruits of this quest for allies were evident with the adherence of the federal league of Aetolia. They had long been enemies of Cassander and had sheltered Polyperchon at his lowest ebb after the defeat of Olympias. Their friendship gave the old adventurer not only the support of several thousand hardy warriors but also access to an invasion route to Macedon that went through Aetolia, outflanking Cassandran defences in central Greece and Thermopylae. By 309 BC, Polyperchon, with Heracles in tow, was at last ready. He had raised an army of 20,000 infantry and 1,000 horsemen and swept through Aetolia. Picking up his allies on the way he reached Tymphaea on the Macedonia-Epirus border and encamped his soldiers. Here in Polyperchon's home principality, his family's influence was still strong, giving the homecoming son the guarantee of a friendly reception.

Cassander had taken no real action against Polyperchon the previous year but now an invasion was under way and the waves of war were washing against Macedonia itself. He recognised that, despite the peace of 311 BC, Antigonus, as the moving force behind Polyperchon, was again taking up cudgels against him. With Macedonia's frontiers threatened, Cassander reacted decisively. The national levy was mobilised at Pella. It would only have taken a few days for the army, using the route down the Haliacmon river, past the royal palaces and tombs at Aegae, to reach the region of Tymphaea.

As long as he could retain the loyalty of his troops, Cassander had every confidence in eventual victory, knowing his Macedonian phalanx was likely to beat even Polyperchon's numerous forces. But the loyalty of the national army began to waver. The presence of Heracles, the last icon of Alexander, in the enemy ranks had its effect on Cassander's men, many of whom would have remembered his father and some even his grandfather. Furthermore, with Polyperchon's subversive work in Macedonia the previous year having its impact, it became painfully apparent to Cassander that he might have difficulty getting his army to fight Alexander's old general.

As so often, Cassander employed cunning where might would not prevail. He sent envoys to open negotiations with Polyperchon and offered some tempting blandishments. These included an appointment as commander-in-chief in the Peloponnese, the return of all his estates in Macedonia and the intriguingly ambiguous promise that he 'would be a partner in everything in Cassander's realm, being honoured above all'.[6] Clearly this cannot have implied a share in the government of Macedonia, as Polyperchon was to return south, but it presumably offered a guarantee of the military and financial support needed to effectively dominate the Peloponnese. It might be assumed Polyperchon had little reason to trust the promises of a man who had earlier been the cause of his ruin but, in an astonishing volte face, he accepted Cassander's proposals. The old warrior, after so many years in obscurity, lost his nerve when real success beckoned. Unopposed pre-eminence in the backwater of the Peloponnese suddenly seemed a more attractive prospect than the risks of real power; this timidity allowed him to agree even to the final shabby condition of the agreement. Cassander demanded, as a seal to their bargain, that Heracles be eliminated. The unfortunate lad was duly assassinated at a banquet especially arranged before the terms of the treaty became widely known.

When the agreement was made public, most of the Aetolians and other allies left in disgust at the cynical manoeuvre. Cassander, anxious to be rid of Polyperchon, paid the first instalment of their contract. He provided 4,000

Macedonian foot and 500 Thessalian horse to bolster what was left of Polyperchon's army and arranged for the general's confiscated land in Macedonia to be returned; little enough to pay to be rid of a man who had, briefly, looked like an awful threat to all Cassander held. The extent to which Polyperchon's prestige had been dented by these events was indicated on the return journey south. This time he took the road down the coast that led through the pass of Thermopylae, the Aetolians having denied him passage through their country, but he found the Boeotians barring his way. Even against this second-rate opposition he could not force his way through.

He eventually regained the Peloponnese that had been his home for so long and remained as an ally of Cassander, being mentioned briefly as fighting in his armies in the four-year war that flared up in Greece later in the decade. By this time, he was nearing eighty and nothing more is heard of him again. He had had a strange and melancholy career. Promoted late in his life by Alexander, he owed his subsequent prominence to the demise of more able men. His short tenure as regent of the empire was an unmitigated disaster. There can be no doubt that he was, at times, a very capable soldier but as a politician he was completely out of his depth. The callous disposal of Heracles was the ugly culmination of a career which had run out of steam and direction many years earlier.

After the failure against Seleucus in the Babylonian War, the Antigonid engine changed its direction from east to west and the man at its head was one of the most charismatic and extraordinary personalities of the ancient world. Demetrius' flawed and unstable nature would be enshrined forever in an analysis constructed by Plutarch and, whatever suspicion we might have about the old moralist's veracity, the bald facts indicate a mercurial temperament and career that is almost unique in Greek history:

> His features combined charm and seriousness, beauty and a capacity to inspire fear, but hardest of all to represent was the blend in his appearance of the eagerness and fire of youth with a heroic aspect and an air of kingly dignity. In his disposition he was equally capable of making himself loved and feared. He could be the most delightful of companions, more voluptuous than any other ruler of his age in his addiction to drinking and other luxurious habits of life, and yet when action was required, he could show the utmost energy, perseverance and practical ability.[7]

Only Alcibiades would seem to offer a match in both youthful promise and the ups and downs of later life but the stage the Athenian strode was far more constrained by geography before the expansion of the Hellenic world under Alexander.

Demetrius had the complete confidence of his father and was able to call on all the assets of the Antigonid realm to outfit his enterprise. His target was to be Athens, a city with which he was to become inextricably linked. Plutarch interprets it as the one morally great act of the Antigonids' lives as he swallows wholesale the claim that the armada from Asia was aiming to free the Greek cities from alien garrisons that kept the citizenry in chains. For him, Athens was an ideal of freedom and culture so for a great power like the Antigonids to come to its aid gave their actions a legitimacy that *realpolitik* could not. This cannot blind us to the reality that the Antigonids' purpose was concerned with a fight for domination and not the traditions of Solon and Pericles. Certainly Greek culture was important; a stamp of worth, a talisman to show it was not self-interest alone that motivated these Macedonian warlords. This small and economically ill-endowed corner of the huge empire the Macedonians inherited still called them back in a way that is only partly explained by affection for a cultural homeland. A more prosaic analysis than that handed down by Plutarch must be given its due. Greece was the greatest single source of first-class infantry outside of Macedon itself. Asia might produce riches, Phoenicia and Egypt shipbuilders and sailors, but it was the cities of Greece, the Aegean and latterly Macedonia that had produced the foot soldiers that dominated every battlefield and remained supreme until the advent of the Roman legion.

The Macedonian element in the field armies of the Successors was vital, they were the battle winners, but they were limited in number. However, if they were a scarce commodity, in the Greek communities there were thousands of men who would turn to soldiering for a good paymaster. For years a mercenary market had been established in the Peloponnese; from there warriors travelled west to fight for the Carthaginians against the tyrants of Syracuse and east to feed the interminable wars of the Successors. By 307 BC, Cassander was well on his way to overall hegemony of the region. He had, by now, sustained himself in the position he had won from Polyperchon and Olympias for almost ten years. Certainly, he had staggered under the blows of his rivals but he had survived. It had been a matter of continual vigilance and oppressive interference amongst those neighbours that were seen as being essential to Macedonian security. Indeed, in 307 BC he was campaigning in Epirus in an effort to ensure the government of that key ally was to his liking when he received news of the threat from the east. The depth of Cassander's control in Greece was impressive. He had the oligarchs of Greece in his pockets, Polyperchon was an ally and Ptolemy's adventure in the peninsula a thing of the past.

This was a situation that neither Antigonus nor Demetrius could contemplate with equanimity and to rock and replace Cassander's dominance was their ojective. Demetrius' expeditionary force was concentrated at the great port of Ephesus, where he took command of a huge fleet of 250 ships, well supplied with marines and a great war chest of 5,000 talents, to be spent on hiring mercenaries and subverting local politicians. The seriousness of Antigonus' purpose can be gauged by the fact that this armada was over twice the size of any previous expedition he had sent to Greece. The invaders sailed for Piraeus, where Cassander's garrison was a vital shackle securing his control of mainland Greece.

The marines began to assault the walls of Piraeus whilst Antigonus' son harangued the crowd who had gathered on the quay. The leading citizens and many of the populace had gathered to welcome what they thought were friends from Egypt and they stayed to listen when the glamorous intruder addressed them from the deck of his great flagship. He told them he intended to free the city from foreign influence, drive out Cassander's garrison and remove his puppet, Demetrius of Phalerum. His oratory found a responsive audience, appealing as it did to the grand memories of those many who resented their obvious thrall to the northern kingdom. Dionysius, Cassander's garrison commander at Piraeus, put up a respectable resistance until the Antigonid soldiers had got inside the walls in such numbers that he deemed it prudent to retreat with his men to the more defensible fort of Munychia. Demetrius of Phalerum had planned to hold the walls of Athens but it became abundantly clear the next day that this was a forlorn hope. With the populace against him, he had no option but to send envoys to negotiate with the invader for the surrender of Athens and safe conduct for themselves. A bargain was easily arranged as the younger Demetrius was in a benevolent mood due to the ease of his victory. Demetrius of Phalerum left the city he had so long dominated under safe conduct to Thebes, where the people had kinder memories of him for his help in rebuilding their city. As it turned out, this was only a staging post *en route* to Ptolemy's court, where he would resume his remarkable career.[8]

Having built a palisade and entrenchment and leaving enough men to invest the Munychia, Demetrius, son of Antigonus, embarked the bulk of his army at Piraeus and shipped it down the coast to attack Megara, where Cassander maintained a considerable garrison. This lightning strike completely unsettled his opponents. The defenders surrendered after a short siege, when it became clear no one was coming to their aid. The whole region from the Gulf of Corinth to the Parnes range seemed ripe for the taking.

Demetrius' firm control over his followers was evident again when, at the behest of the Athenians, he halted the systematic looting of Megara and prevented wholesale destruction. A story is told about the most famous resident of the town, the philosopher, Stilpo, who had retired there for a life of contemplation. He is little remembered now but then enjoyed a reputation as a great philosopher. Known in his youth as a drinker and womaniser, he had transformed himself into an exemplar of personal probity, in the process acquiring the kind of unlikeable pomposity typical of reformed reprobates. The most formidable debater of his day, his reputation brought other great names to his school, including Zeno, the founder of the Stoic school and Crates, the Cynic. Acclaimed as an authority on politics, Stilpo had deftly avoided attaching himself to any of the Macedonian dynasts who courted him. Ptolemy, in 308 BC, had tried to take him off to Alexandria but Stilpo was his own man and decamped temporarily to Aegina to avoid these advances. Now his search for peace was again rudely interrupted and he was not in good temper when Demetrius had him brought into his presence. As when Alexander encountered old Diogenes in his barrel, this thinker was prickly when confronted with the power and influence of the material world. When asked if anything of value had been stolen from him, Stilpo replied with an academic's disdain: 'I have seen nobody carrying away any knowledge'.[9]

Another, though less famous, comment is more revealing of the times. After Demetrius declared Megara free of its foreign garrison, Stilpo sarcastically remarked that his campaign of liberation had truly left the town a city of free men, because the Antigonid soldiers had stolen all the slaves. This not only shows that the contradictions inherent in a society based on slavery, yet exulting an ideology of freedom, were well understood at the time, but also gives an insight into what a soldier's plunder consisted of in the ancient world. When an enemy city was sacked, it was not so much gold, silver or works of art that were the victor's spoils, but trains of slaves destined to be sold for cash.

While the siege of Megara was in progress another colourful incident had occurred. It involved Cratesipolis, that resourceful and apparently beautiful woman who had retired from public life the previous year after selling off her interests to Ptolemy. Unable to resist the lure of her reputation, Demetrius left the camp outside Megara and set off with a few attendants to make her acquaintance. They arranged to meet at a secret rendezvous, where he pitched his tent away from his guards so Cratesipolis could visit him unobserved. However, some of Demetrius' enemies got wind of what was happening and suddenly attacked the camp forcing him to flee ingloriously, wrapped in a shabby cloak. As for Cratesipolis, the sources tell us frustratingly little about this enigmatic figure and after this she fades completely from history.

With these adventures over and much achieved in Attica, Demetrius returned to the siege of Munychia, a fort that had kept the Athenians chained to Cassander's will for twelve years. Antigonid engineers had been hard at work. Siege machines had been built and gathered in a park near the hill where the Munychia stood and, already, catapults were harassing any members of the garrison that dared show themselves on the battlements. With the return of the main army, an all-out attack was launched. The assault troops must have taken considerable casualties from the bolts, arrows and spears fired down amongst them but morale built on success was high. The defenders had been under siege for months, short of provisions and with no sign of relief from the north. The Antigonids broke into the fort and drove the garrison back until they soon had no option but surrender.

With immediate military aims accomplished, Cassander's power eradicated south of the Parnes and the weather indicating the onset of winter, Demetrius finally allowed himself the pleasure of a triumphant entry into Athens itself. The city's power in the world was a shadow of what it had been a hundred years before but the reputation of her citizens' achievements still held the Hellenic world in her spell. Demetrius was not immune to Athens' reputation for both high culture and low entertainment and the people welcomed him in style.

The assembly, reconstituted in its ancestral form, voted Demetrius an avalanche of honours. He and his father were hailed as kings. They were raised up as saviour gods of the city with gold statues of them set up at public expense. Two new tribes were created in the citizen roll and named after them, as were two sacred triremes. Demetrius was given the status of an oracle whose dictate must be obeyed. One of the months of the year was even renamed after him. Temple women were put to work weaving the image of the Antigonids into the fabric of Athena's holy mantle and athletes and artists adjusted their calendars to incorporate the new games dedicated to these most junior members of the local pantheon.

Though Demetrius soaked up these extraordinary sycophantic antics with relish, it did not deter him from the practical construction of a power base in the city. In his absence over the summer, Aristodemus had been grooming a politician, Stratocles, an old assembly hack who had made his name acting against Demosthenes years before, to orchestrate Athenian policy to an Antigonid tune. Not content to arrange a sympathetic administration,

Demetrius insinuated himself into the traditional ruling class by marrying Eurydice, a descendant of the ancient and aristocratic family of Miltiades, hero of Marathon, thus grafting his family's cause onto the stem of Athenian history.

Antigonus had received the news of his son's progress in Europe with great pleasure. Athenian envoys had travelled to his headquarters, with all ceremony, to thank him for delivering them from oppression and to relate the roll of honours the city had bestowed on his family, a love feast from which these new clients of the Antigonids benefited in a grand manner. Antigonus sent the Athenians food and money as well as timber sufficient to build 100 warships, a gift that encouraged a resuscitation of ancient naval might and offered the promise for Demetrius of a useful seagoing auxiliary. Imbros and Lemnos were also returned to the city, north Aegean islands and former Athenian colonies that had been considered important enough for some years to have been secured with Antigonid troops.

Antigonus enjoyed these European triumphs but they failed to deflect him from deeper objectives. Since 315 BC, control of the sea had been the cornerstone of his western policy. Without the great fleets and ports he controlled, what had been achieved in Greece could not have even been begun. Ptolemy's Egypt, the other great maritime power, loomed large in his mind and though the Lagids had not interfered so far against Demetrius' invasion, their potential to do so was worrying. This surely explains his apparently strange decision not to allow Demetrius to assault Cassander at what must have been the Macedonian ruler's lowest ebb.

The cockpit of the new war was Cyprus, where Ptolemy had long been the dominant power. Antigonus had campaigned there in the Perdiccan wars and for years had been trying to undermine the allegiance of the petty rulers of the island. He now determined that Demetrius should directly confront his enemy. If he could secure Cyprus it would give him uncontested control of the seaways from the ports of Palestine and Phoenicia to the Aegean, depriving Ptolemy of the base from which he had so destructively attacked Cilicia, Caria, Lycia and Syria.

Whatever the risks of Demetrius' enterprises, his father had kept his old bones in Syria, distracting himself with the architects, masons and surveyors who were planning out the new city of Antigonia. Cassander had his Cassandreia; Lysimachus had built a new seat of government in the Thracian Chersonese, where Cardia had once stood; and Seleucus was in the process of founding Seleucia on the Tigris to replace a battered Babylon; Antigonus was determined not to be left behind.

Geography and trade made northern Syria the natural choice for the site of the great foundation. From there, Antigonus could control the lands to the south, where the cities of the Levant had prospered for generations as the Mediterranean terminus of eastern caravan trails, and the spice routes from India and Southeast Asia. Antigonia was also a focal point on the great road network that led west to Anatolia and east to Mesopotamia.

Convening great councils, handing down Solomonic judgements, even achieving bloody victories in battle, could all be ephemeral, but a city with temples and festivals to glorify the name of its founder – this was immortality.[10] The city is gone, the story of Antioch subsuming all trace of this earlier foundation, but that should not obscure how great the expectations for Antigonia were at the time.[11]

During the construction of what was seen as a timeless metropolis Antigonus received news of Demetrius' spectacular triumph at Salamis, the like of which Antigonus had not known since the defeat of Eumenes. All seemed auspicious and in a year of victory the old marshal took a step he had been contemplating for some time. The reputation of Philip and Alexander held a magic that never failed to exert a hold on the imagination of the people of the Greek world. But nearly twenty years had passed since the latter's death; the legitimacy of their dynasty had withered and Alexander IV, the last of their blood to sit on a throne, had been eliminated. Antigonus had been acclaimed king by his non-Hellenic subjects for years and from hindsight the extension to all his dependants seems inevitable. He had possessed an empire, in reality, for over a decade but naked power as ideology is never comfortable for long and the need existed to construct a legitimate foundation for the future of Antigonid rule. 'And when Antigonus heard of the victory that had been gained', writes Diodorus, 'elated by the magnitude of his good fortune, he assumed the diadem and from that time on he used the style of king'.[12] To secure the succession, Demetrius was elevated with his father while still involved in the task of pacifying Cyprus. With the diadem came a summons to return to Syria that was immediately obeyed. He sailed for the port of Laodicea before the onset of autumn weather made fleet movements dangerous, to a meeting with his father where the lustre of victory and newly-acquired royalty were mixed in great show.[13]

Ten years of autocratic rule made a king as much as any blood or constitution. But if the move to monarchy was such a comfortable solution, the question is why it was not taken years before. What is crucial in understanding this development is to discover the audience it was aimed at. It was certainly not done to simplify relations with the Greeks, in a sense it only complicated these. Being a city's saviour god might facilitate the problematic question of constitutional authority but a royal title did not. Kingship was either ridiculous or threatening to most Greeks. For the peoples of the old Persian empire it was just an explanation of a truism. Those the new title was meant to impress were exclusively the Macedonians, indeed Antigonus' own Macedonians, who won his battles and governed his empire. To offer them a framework that satisfied their material and psychological needs it was the only answer. For them, proper authority had to be monarchical, which could legitimise their own positions, the property and authority they had received from the patronage of their leader. It was a step that was natural but nonetheless still entailed dangers.

Antigonus was substituting his own dynasty for that of Alexander. He knew his rivals would not accept, without force, the authority his new status made claim to. Indeed, soon after these diadems were first conjured up in Syria, Cassander, Ptolemy, Lysimachus and Seleucus were falling over themselves to assert their kingship. Their claims for the moment were specific to their own territories but what soon became clear was that Antigonus, the man who harboured ambitions to unify the Macedonian world under his rule, had started a fashion that looked set to institutionalise its division.[14]

With Ptolemy now at his weakest after the disasters of Salamis, Antigonus decided to deal with him once and for all. But, as we have seen, the invasion of Egypt turned into something of a fiasco as the natural defences of the Nile coupled with Ptolemy's resourceful tenacity denied him. Although little weakened, the retreat from Egypt marked the end of the great days of Antigonid power as the old general's ambitions became more limited in scope and enterprise.

The semi-retirement of the head of the Antigonids contributed to a sea change in strategy. No longer were campaigns directed to the swift and total elimination of rivals; the other *Diadochi* had a real strength that needed to be worn down, since they could not be crushed in blitzkrieg assaults. A cautious note enters policy that was not noticeable before, military offensives were not abandoned but they became more limited in scope. The total strength of the kingdom was not again committed to the gamble of war until the last act of Antigonus' life. Formidable armies would be mobilised but they were led by the son, not the father. At the height of his powers, still under thirty, Demetrius was only too willing to shoulder the burden and the next few years saw him ranging like a titan across the Aegean world in the Antigonid cause.

Ptolemy was vulnerable in his wallet; a considerable amount of his disposable income came from the profits of commerce and, with his navy in dire straits, this seaborne traffic was ripe for attack. The normal hazards of weather and piracy made ancient navigation risky in ordinary circumstances, and the Antigonids intended that additional dangers should be organised against Ptolemaic shipping. The recent acquisition of Cyprus, combined with a dominant position in the Aegean islands and the control of the coast of Asia Minor, meant they could almost establish a long-distance blockade against any rival. The nature of fourth-century BC sea travel ensured that this embargo could never be total; ancient warships were not capable of cruising the sea-lanes to stop all commerce. Yet if Antigonus could control most of the landfalls on the important routes, life would be extremely difficult for merchant captains sailing from Alexandria and the other Ptolemaic ports of North Africa. But there was a missing link: the island of Rhodes. Without this republic's cooperation the chances of squeezing Ptolemy's economy were much reduced.

During the years of the succession struggles, benevolent neutrality had been a profitable posture. Rhodian shipyards had built many of Antigonus' warships and her populace had found employment in his expanding navy. Egypt was also a major trading partner both as customer for goods bought in Rhodian ships and as a source of essential imports for the island, while Rhodes also served as the middleman for Egypt's grain trade with Greece.

Antigonid pressure on the island was cumulative. During the Salamis campaign an attempt had been made to force them into an alliance against Ptolemy. When the end of winter allowed ships to put to sea, Antigonus sent a small force to disrupt Ptolemy's trade with the island and to force the recalcitrant populace into line. The squadron met with little success and was eventually driven off. Even so, threats of retribution caused the Rhodians to immediately despatch envoys. Unfortunately, these ambassadors would not agree to join the war against Ptolemy. Frustrated by their obduracy, Demetrius was delegated to lead a great fleet and army to enforce compliance on the island.

The expedition was assembled at Loryma on the Carian mainland, almost directly opposite Rhodes city. The island sent more envoys to explain that they had rethought their position and were prepared to join the alliance as required. Demetrius demanded they hand over 100 leading citizens as hostages and that he be allowed to enter Rhodes harbour with his fleet to collect them. This proved the last straw for the proud republic; the envoys withdrew and the island determined to resist the invader.

It was here that Demetrius would earn the epithet 'Poliorcetes' (besieger of cities). His ambition and inclination placed him well in sympathy with an age of architects and builders when so many of the monuments that would be acclaimed as wonders of the ancient world were built. The Mausoleum at Halicarnassus, the Colossus of Rhodes and the Pharos at Alexandria were all built within a couple of generations either side of the year 300 BC. Demetrius embodied the spirit of Hellenistic gigantism, spending prodigiously from his father's resources to construct huge warships with more and more men to each bank of oars and massive siege towers, battering rams and missile throwers to attack the walls of enemy cities. The siege of Rhodes was one of the epic contests of this age and in it Demetrius would hit high notes of engineering ingenuity.

Demetrius brought with him 200 warships and 170 transports, decks crowded with over 40,000 soldiers and pirate allies. It is also claimed there were almost another 1,000 yachts and trading craft owned by maritime entrepreneurs eager to join in the looting of Rhodes. They sailed round the coast and landed where they were well placed for attack, but distant enough to avoid harassment by the city's artillery. A breakwater was rapidly constructed to protect the precious ships, while the soldiers built a palisaded camp to defend themselves against enemy raids.

The initial plan was to capture the harbour and blockade the city. A naval task force failed to get inside the harbour walls, but won a small foothold on the mole that protected the harbour, only to be driven back after eight days' bloody fighting. The Antigonids drew away to regroup. The second offensive, a week later, was carelessly handled and three Rhodian ships inflicted great damage on the Antigonid fleet until numbers overcame them. The weather then intervened and in the ensuing chaos the Rhodians captured the garrison on the mole. Demetrius prudently withdrew to the shelter of his artificial harbour.

This was to be the last onslaught by Demetrius in a miserable season in front of Rhodes' walls and his disappointment was further compounded by the sight of reinforcements. 650 mercenaries (some of them Rhodians), sent by Ptolemy and other friends in Crete, sailed into the port he had so singularly failed to close. Winter storms now threatened, ending any possibility of continuing the assault and the Antigonids resigned themselves to wintering on the island.

Failure both to capture the port and cut off the supply of reinforcements caused a change of tactic in 304 BC. Demetrius turned his attention from the harbour to the land walls of the town. As soon as the weather allowed, soldiers built trenches and palisades, miners began the tunnels that would snake under the walls and his engineers uprooted every tree on the island to construct the machines that would directly assault Rhodes' defences. The main curtain wall was soon undermined and, after fierce fighting, collapsed completely. But Demetrius' forces now found to their chagrin that the enemy had built another wall behind the first and were even engaged in building a third wall.

Over a year of endeavour, increasing physical hardship for his troops encamped on the small island and the competing demands for his presence elsewhere made it clear to Demetrius that time was running out. He organised his best men for a risky but potentially-decisive night escalade. The 1,500 soldiers managed to reach the theatre in the city but were halted and counterattacked by the reinforcements from Ptolemy. Trapped, all were eventually killed or captured.

Antigonus finally intervened and ordered his son to make peace with the brave islanders. The arrival of an Aetolian delegation urging him to come to Greece to oppose Cassander served as the rationale, allowing the defeat to be disguised as an act of policy. The peace terms agreed left no doubt about who had prevailed. The treaty between the republic and the Antigonids specifically excluded any duty on the island's people to take up arms against Ptolemy.

It was Rhodes' greatest hour. Just over 7,000 defenders, some of them slaves freed for their gallantry during the siege, had staved off one of the largest amphibious enterprises of the era, an extraordinary achievement that the maritime republic celebrated with a rash of statues to her royal benefactors (Ptolemy meriting pride of place, as described previously).[15] The Colossus of Rhodes was begun at this time as the final exhibition of civic pride. The least known of the seven wonders of the ancient world was an enormous bronze statue of Helios, the sun god. Over 110 feet high, it was three times taller than any other Greek statue at the time and all funded by the dismantling and sale of the siege machines Demetrius left behind. We have no precise idea of what it actually looked like or even where it stood during its short life of less than seventy years before an earthquake in 226 BC toppled the giant at its knees. For 900 years it remained a sad if impressive ruin until in 654 AD the Arabs, after taking Rhodes, dismantled the remains and transported the fragments back to Asia.[16]

Another city had defended its independence less well than Rhodes in these dangerous days of Macedonian power. The changes Athens had gone through since the death of Alexander had been driven from outside. The exclusive experience of Athenians to the year 307 BC had been the oligarchic, pro-Macedonian tutelage, from Antipater's stooges to Demetrius of Phalerum. Even when that year saw the foreign garrison turfed out of Piraeus it was through the agency of another outsider. Yet when Demetrius Poliorcetes resurrected the old constitution and re-enfranchised ten thousand citizens, he kick-started a kind of political activity quite different from that of the Phalerian's day.

A belligerence and vitality was recovered at the heart of Athens that cannot help but appeal to us. The imagination paints a picture of the new voters walking from workshops in the city, from smallholdings outside the walls and from Piraeus to the Assembly at the market place or the hill of Pnyx. Many travelled through the dark to meetings that started soon after daybreak, where thousands gathered to decide on questions that alone were the province of the whole citizen body.[17]

Selection by lot ensured involvement and the political lifeblood of the state flowed to the music of pebbles clattering through the sortation machines. Free, enfranchised men were picked by chance to sit on the committees of five or ten that administered the minutiae of civic life or as jurors to decide on the disputes of an increasingly-litigious people, and in the boule of 600 that determined the agenda of the assembly.

All so much more admirable than our own arrangements that claim both the title of democracy and an ancestral line back to ancient Greece.[18] The involvement of modern citizens in the running of their lives is minimal, the politics of government an incubus and its participants regarded as high-status hucksters, while a mass vote once in half a decade only mandates rough parameters for a ruling elite. Sovereignty of the Assembly and sortation mark Greek democracy out as a totally different thing from its by-blows representative government. As a human event, the Assembly at Athens was far nearer to union meetings held at Longbridge or the pithead before the Tory laws of the 1980s' than the anodyne tomfoolery played out in the Houses of Parliament.

Yet the lot did not dominate every corner of city life. The Athenian board of generals, constitutional commissions and diplomatic legations were elected directly by the Assembly through a system that, though it tried to ensure representation from all the tribes, allowed the re-election of the same person year after year. With these key positions not subject to lottery, direct democracy was no guarantee against the corruption of privilege. High offices, through the centuries, tended to be filled from aristocratic families. Butchers, tanners and innkeepers seldom became generals, leading diplomats or faction leaders, but sortation did ensure the poorer classes were deeply involved in city administration.

Still, it was not the new political vigour south of the Parnes Mountains that concerned Cassander's administration at Pella. News was reaching them that the energy and wealth pent up during the peaceful rule of Demetrius of Phalerum was being spent prodigiously by his successors in preparation for war. A new generation of Athenians, unbowed by memories of the Lamian debacle, were taking up the burden of militant civic activism. Contemporary inscriptions attest that a property tax was imposed and that foreigners and metics were squeezed for considerable 'gifts' to produce the exceptional revenue required for a thoroughgoing refurbishing of the state's defences.[19]

The four year war began with Cassander moving south through Thessaly, where garrisons safeguarded the road, past Thermopylae, which was well held by his supporters. Boeotia came over onto his side and persuasion or intimidation smoothed the passage to the foothills of Mount Parnassus. The Athenians were desperate for allies and despatched Olympiodorus to sail to Aetolia and approach those other inveterate belligerents of the Lamian War for help. They needed little persuasion to enter an alliance but, for the moment, this could not prevent the Macedonian army breaching the northern frontier of Attica. After forcing the Parnassus passes, however, Cassander was able to make little headway.

With the Aetolians threatening their land communications, the invaders withdrew. Cassander returned to the offensive the next season and his armies were once more in the south. Frustratingly little is known of the course of the war but fighting took place around Elatea, the second city of Phocis (after Delphi), which controlled the road to south and central Greece.

That Elatea, to the north of Chaeronea, was the focus of the war in 305 BC adds considerably to our understanding of the balance of power in that year. Cassander's enemies were not this time confined to just defending Attica. The Boeotians were first persuaded to a truce and then to joining the Athenian-led coalition. So it was in considerable strength that Olympiodorus marched to the relief of Elatea. The details of the successful campaign are lost but the Elateans dedicated a bronze statue of Olympiodorus at Delphi in gratitude for their deliverance. The Cassandran army was forced to turn tail for a second successive year. Yet, like twenty-years before, the Athenians were to find a Greek coalition impossible to sustain.

The year 304 BC saw a change in Macedonian fortunes. Aetolia and Phocis fell away from Athens and Boeotia switched sides again. Now with no obstruction to impede his progress, Cassander was soon within twenty miles of Athens, capturing the Phyle and Panactum forts that dominated the passes from Boeotia to Attica. Athens' woes mounted when Cassander mobilised the Macedonian navy and used it to shattering effect against the Athenian fleet. Amongst the prisoners from the battle were islanders from Salamis. Being set free without ransom, they surrendered the island to Cassander out of gratitude. With a new enemy so close, the Athenians found themselves virtually blockaded. The seaways to Piraeus were cut, fickle allies had left them in the lurch and, to round off the sense of encirclement, Cassandran forces had taken Corinth and were ravaging the Peloponnese, so no help could be expected from that quarter. Athens was alone, facing, for the first time in almost a century, an enemy outside her gates, bent on her destruction.

There is no doubting the Macedonians' seriousness of purpose; their senior military establishment had descended on Attica in force, as graphically evidenced by the recent find of an Athenian lead curse. Discovered in a grave near the Dipylon Gate on the city walls the tablet was supposed to activate the dead person's ghost to harm the cursed. The names contained are those of Cassander, his brother Pleistarchus, Demetrius of Phalerum and Eupolemus (Cassander's general, formerly active in Caria).[20] One of these four officers, far from having his spirit undermined by this conjuring, nearly finished the campaign at a stroke. Pleistarchus almost got his corps within the city walls in an early assault and was only repulsed after a very hard-fought encounter.[21] After this near run thing, Cassander settled down to a regular siege.

While Cassander camped beneath the walls of Athens, Demetrius moved with great alacrity, a shocking development for those who had become used to Antigonid military might being bogged down in Rhodes. He visited islands on the way to reassure friends and overawe dissidents and then headed for Boeotia, entering the Euboean channel and landing at Aulis. From this base, Demetrius looked set to clamp himself across Cassander's road back to Pella.

Athens, for Cassander, now looked decidedly marginal. With summer on the wane, the threat of being cut off from Macedonia for the winter was very real. The army broke camp and was hurried north through the passes into Boeotia, hoping to get through the gates at Thermopylae. In fact, it was blocked and Cassander was forced to take his men west of the Kallidromo Mountains. Here they were caught and a running battle cost Cassander 6,000 Macedonians who deserted after the fight, while the rest escaped to Thessaly and home. Demetrius did not follow but re-established himself by making an alliance with the Boeotians and retaking the forts at Phyle and Panactum, before wintering in Athens.

When the city fathers welcomed their deliverers, this time it was the antics of the visitors that bought a blush to the cheeks of the citizens. Demetrius billeted his headquarters' staff in the Parthenon itself, claiming his right as saviour god to live in Athena's house. The blasphemy of filling the Holiest with soldiers and prostitutes and the debauching of Athenians of both sexes by the king is lovingly detailed by Plutarch, though nothing is heard of it from Diodorus. No doubt, Demetrius enjoyed himself with vigour and was not over tender with the sensitivities of the citizens, but this alone was not the cause of the tensions that surfaced. The reality was that not everybody was as happy as Stratocles that Demetrius' military might made him arbiter of Athenian fortunes.

It was only after the army left for the Peloponnese that the lid blew off this pot of troubles. Demetrius, from his camp, demanded immunity be given for a friend convicted by an Athenian court. The people reacted with outrage and banned any further involvement of the king in domestic matters. This bid for real independence was not, however, a practical possibility. It was not just a matter of Demetrius' power to coerce; the Athenians needed him in order to remain out of the clutches of Cassander. So when Demetrius stamped his feet it was only a matter of time before the citizens reluctantly acquiesced.

In the spring of 302 BC, Demetrius began an astonishingly complete attempt to secure hegemony in mainland Greece, activity that belies the tradition of his degeneration into an irresponsible debauchee at this time. He decided an attack on Cassander's kingdom would be a formidably difficult enterprise, and before trying he would need to secure his rear and weaken the enemy by the indirect approach.

Those veterans, Polyperchon and Prepelaus, defended Cassander's cause in the Peloponnese, but the situation was complicated by the presence of a rump of Ptolemaic power at Sicyon and it was there Demetrius struck. With a secure bridgehead at Cenchreae, taken two years previously, he was able to turn the defences at the Isthmus. Disembarking there with the Acrocorinth looming on their right hand, the Antigonid army had an easy day's march to Sicyon.

Demetrius' army broke through the walls in a night escalade and the citadel garrison surrendered on terms that they could ship back to Egypt unmolested. Now he turned southeast aiming at Corinth with its mountain citadel, where Prepelaus commanded. That should have proved a tough nut even for Poliorcetes, but when he led his army down the road towards the city gates the Corinthians let him in and, without pause, the attack was directed against the Acrocorinth.

Some of the city garrison had not been able to reach the craggy top of the Acrocorinth but had prepared a defence down the slopes at an outwork called Sisyphium. Here the defenders stood but Demetrius' men poured over them. Many of the Antigonids were wounded in the assault but their impetus was unstoppable. Men who escaped reached the citadel at the top, where, far from being an asset, they panicked the others. When they saw the enemy columns with their siege engines pass over Sisyphium and up towards them, the garrison's nerve broke. They surrendered or fled as best they could down the precipitous far side.

Demetrius now moved west into Achaia. Cassander's garrisons at Bura and Scyrus put up a stern fight before they were evicted. At Orchomenus the defenders hurled insults at Demetrius when he arrived beneath the walls. The young king disliked his dignity being mocked at the best of times so there was no question of waiting to besiege the place. Again, the assault parties took the defences after bloody fighting and the commander and eighty men were crucified in front of the town to relieve Demetrius' bile.

Demetrius had been hitting the high notes of success since he entered the Peloponnese and now all opposition in the area crumbled. Celebrations were in order and the festival of Hera provided the setting. Here he married the sister of Pyrrhus, Deidameia, previously betrothed to Alexander IV. Not only did this advertise Demetrius' claim to the throne of Macedonia, but was potentially a coup to forge an axis with the Epirotes against Pella itself.

Demetrius had now built a power base that would prove to have real strength when tested by catastrophe. In 302 BC he arranged his masterstroke. The Isthmus festival was turned into a great assembly of the communities of Greece who had come over from allegiance to Cassander. There Demetrius created a new league of Corinth that encompassed most of Hellas south of Thessaly, with the most notable and predictable exception being Sparta. All members were assessed for their military contribution and default was severely punished.

Cassander, whilst instigating countermeasures in Asia, decided on a holding operation against the new Greek alliance. He marched down through Thessaly, intending to defend Macedonia at a distance. His army of nearly 30,000 infantry and 2,000 horse posed problems by holding the passes and roads north. But Demetrius took his forces to Chalcis, in Euboea, and then embarked for Larisa Cremaste on the mainland, near the northern mouth of the Euboean channel, outflanking Cassander's defences.

Cassander had known the communities here were weak links and tried, but failed, to move their populations to more defensible sites. Now his prescience was proved when, after the invader's initial success, several more towns in the vicinity went over to Demetrius. Poliorcetes was now in a position to attack Thessaly itself and marched against two of the most important cities, Thebes and Pherae. Cassander rushed back to protect them.

Showing real perseverance, Cassander resumed a waiting game in anticipation of news from Asia. Against an invading army of 8,000

Macedonian pikemen, 15,000 mercenary foot, 8,000 light-armed auxiliaries, 1,500 horse and 25,000 Greek troops from the league, he could not risk a battle. So he dug in to try and hold them up. The stalemate seemed set to last, until, after several weeks, some disaffected citizens from Pherae offered Demetrius an opportunity for action. He led part of his army to Pherae, entered without opposition and assaulted the citadel. The garrison surrendered and, with the town secured, the road north to Lake Boebe and into Macedon itself was once more open. Cassander's strategy seemed to be in tatters, his hold on his kingdom balanced on a knife-edge.

Once again, however, the direction of Demetrius' endeavours was put out of joint by his father's diktat. Messengers came to call him back from the brink of triumph to support the war in Anatolia. Cassander's gamble had just paid off. Both sides knew that the future of Greece and Macedonia was to be decided in Asia.

Chapter 9

Ipsus

At a later period after Antigonus had been killed in battle, and those who had taken his life had begun to oppress and tyrannise over their subjects, a peasant in Phrygia who was digging on his farm was asked by a passer-by what he was doing, and replied 'I am searching for Antigonus'.[1]

Before the advent of Alexander the world of both Hellene and 'barbarian' had, for almost two centuries, conformed to a stable general pattern. On the marches between these two worlds there might be changes, disputes over the control of Aegean cities or national revolts in Egypt, but, in the main, Hellenic society clung to the narrow confines of mainland Greece, the islands and the extreme edge of the Asian land-mass, whilst the Persians ruled the vast heartland of Anatolia, Mesopotamia and Iran. Each felt the need to frequently meddle in the domestic squabbles of the other but not since Xerxes had either civilisation tried to completely overthrow the other. Alexander's conquests had ruptured this pattern completely but he had not lived long enough to establish a new one in its place. After the two decades of bloody and destructive strife that followed his demise, it seemed at last as if a new design had emerged. Antigonus was established in Anatolia and the Levant, Ptolemy held Egypt and Seleucus was monarch of inner Asia, whilst between them Cassander and Lysimachus ruled the European provinces of Greater Macedonia that Philip had created.

In fact, it was not to be; the incurable bellicosity of the first Hellenistic monarchs would smash this arrangement almost as soon as it was established. Another twenty years and the trauma of a brutal invasion from central Europe would be needed before the kaleidoscopic picture of the Hellenistic world finally settled into place. The events that threw into confusion these new-found kingdoms were some of the most dramatic of ancient history. Four of the kings would come to battle in the heart of modern-day Turkey in an epic conflict, where the number of combatants would assume almost twentieth-century proportions. One would lead a march that makes Hannibal's journey from Spain to Italy pale into insignificance and huge armies would coordinate their movements from starting points thousands of miles apart, with no more sophisticated means of communication than messengers on horseback.

The principal catalyst of these events was Antigonid aggression. Failures in Egypt and Rhodes had offered some consolation, but still the other *Diadochi* were convinced Antigonus and son intended to unify the Macedonian empire under their rule. As the last decade of the fourth century BC ran down, it was Cassander who was directly threatened. In Demetrius' first foray into mainland Greece, the ruler of Macedon had seen his dominant position there undermined, but on his second visit the young king seemed set to attack Macedonia itself.

Initially, Cassander attempted to diffuse the impending deluge by diplomacy. He outfitted an embassy that travelled all the way to Syria, only to find 'Antigonus replied that he recognised only one basis for settlement – Cassander's surrender of whatever he possessed'.[2] With war the only alternative, early in 302 BC Cassander invited Lysimachus to visit him at the Macedonian capital, Pella.

There is a story that this Lysimachus, destined to be the penultimate survivor of Alexander's marshals, was not truly a Macedonian but came from Thessaly. His father was reputedly a peasant from around Crannon who came to the attention of Philip II when he was campaigning thereabouts. If there was any truth in this, the rest is even more improbable: that he insinuated himself into the Macedonian king's affections by flattery. The more likely explanation is that he gained notice for the same warrior qualities of courage and tirelessness that characterised his son. Lysimachus himself is known to have been born in Pella a couple of years after Alexander, when his father, Agathocles, was a leading light at Philip's court. His peers considered Lysimachus unimpeachably a Macedonian insider and no comments on his origin, like those against Eumenes of Cardia, are recorded. This is particularly telling as any hints would surely have been passed on by Hieronymus, who was only too willing to blacken Lysimachus' name in the service of the Antigonids.

Antecedents aside, his social position was sufficient to win a place as one of Alexander's bodyguard, an honour open only to warriors of the highest status.[3] In this capacity, the young soldier attended closely on the king during all the great campaigns, though he was never granted independent command. A tale from Plutarch suggests how close a bodyguard stayed to his master. He tells us that when a chronicler of Alexander, many years after the alleged event, informed Lysimachus of the visit of an Amazonian queen to that king's court, he replied 'I wonder where I was then', indicating that, if he had not witnessed it, there could be no truth in the claim.[4]

Lysimachus is first mentioned when a brother steals the headlines. When chasing down the warlord, Sisimithres, in Sogdia, Alexander pursued closely with his cavalry but the forested hills were rough and the pace so hard that many of the king's followers broke down their mounts. Lysimachus' brother, Philip, was one of these, but refusing to remain behind like the other dismounted troopers he kept up with the pursuit on foot. Supposedly, he repeatedly refused Lysimachus' offer of his own horse to ride, even though the chase was pushed hard for over fifty miles. After catching up with the enemy, Lysimachus and his brother fought Homerically, protecting their king with their bodies. When the Sogdians were overcome, Philip died cradled in Alexander's arms, not of battle wounds but of exhaustion.[5]

From this time, Lysimachus is lost to sight until the grand army traversed the Hindu Kush into India. There he, too, crossed the flooding river in Alexander's boat to confront Porus. At the Hydaspes he came off unscathed but, not long after, was severely wounded when battling the Cathaei, whose capital was at Sangala (near modern Amritsar). As an invalid, he was sent back with Craterus and was spared the ordeal of the Makran desert.

It was not only in battle that Lysimachus and the other young aristocrats who guarded the king were kept on their mettle. The affair of Cleitus the Black shows them in attendance at evening entertainments. Lysimachus was one of those who helped disarm Alexander when he first grabbed a spear, though, like the rest, he was powerless to intervene when the second, fatal, assault took place. Not that all his behaviour at court reflected so well on his reputation. It is claimed his negative reports were at least partly responsible for the doom of Callisthenes, nephew of Aristotle in the aftermath of the pages plot.[6]

Lysimachus was also noted as the particular disciple of Calanus, the Indian guru who joined the army at Taxila, when Alexander was winning friends and allies before marching against Porus. Calanus had got through the desert march of Makran when men half his age had died of exhaustion, but it had irreparably damaged his health. He decided to die rather than drag out his days as an invalid and burden on his friends. A great funeral pyre was constructed in front of the army and court and he proceeded to mount the structure to be burnt alive in the flames. As he did so, bidding goodbye to his intimates, he bequeathed his richest possession, a fine Nesaean horse, to Lysimachus.[7]

After this, little is heard of Lysimachus during Alexander's life, though he is attested as attending the fatal party at Babylon, hosted by Medius. His support for Perdiccas, which came naturally enough against the outsider, Meleager, won a place in the pecking order that was perhaps not presaged by his record under the dead king. In the settlement of 323 BC, Lysimachus did not garner one of the plum provinces; yet his reward was of such strategic importance that he must have been thought a dependable friend. He drew as his portion the border satrapy of Thrace and, as far as is known, when he took the road out from Babylon it was the first time he had held independent command. The escort that accompanied him was not large, 4,000 infantry and 2,000 cavalry to control an area that was large, populous and likely to be resistant to his government.

His troubles began as soon as he ferried his small army across the Hellespont. In the centre of what is now modern Bulgaria an aggressively independent state, the kingdom of Seuthes III, arose and was to give Lysimachus much trouble in his early years of power. The Odrysian kingdom was centred on a Thracian new town, Seuthopolis, near Kazanluk.

The Thracians marched down to meet the enemy in the Chersonese. A long and bloody battle was the result and both sides sustained heavy losses. To avoid further conflict the king and the satrap negotiated a treaty in which Seuthes kept his title and position but as the friend and ally of Lysimachus, an arrangement bolstered by marriage to an Odrysian princess (who bore Lysimachus at least one son, Alexander).[8] Lysimachus had been lucky; the campaign had been far from a complete success yet he was, at least, able to claim control of the province. Crucially, his writ did not, as yet, run to the rich Greek cities of the western Pontic coast, though by 315 BC he maintained garrisons in several of them.

For a few years, factional feuds, tribal politicking and dealing with the Greek communities, who had been so long planted in the region, filled Lysimachus' working days rather than involvement in the grand designs his fellow dynasts were acting out elsewhere. But the siting of his satrapy on the European shore of the Hellespontine crossing from Asia meant he could not expect to be long left alone as the Macedonian world erupted into civil war. Loyalty to Antipater, as Alexander's last effective viceroy in Europe, was forced on him by geography and this state of affairs was formalised when he married Antipater's daughter Nicaea, the widow of Perdiccas.[9] Lysimachus did not contribute to either the Lamian campaign or the war against Perdiccas, but a posture of co-operation guaranteed he retained Thrace in the carve up at Triparadeisus and his growing status was reflected in the naming of his youngest brother, Autodicus, as one of Philip Arrhidaeus' bodyguards. When Polyperchon succeeded Antipater and became embroiled in a war against Cassander, the Thracian satrap stood aside, though the warmth of his later relationship with Cassander might suggest he was not displeased with the eventual outcome in the power struggle. The assassination of Cleitus, the admiral, by his soldiers implies a more formal commitment.

By 316 BC the ruler of Thrace was most certainly allied to Cassander, though, in the years since Antipater's death, a sea change had occurred in his relationship with Pella. Any suggestion of suzerainty owed to the ruler of Macedonia had disappeared and Lysimachus demanded an equality of standing with Cassander that he would have hesitated to claim from his father. Lysimachus had secured his own position in the seven years since he arrived and the ruler in Macedon had been weakened in the wars fought to eliminate his rivals. It was as equal partners that they turned to face the larger danger of Antigonus.

Lysimachus' envoys joined the coalition negotiating party sent to test out Antigonus' intentions by demanding a share of the spoils of his victory over Eumenes. The glimmering of future policy is clearly shown when the portion Lysimachus demanded was Hellespontine Phrygia, a province that would have given him firm control of both sides of the crossings between Europe and Asia and the trade lanes from the Black Sea and Sea of Marmara.

War came but for a long time the Thracian ruler would not confront Antigonus in person. It was to the north that events dragged Lysimachus. His garrisons by now occupied most of the Greek cities of the Black Sea coast but his rule was far from popular. Several communities secretly formed a league and sent to nearby Thracian and Scythian peoples to support them in rebellion. Probably funded by Antigonid gold, the towns of Callatis, Istria and Odessus all expelled their garrisons. No such concerted threat had been faced by Lysimachus before and Lysimachus' response matched the gravity of the situation.

He made Odessus his target after descending to the coastal plain from the Haemus Mountains. A garrison was left to hold the town as the army moved north to Istria. Here, as at Odessus, the citizenry, without support from their dilatory allies, were not prepared to hold out.

The Scythians had taken some months to muster their forces but finally these formidable horse-archers had entered Lysimachus' lands in great number. Hearing the Danube had been crossed, Lysimachus turned back to face this new threat. The Scythians accepted battle but, outside their native steppe, Lysimachus' superior technique and more balanced forces were too much for them.

Lysimachus pressed on to Callatis. Here, where the revolt had begun, the citizens were determined to resist. Lysimachus' officers had hardly opened the siege lines when he heard that Antigonus had sent an army, under Pausanias, to southern Thrace. He had managed to subvert Seuthes III, who now sent his forces to hold the passes through the mountains.

Lysimachus again responded decisively. A skeleton force of veterans was left to block up Callatis while the main army drove on to clear the enemies from southern Thrace and the route to Macedonia. Undaunted by the mountain defences, the Macedonians attacked as soon as they arrived. Lysimachus drove his pikemen forward again and again, losing many of his best veterans before the Thracians eventually gave way. Seuthes' men were slaughtered, trapped in mountain passes at the mercy of a victorious enemy.[10]

The Antigonid army in southern Thrace fell apart when they heard that Seuthes' men had been dispersed. Pausanias fled, but was ruthlessly pursued and killed. As if 313 BC had not been full enough for Lysimachus (he had conquered six enemies so far), late in the summer news arrived that Antigonus himself was approaching with his main army.

With Antigonus intending to use the northern route to Europe, Byzantium was the key and Lysimachus sent agents to urge the citizens to refuse Antigonus any crossing of the Bosporus. They had money and arguments that both gelled with the city fathers and Antigonus' progress of conquests was halted; he had to winter in Asia rather than in Lysimachus' Thrace.

The following spring Antigonus found himself occupied with other matters and it became clear Lysimachus had survived a most extraordinary deluge of dangers. He had overcome everything thrown at him and his reputation as a general of energy and daring was established. The extent to which the ruler of Thrace had made his name was reflected two years later. One of the main parties in the peace of 311 BC, his ambassadors were active in this abortive attempt to order the post-Alexandrine world by negotiations, rather than a fight to the death. In this the alliance with Cassander remained the cornerstone of policy and, when the frailty of the peace of 311 became clear, the importance of the axis was highlighted. Lysimachus showed no concern over the disposal of Alexander IV and Roxanne; he had long since lost any residual loyalty to the old royal family, and it had the advantage of simplifying his own legitimacy.

The years between the peaces of 311 to 302 BC are a virtual blank for Lysimachus. We know that in 309 BC building work was begun on his permanent capital, Lysimacheia, on a site slightly inland of the Hellespontine shore. Two years later, in 307 BC, Lysimachus followed Antigonus, Demetrius, Cassander and Ptolemy and assumed the title of king. The bodyguard, who Alexander never allowed independent command, had acquired the same title as his late master possessed. Lysimachus also sponsored some supplies for beleaguered Rhodes but that is the sum of our meagre sources. Yet it was he who became the undisputed leader of the coalition that set itself to bring down Antigonus. From the margins to the very centre almost overnight; this, however, is an extreme impression born of the sources available to us. Despite his activities apparently being of little interest to those who wrote the story of the era, the status of the strong man from Thrace was not in question amongst his peers. His generalship was proven and his military resources second to none, bar the colossus, Antigonus himself.

Cooperation and friendship had been the keynote between Cassander and Lysimachus for some years but the new situation in 302 BC was to bring a qualitative strengthening of their relationship. Lysimachus had no illusions that, if Demetrius overthrew Cassander, a reckoning with him would not be long in coming. From this moment on, these kings in Europe would act as one against their common enemy, combining their armies and resources for a fight to the death. Both had for years been part of a loose and sometimes ruptured coalition with Ptolemy and Seleucus but this time they knew that they must directly involve these powers in an assault on Antigonus. Close friends of the kings were despatched as envoys to the court of Ptolemy in Egypt and to Seleucus, in the heart of Asia.

It would be some months before Cassander and Lysimachus knew the results of these embassies but, in the meantime, they could between them mobilise a formidable army. Lysimachus ruled over a people who could provide peltasts (light infantry) and aristocratic cavalrymen in abundance and his links with the Greek settlements alongside the Aegean, Black Sea and Propontic coasts assured him of a useful supply of mercenaries. He only lacked first-class Macedonian phalangites, but Cassander could fill this gap.

Many thousands of these formidable pikemen were seconded to the king of Thrace under the command of Cassander's capable diplomat and general, Prepelaus. The kings' strategy was partly dictated by geography and partly by the present threat of Demetrius. Cassander would march south to hold off Demetrius with the remainder of his forces whilst Lysimachus and Prepelaus would invade Asia and take the vital Aegean cities from Antigonus. Then, with support from the armies of Seleucus and Ptolemy they could force a decisive battle on Antigonus in his own backyard. The old warrior would then have to recall Demetrius from Greece. It was a high-risk strategy and, although he was not to be present at the final denouement, it was clearly Cassander who was staking most on the outcome. By denuding Macedonia of Prepelaus' troops he was putting himself in severe danger from the rampant Demetrius.

This was the first time that Lysimachus had taken the offensive against Antigonus and invaded the Asiatic side of the Hellespont. While he had been wined and dined by Cassander in Pella, his agents had been preparing the way. The citizenry of the towns along the Asiatic shore had been lobbied and bribed to good effect. Lampsacus and Parium opened their gates to his soldiers and their cooperation proved vital in ensuring an uncontested crossing of the army from Europe.

Lysimachus was a cautious commander and, with the latest information putting his enemy away in Syria, he decided to secure that Hellespontine territory that abutted his own kingdom. Not all the communities there had been inclined to swap a distant association with the Antigonids for that of a king whose capital was just over the water in the Thracian Chersonese. And others chose resistance, within age-hallowed traditions of civic rivalry with those cities that supported Lysimachus.

One to resist was Sigeum, lying at the mouth of the Hellespont, and Lysimachus was required to storm its defences and install a garrison. Abydos was another and they successfully resisted him. Fortunately for Lysimachus, the Abydos example was not followed in the rest of Hellespontine Phrygia and that failure looked less important as, in the south, Prepelaus had cleared the way for further conquests.

In Aeolis and Ionia, Cassander's officer had achieved much. Adramyttium opened its gates to him and Ephesus had succumbed after threats of devastation. Here he burnt the fleet he found so that it could not fall to Demetrius, and he boosted relations with Rhodes by releasing the 100 hostages held there by the Antigonids from the time of the siege of that courageous town. Other places on the coast held out with support from Demetrius' fleet as Prepelaus decided to head inland against Sardis, the Antigonid regional treasure house and once the capital of Croesus' Lydia. The Macedonian marched his men from the coast up the valley of the Hermus for several days before he sighted its walls. In the end, he did not need to test the stern defences as he had purchased the garrison commander, Phoenix, who opened the gates, intent on an assured future under a new master.

Lysimachus, informed of his ally's successes in the south, determined to utilise what was left of the season. He aimed to establish himself in the highlands of central Anatolia before the foul winter weather made further campaigning impossible. His objective was the city of Synnada, in the southwest of Phrygia. Lysimachus' army had a long and arduous march to reach its destination. But, once again, when they eventually reached Synnada treason had smoothed the way.

The commander, Docimus, had been Perdiccas' satrap of Babylon before joining the other Perdiccan fugitives in Pisidia. Captured by Antigonus, he had betrayed his comrades to wheedle his way into Antigonus' good graces and command at Synnada had been one of his rewards. Given his pedigree, it comes as no surprise that he once more turned traitor and betrayed Synnada and other fortified treasuries in the area to Lysimachus.[11]

It had so far been a year of considerable success for the coalition commanders; local divisions and the conveniently-treacherous inclinations of so many of Antigonus' commanders had eased their path to a point where they controlled very large areas of Antigonus' Anatolian possessions.

Lysimachus, not unreasonably, expected a period of respite before the Antigonid main army arrived from Syria. Antigonus was now eighty and the invasion cannot have been anticipated. So Lysimachus came in for an unpleasant surprise when messengers conveyed the astounding news that the man himself was not far away, marching at great pace with a massive army, determined to bring on a battle.

When the events of 302 BC had begun to unfold, Antigonus' court was enjoying the fruits of security and prosperity in the new capital, Antigonia. A tithe on the commerce of west Asia and the eastern Mediterranean, which the city's central position allowed, was more than sufficient to fund the prestige projects conceived by the king and his friends to breathe life into their new foundation. Through the ages, patronage of sporting and artistic activities has been as much to do with personal and national prestige as with entertainment, and never more so than in this era. Antigonus had set in motion a competition to be held at Antigonia, where the number and quality of the participants was meant to bear comparison with the great and ancient festivals of Greece.

Sportsmen and artists from the whole of the Hellenic world had been attracted by generous prizes and most of them were already in the city billeted in inns or the homes of friends, when the news arrived of Lysimachus' invasion. It was with great reluctance that the old man realised he must cancel the event and once more take the field in person. Generosity was an important quality for a civilised ruler and his guests, if they could not perform, must not be allowed to depart empty-handed. A total of two hundred talents was laid out to compensate the redundant contestants who received invitations to return when the present crisis had been resolved.

Once the decision was forced on him, Antigonus showed all his old energy; the resting giant had been stirred and was now prepared to vent his anger on those who had disturbed his retirement. The field army was concentrated in camps around Antigonia; most would have been looking forward to attending the festival, so little time was lost in preparing for the long march to the northwest. Syria was left behind and the army moved first to Tarsus in Cilicia, where final preparations were made. The army received three months' pay from the camp treasury and from Alexander's old depository at Cynda; Antigonus also took 3,000 talents for expenses for the upcoming campaign. The army marched on the age-old route through the Cilician Gates and then crossed the Taurus before they could bivouac in Cappadocia. All along the route his garrisons and local peoples were forced to reaffirm their loyalty now that he was amongst them. They crossed Lycaonia and Phrygia, where travellers and agents from the west began to bring him up-to-date news of Lysimachus' movements. He knew his enemy had taken Synnada but the latest word placed him forty or so miles east of Dorylaeum, encamped in the rolling plains of the Anatolian plateau. Winter was threatening but Antigonus determined to strike, immediately marching his men at top speed after his prey.

When the coalition leaders realised that Antigonus was, at best, only a couple of days' march distant they called a full council to decide on their response. They were exposed, certainly outnumbered, and a defeat here in the interior of Anatolia could be disastrous. They decided to neutralise Antigonus' numerical superiority by digging in and refusing battle and then gradually withdraw north, in an effort to rendezvous with Seleucus. Antigonus chased them from entrenched camp to entrenched camp. Lysimachus was just about able to hold his own for a few weeks, but his position ultimately depended on supplies holding until Antigonus was forced by the weather to give up the contest. The old king finally surrounded his quarry and looked set to bag them. But the first storms of winter allowed the coalition army the cover they needed to slip away. The tracks of both armies soon became seas of mud. Antigonus realised he could not manoeuvre his army in this morass, to bring his enemy to battle was impossible and to continue the chase would cause losses from exposure and desertion.

The two kings had been sparring across the Anatolian plateau for weeks but no decision had been reached and now both looked for winter quarters. Lysimachus kept marching north; he had a long journey before his men could disperse in security in the friendly environment of Bithynia. Antigonus, disappointed, turned south and returned to Phrygia and his old capital, Celaenae Apamea.

It was during this dramatic contest with Lysimachus that Antigonus first received word that Seleucus was on the march from the east to join the enemy coalition ranged against him. The fact of Seleucus' imminent arrival was hard to believe and only a number of impeccable sources eventually convinced him it must be true. When the envoys of the European kings found Seleucus' court, in 302 BC, he was deep in the eastern half of his dominions. He may have been on the borders of India with the 500 war elephants gifted to him by the Indian king Chandragupta as part of their peace pact. They found a monarch who was extremely receptive to their suggestions. His eastern frontiers were temporarily settled, which allowed him to use his considerable power elsewhere. To persuade him to deploy it against Antigonus was not difficult; he had been in bloody conflict with the man only a few years previously in Babylonia.

Even so, the decision Seleucus took when the envoys had explained their mission was one of the most remarkable strategic gambles ever taken in that era or any other. He was prepared to risk everything on a desperate enterprise against Antigonus. If it failed the dangers to his own position would be immense. But, by the same coin, if it succeeded the demise of the Antigonid empire in the west would open up exciting possibilities. The cautious approach would have been to nibble at the old king's Levantine positions while he was involved in defending Asia Minor, but this would have been to throw away the chance to face and finally defeat Antigonid power on almost-equal terms. Seleucus might command first-class cavalry and numerous elephants but he did not have access to veteran Macedonian and Greek infantry. If he combined with Cassander and Lysimachus, this paucity of front-line infantry would be rectified and make a crushing victory in the field a real prospect.

To understand the daring of the choice he made it must be realised what a vacuum of intelligence he operated in. The news he had of events in the west was already many weeks old and by the time he reached the scene a whole campaigning season would have passed and the decisive battle, possibly, already fought. Little is known of his march from the highlands of Iran to join his allies in Anatolia, but were it documented it would undoubtedly hold a place as one of the greatest feats of the ancient world. Seleucus took with him 480 elephants and 100 scythed chariots as well as 12,000 cavalry and 20,000 infantry over a huge distance. From the rugged hills and deserts of Iran, over the high mountains of Armenia, the country he had to cover was consistently wild and dangerous, often peopled by tribes who had never bent their knee to the great king of Persia or even Alexander; a journey of over 2,000 miles and at an inopportune time of the year with winter approaching. Elephants had completed the journey from India to the West before; Craterus had brought many with his veterans, but this had been over several years and they had been able to take an easier way. These animals had traversed the well-travelled route up the rivers of Mesopotamia to Syria, through Cilicia and over the Taurus; an itinerary not available to Seleucus because of Antigonid garrisons holding the lands west of the Euphrates.

It was a travel-weary army that eventually appeared in Cappadocia; Seleucus had ensured against serious erosion of his strength by making steady, but slow, progress and it was already late in the season when he arrived. He heard Lysimachus had found winter quarters near Heraclea, on the Black Sea, and he adjusted the line of his march accordingly. He led his footsore band into the Salonian Plain near modern Bolu, where the majority of his allies were bivouacked, and gave orders to his relieved followers to finally halt and build the huts where they could recuperate over what was left of the winter.

Seleucus and Lysimachus had not met since those dark days at Babylon, over twenty years before. Then they had been minor players in the drama, now they were main protagonists. They would have had much to reminisce about, but even more to plan, and for Seleucus there was the satisfaction that his great gamble had paid off and he had arrived in time.[12]

The officers and men were able to depend on a friendly environment here on the temperate coast of northern Asia Minor. Heraclea was the most important place in the region, a port city that had grown fat on the local trade in corn and mineral ores. Well defended with a small but efficient fleet, it was ruled by Amastris, the widow of Dionysius, the former tyrant.[13] A niece of Darius, she had been married to Craterus at the Susa weddings but had been put aside when he allied himself to Antipater and married Phila. She had then wed Dionysius, made herself regent for his children and ruled Heraclea ever since his death. A powerful widow of her aristocratic lineage did not lack for suitors and one such was Lysimachus, eager to further his ambitions in the Pontic region. They had recently married and now the dividends of this domestic arrangement became obvious.

The confirmation of Seleucus' arrival had shaken Antigonus to the core and for the first time he was convinced of the potentially-fatal threat posed by the coalition of his enemies. Every Antigonid spear and sword was needed in Anatolia and messengers were sent to Demetrius, in Greece, with orders that he hurry back to his father's side. Now the best of his army had to be shipped out with all the warships he could muster. As Demetrius looked back over his shoulder, it was only ramshackle arrangements with Greek allies that would sustain his cause once the Antigonid army left. The best hope was to quickly aid his father to victory in Asia and return west before all he had created crumbled away.

Demetrius' Asian landfall was Ephesus. He bullied the Ephesians into returning to their former allegiance and gave terms to Prepelaus' garrison to save a protracted siege. Demetrius replaced them with his own troops to ensure a safe base for the fleet while he took the road north. At breakneck speed the army marched up the coastal route towards Hellespontine Phrygia. The army was kept light and supplied from the fleet cruising along the coast.

Almost the mere fact of the arrival of the army on the Hellespont reversed Lysimachus' first triumphs in the area. Parium was retaken easily; this lightning strike had secured one of the major crossing points to Asia but Demetrius intended to close off the other route too. As it was not far to the Bosporus he still had time to reach there before winter weather set in. Once he reached the straits on the Chalcedonian side of the water, he constructed a strong camp. Three thousand infantry were left to man it and thirty warships to patrol the crossing points and the adjacent waters of the Black Sea.

When Cassander was sure that Demetrius had left Greece he released more of his men to reinforce Lysimachus. He, as usual, stayed in Europe and sent his brother Pleistarchus in command. There could be no doubting Cassander's commitment to the coalition as the force entrusted to his brother was a formidable one: 12,000 infantry and 500 horse, a large section of what remained of the Macedonian army. With the enemy commanding the seas, they would have to take the overland route through Lysimachus' Thrace. The Hellespont was too well held by Demetrius and it seems probable the intention was to cross further north near Byzantium, a longer journey but one that would allow them to disembark not far from Heraclea. But, on nearing the Black Sea coast off Thrace, it became plain the Bosporus was also closed off by Demetrius' men. Pleistarchus now endeavoured to ferry his men by sea along the Black Sea coast. The transports that were gathered in Odessus were insufficient to get the army to Heraclea in one journey and Pleistarchus risked the crossing in relays. The first arrived safely, but the second was not so lucky and they were almost all bagged by the enemy guard flotilla and the third was struck by a tempest. Only a couple of vessels limped into Heraclea, the rest were sunk and Pleistarchus' flagship went down with only thirty-three men surviving. Cassander's brother at least had the good fortune to be one of these, though it could have seemed little enough consolation when he was cast ashore, more dead than alive, with the barest remnant of the men his brother had entrusted to him.

The survivors soon made their way to Lysimachus' headquarters. He had hoped for much greater reinforcements than these few and, more than this, the adventures of Pleistarchus showed communications with Thrace were completely blocked. Even the arrival of Seleucus could not deflect from the vulnerability of the coalition army now that it was, to all intents and purposes, cut off from Europe, a situation that was soon common knowledge in the army and led to mounting desertions. During the winter of 302/301 BC, both Lysimachus and Seleucus must have had some inkling of what an epochal year was about to unfold. Four kings, three of whom had commanded under Alexander, were set to force a decision in the interminable wars that had followed the conqueror's death. Soldiers were in arms from as far west as Illyria and Epirus, from as far east as Bactria and Sogdia, whilst between them the armies fielded half a thousand elephants that had begun life in the valleys of the Indus and Ganges. That the allied army had rendezvoused successfully, apart from Pleistarchus' mishaps, had been extraordinary enough but that was but a prologue. What exact plans were made by Lysimachus and his allies in the comfort of Heraclea are unknown, but it is clear they were set on an immediate offensive to bring on the decisive encounter. Lysimachus was in command but, with great officers like Seleucus, Prepelaus and Pleistarchus at the head of their own units, he was coordinating a committee of almost equal partners. To sustain unity would be difficult and the longer the campaign lasted the more opportunity there would be for fractures. As with the leaders, so with the men; warriors whose homelands were thousands of miles distant from each other and who had not fought together before were likely to find much to quarrel about if the campaign proved protracted.

When spring was so advanced that the mountain passes were clear, the allied army marched south, up onto the rolling steppe of what is now west-central Turkey. The strategy of invasion was risky; the soldiers would have a long march before encountering the enemy in his own backyard, where defeat might mean annihilation. In the same country, the year before, Lysimachus had retreated from Antigonus but now, strongly reinforced, he was in a position to face him in open battle.

Antigonus awaited the arrival of the enemy; he also welcomed a decisive contest. Demetrius had joined him at winter camp with the bulk of his army, leaving only garrisons to hold the main crossings to Europe. The two Antigonid monarchs mobilised their armies in preparation while they waited for firm news of the enemies' movements so they could march to intercept them. Ipsus, where the final clash occurred, was about fifty miles northeast of Synnada and Lysimachus had directed his march there to threaten Antigonus' communication to the east and so draw him into a fight. This manoeuvre against the road back to the Levant was a persuasive factor for the old king.

There are stories in Plutarch that suggest Antigonus had premonitions of disaster that affected his confidence but these can be dismissed as examples of hindsight. Nothing in his actions suggests a failure of nerve. The old man had marched from Syria to Anatolia, while Demetrius had conquered from Greece to the Hellespont. Antigonus, at eighty, intended to lead his army as of old. He and his son had confidence in the number and quality of their forces and planned to take the tactical offensive once the battle unfolded. The Antigonid army was almost as large as the one they had led against Egypt and most were seasoned veterans. Macedonian phalangites and the best mercenaries money could hire were at its heart. They also had excellent light infantry from Anatolia and unit after unit of aristocratic horsemen drawn from half the Hellenistic world.

The great misfortune of this, the most important and decisive of all the Successors' battles, is the paucity of information available. Little enough is known of the site of the battle, except that it was a wide open plain, a vast arena where these two huge armies could manoeuvre unrestricted.

On the Antigonid side, 70,000 infantry were deployed conventionally in the centre of the battle-line. Perhaps as many as two thirds would have been armoured pikemen of the phalanx, while the light-armed men guarded the elephants and provided the flexible connection with the cavalry on the flanks. Ten thousand cavalry were divided between the two wings, with the greatest number and best quality on the right flank under Demetrius. Distributed along the whole of the front were seventy-five elephants, whose role would be to try and counter the far greater number of beasts the enemy could deploy.

The dispositions in the opposing camp are less clear but enough is known to draw a few conclusions. The allies fielded 64,000 foot; although over 20,000 must have been light infantry. In cavalry, they fielded 15,000, divided evenly on either flank of the phalanx.

By the time Demetrius gave the order for his horsemen to advance, the dust kicked up by the myriad of animals' hooves and human feet must have made visibility all but impossible. In this murk, Antigonus' son pressed his charge with such élan that his opponents fled. But Demetrius failed to keep his troopers in hand as they swept away in pursuit.

In the centre, the contest had begun with duels between the elephants but this was a preliminary to the main clash of the phalangites. The push of pike began and veterans settled down to the process of jabbing and shoving. Now was the moment for Demetrius' victorious troopers to return and take the enemy phalanx in the rear. He had eventually reordered his squadrons to reenter the fray but he found that his way was blocked by 300 elephants in a great line across his path, an enemy ploy that was to prove disastrous for Demetrius' father.

The Antigonid right had been exposed when Demetrius charged away. Harassed by horse archers and javelineers who fired into their packed ranks and threatened to charge against their exposed side, morale began to fail and some warriors started to go over to the enemy. Antigonus attempted to rally those he could reach but more and more of the enemy were closing in on the old man himself, his guards were falling around him and in the confusion he was hit by several javelins. He succumbed to wounds inflicted by the spears of what were most likely Seleucus' men, fulfilling the prophecy of Chaldean astrologers that it would be Seleucus who brought Antigonus' downfall.

Demetrius witnessed the final disaster from too far to help and bitterly accepted defeat. He rode off with his cavalry and some other remnants to Ephesus, where he risked a respite. One of these refugees was Pyrrhus, the 18-year-old exiled king of Epirus, who had fought valiantly in the battle. But, if something had been saved, it would have been of little comfort for the filial Demetrius when during the retreat he received news that Antigonus had neither escaped nor surrendered but died on the field of battle.

At last, this octogenarian who had been a contemporary of Philip II was a corpse; the last of a generation. Few other examples can exist of a man of whom virtually nothing is known until he reached his fifties but who then set the world on fire for over twenty years by explosive energy and ambition. Since overcoming Eumenes, his power had been at the hub of the Hellenistic world constellation, whether the stars within in it were pulled towards his centre of strength or forced apart by fear of it.

Full of contradictions, he was vain enough to kill a man who ridiculed his missing eye, noted for arrogance and a failure to consider the advice and weaknesses of his followers. Yet, he could laugh at the sycophants who littered his headquarters and enjoyed a home life that in no way suggested megalomania. He was apparently a faithful husband and the close and trusting relationship he had with Demetrius was legend.[14]

The first Antigonid led the way in so many things: first to set a trend to kingship, the first to fully milk the propaganda benefits of claiming the title of defender of Greek autonomy. And he alone, after Perdiccas, held out the promise and had the ambition to regain the entirety of Alexander's empire. A warrior all his life, since Philip turned his class into a purely military elite, Alexander made him and his peers the most successful soldiers and powerful rulers in the world. So when he was able to express his own aspirations it was hardly a surprise they came in imperial form. The most aggressive of the successors, his response to the invasion of Lysimachus was the hallmark of a man not dulled even by advanced old age. Antigonus had answered the challenge by mobilising the whole resources of his kingdom and gambled everything on a final reckoning.

Everything about Antigonus' final defeat leads us to see it as epochal. It came chronologically almost at the turn of a century and is the point where the one detailed dependable source runs out, so all that comes after is seen through a different and fractured lens. However, common sense should give us pause. In his eighties, if he had drawn or even won the day, he could not have reasonably expected to have time to build on the achievement. But, even with defeat, his empire was far from wiped out at Ipsus.

Chapter 10

Ptolemaic Revival

Demetrius Phalerum persuaded King Ptolemaeus to get and study such books as treated of government and conduct; for those things are written in books which the friends of kings dare not advise.[1]

The crushing defeat and death of Antigonus at Ipsus, though it had not directly involved Ptolemaic arms, nonetheless turned Ptolemy's world around. Not since the death of Alexander had the political firmament changed so completely and what for a decade and a half had seemed the natural order of things was swept away. Absent from the decisive battle, Ptolemy was excluded from the arrangements that followed it. Much of the disposal of the Antigonid empire did not involve him, only when he heard that Seleucus and not he had been granted title to Coele-Syria were his vital interests touched. Seleucus arrived in the Levant late in 301 BC to find Ptolemaic garrisons well entrenched in the country south of Aradus and that their commander clearly had no intentions of voluntarily withdrawing them. Ptolemy justified his retention of these lands as recompense for his part in the war against Antigonus, which he claimed had been substantial. In the event, Seleucus held back from conflict with the man who had sheltered him as an exile and, while not relinquishing his claim to the province, for his lifetime he refrained from pushing the matter. Over the next 140 years six wars would be fought between the descendants of these two monarchs over Coele-Syria but, while these veterans of Alexander lived, there was peace.

One of four old kings who had survived from the days of Alexander, Ptolemy was in his sixties by this time. The man he saw as the key to his own security in the new century, when an Antigonid Asian empire no longer existed, was Lysimachus. The Thracian king had gained much from the campaign of 301 BC and now controlled a fiefdom that stretched far on both the European and Asiatic sides of the Hellespont. Much of Anatolia was his and these new lands, combined with those of his original Thracian empire, made him arguably the most powerful of all the remaining kings.

The logic of geography made Lysimachus particularly susceptible to Ptolemy's advances as on two sides he shared with the Egyptian ruler powerful potential enemies. To his east (apart from the feeble brother of Cassander in Cilicia) were the newly-won possessions of Seleucus, whose expanding foundation of Antioch gave abundant evidence that his eyes were turned to the Hellenic West and not to Iran and India, where he had concentrated so much of his efforts before Ipsus. Lysimachus' own concerns matched Ptolemy's for Coele-Syria and this alone would have been grounds for an alliance against an Asian king whose domain stretched from Afghanistan to Syria. But this was not the only sphere where their interests coincided. Lysimachus was the deadly rival of Demetrius, who still retained holdings in mainland Greece and on the Anatolian coast and was virtually undisputed ruler of the waters of both the Aegean and eastern Mediterranean. Ptolemy, with his ambition to contest that thalassocracy and regain his control of Cyprus, was a natural ally in the continuing war against Antigonus' son.

In 300 BC the axis between the courts of Lysimacheia and Alexandria was consummated by the marriage of Lysimachus to Ptolemy's daughter, Arsinoe. Her dowry cost was soon shown to be well spent when the alliance of Seleucus and Demetrius raised a spectre of the two kings acting in cooperation. What confuses any neat classification of Lagid policy is that later in the year 300 BC or in 299 BC, Ptolemy entered an arrangement with this same Demetrius, facilitated through the good offices of Seleucus.

The Egyptian ruler, spraying out his offspring like confetti, offered yet another daughter to this new friend, while Demetrius reciprocated by sending his young lieutenant, Pyrrhus, as hostage to the court at Alexandria. The marriage was not celebrated for thirteen years and the misalliance itself was short-lived. The motives behind this odd love-feast are difficult to unravel; to befriend the two powers who were bound to be his rivals at the risk of alienating Lysimachus seems the act of a considerably less adept diplomat than Ptolemy. Whatever, with no internal logic, it quickly collapsed and had virtually no impact on future Ptolemaic policy. The attack on Samaria by Demetrius soon after and the beginning of a Cypriot war showed how little the arrangement constrained these monarchs' treatment of each others' spheres of influence. Hostility was inevitable when the thrust of Ptolemy's efforts was to exploit Antigonid weakness and win back what had been lost in the disastrous year of Salamis. The whole of the Ptolemaic claim to first-rank status depended on sea power and it is no mere happenstance that the dynasty finally went down in a naval disaster at Actium over two and a half centuries later.

Since 306 BC, the Egyptian navy had been gradually reconstituted in the shipyards of Alexandria and Pelusium. The target of their first efforts was predictable: the island of Cyprus. There are no details of the campaign but by

294 BC they were in control of the countryside and cities outside of Salamis itself. The city was a stronghold of the Antigonids; Demetrius' mother, Stratonice, had withdrawn there from Cilicia when her husband died at Ipsus. The defence of the town was conducted by this formidable woman, who had been in a strong enough position the year before to send a squadron to beef up her son's navy for the assault on Athens. But without succour and after a considerable siege, she finally had to admit defeat. The news reached Demetrius in the midst of the manoeuvres that led to the take-over of Macedonia. While he had taken a kingdom, his mother had lost an island, but one that had been central to sustaining Antigonid maritime hegemony. Yet Cyprus had not been the only place where Ptolemy had looked to test Demetrius in these years.

The setting was Athens, where the people had brought on the wrath of Demetrius by acquiring a new supremo, Lachares, who was known to be committed to Cassander's camp. The Besieger himself sat down in front of Athens' walls in 296 BC and the citizens commenced one of the worst experiences of their eventful history. The initial mood was buoyantly defiant with the Lachares-controlled Assembly decreeing death for anybody who even dared to propose treating with the enemy; this despite the fact that exiled opponents of Lachares were holding Piraeus and cooperating with the besiegers. In addition, Eleusis and other outlying places had been occupied by Demetrius' soldiers, ensuring that all lifelines to the city were blocked.

Life inside the walls rapidly became very hard indeed and only once, as the siege ground on over the winter, did it seem help was at hand. When Demetrius crossed from Asia in 296 BC his fleet had been badly damaged by a great storm off the Attic coast and this encouraged the king of Egypt to take a hand. The desperate and starving Athenians received news, early in 295 BC, that a Ptolemaic fleet of 150 ships had been sighted off the island of Aegina, close to their coastline. It seemed the man who had succoured the Rhodians when the Besieger was at her gates was intent on repeating the service for them.

But conditions were very different; this time the port was closed and the siege lines drawn tight round the victim. To bring in supplies or raise the siege would require stiff and determined fighting. If the head of the Demetrian juggernaut could be erratic, his officer corps was clearly very efficient. By bringing in squadrons from the Peloponnese and Cyprus they got together 300 fighting ships and as the sight of their number hove into view, the Ptolemaic armada cut and ran as fast as their sails and oars would propel them.

Concurrent with these events, factors were at work in the Balkan Peninsula that seemed set to change the patterns of power irredeemably. Athens fell to

Demetrius in 295 BC, after Lachares dodged out of the doomed city to exile in Thebes. Those left behind opened the gates and found to their relief that Demetrius, who had breathed fire before, was comparatively lenient, only ensuring Stratocles was reinstated in power. He was to be backed by a garrison at Piraeus and another occupation force in the Museum, which had been decked out as a fortress and part of the very fabric of the city walls. Then the crown of Macedonia itself had fallen to Demetrius like a ripe fruit from the rotten branch of Cassander's house. The sea lord had become one of the great landed monarchs and Ptolemy's plans to erode his thalassocracy looked very ragged now his rival had overnight multiplied the money, men and territory at his disposal.

Yet Ptolemy refused to throw in his hand. Too overmatched to fight it out, he had other options that his imaginative mind extensively explored over the next half decade. One particular seed he had already planted flowered into a forest of troubles for the new tenant at Pella. Pyrrhus of Epirus, sent to Alexandria as a token of good faith by Demetrius in 299 BC, had worked hard to find the levers of influence in the court of his host. Berenice, one of Ptolemy's wives, was buttered up to the extent that she betrothed her daughter (by a previous marriage) to the twenty-year-old prince and badgered the king to aid the exile in regaining his lost throne. Twice in his young life Pyrrhus had been kicked out by his turbulent subjects, but the branch of the royal house he represented retained support amongst the political classes of the volatile kingdom. Boats and soldiers were provided by Ptolemy in 297 BC for a descent on the Adriatic shore and the future terror of Rome and Carthage was reinstated in power at Dodona. Initially, the arrangement was that he shared the throne with Neoptolemus, the incumbent, whose supporters had thrown Pyrrhus out before. This proved as unworkable as a similar experiment soon to be tried in Macedonia. He eliminated his colleague and began the reorganisation of the Epirote state that would make it a powerbase for the quarter century of mayhem he would wreak on the central Mediterranean world. Almost immediately he began to harass Demetrius. While Epirote armies with their Aetolian allies became one major distraction, Ptolemy's hands were also seen to mix the stew of discontent elsewhere in Greece. His agents encouraged dissent in Boeotia, where Thebes itself twice staged anti-Macedonian revolutions that at key moments forced Demetrius away from far fonder ambitions. These techniques of intervention by proxy were the mould for Ptolemaic strategy in Greece for generations to come, when the sons and grandsons of Demetrius and Ptolemy Soter would pursue their rivalries.

Virtually nothing is recorded and no illuminating epigraphic or papyrological evidence has been found relating directly to Ptolemaic military activity for the six years from 294 BC. Yet, by 288 BC, the expansion of Lagid maritime influence was working up a real head of steam and Ptolemy was prepared to enter the coalition against the perennially dangerous king of Macedonia. Lysimachus, Seleucus and Pyrrhus were all involved and there was a major role envisaged for the Egyptian fleet. In what numbers it came north is unknown but it must have been considerable. Assuming the 150 vessels that had turned tail in 295 BC had been the bulk of the Egyptian fleet, with the adherence of Cyprus (who alone had provided 120 warships for Alexander at the siege of Tyre) they may have been able to field 300 or so. Certainly it was in full panoply that, for once, Ptolemy, himself, sailed. He probably travelled via Cyprus; the urge to visit Salamis and symbolically bury the memory of his earlier defeat must have been irresistible. From there he entered the Aegean but the effect of his dramatic intervention is difficult to judge. The battle against Demetrius was won on land, yet the danger of Ptolemy's fleet hovering on the eastern horizon, intent on raising the Greek cities against the king of Macedonia, must have had some impact.

With the Macedonian war won, Ptolemy did not personally remain in Greek waters. But, while he returned to Egypt, he left his admiral, Zenon, to continue the forward policy in the Aegean with a flotilla based on the island of Andros. He pops up as a significant factor when the Athenian kettle boiled over again in the spring of the following year. The government left by Demetrius in 295 BC had mutated in an even more oligarchic direction. Though Stratocles had died, the men in charge were still so compromised by their dependence on Demetrius that they held on to power with an ever-thinning confidence. Their overthrow was well planned. Olympiodorus organised the democratic effort to challenge the Demetrian garrison at the Museum. Success was assured when the second-in-command of the garrison, Strombichus, deserted his commander and led a good number of his mercenaries over to the Athenian side. A streetfight led to defeat for the rest, who were driven back, overrun and forced to surrender.

But this was only the start of things. The garrison at Piraeus remained a danger and Demetrius himself, somewhat reconstituted from the debacle in Macedonia, was not far off in the Peloponnese. The Athenians needed help and it came in the spring when Zenon's fleet of 100 un-decked ships, based at Andros, ferried over to Attica 1,000 Ptolemaic mercenaries under the command of Callias. With Zenon's help, he brought the harvest into the city in the face of the Piraeus garrison, who were trying to destroy the crop. Then, when Demetrius set up siege lines round the town – beleaguering Athens seemed to have become a something of a hobby for him – Callias led his mercenaries out to battle, hurling them against the enemy with such abandon that he managed to get himself wounded.

Ptolemy was committing himself. He gambled his prestige on the involvement of Sostratus of Cnidus, one of his most senior councillors. A hugely-wealthy Greek from Caria, he is best known as the financial sponsor of the lighthouse on the Pharos at Alexandria but, in fact, he had a plenipotential career that continued well into the reign of Ptolemy's son. Sostratus arrived at Piraeus intent on notching up Ptolemaic influence in mainland Greece. The Besieger had only been dug in before the city walls for a few weeks and was distinctly susceptible to persuasion. Demetrius was both aware how fragile was his own power and that time was running against him if he was to act out the last desperate fling in Asia that had already formed in his mind. With the man across the table eager not to be bogged down in Attica, it was easy for Sostratus – with Callias holding his coat – to facilitate a peace conference between the warring parties. Pyrrhus was included in the arrangement as well and undoubtedly the presence of his troops encouraged pliability on Demetrius' part. The Besieger agreed to withdraw from Athens' walls and, though he left garrisons at Piraeus, Eleusis and the Attic forts, the man himself drew off for what would turn out to be his final campaign.

The year that followed vindicated Ptolemy's patient policy. It was a tense time for the old man in Alexandria, waiting like a vulture in the wings for the last twitch of life in the battered body of Demetrian power. Events broke sometime in 286 BC when contact was made with a man in Miletus, a prince of Sidon called Philocles.

The Demetrian armada, with Philocles as one of its most senior admirals, had shipped across the Aegean from Attica to the great Asian port of Miletus. There the assembled sailors and mercenaries watched their commander-in-chief celebrate a long-delayed marriage to Ptolemais (Ptolemy's daughter by the exiled Eurydice), who had been promised to him in their treaty of 300/299 BC. When he plunged off into the interior of Anatolia, the fleet stayed laid-up in Miletus harbour, only able to wait on events now Demetrius had committed himself to an exclusively-terrestrial struggle. These were loyal men - many had served the Antigonids, father and son, for three decades - but they were not completely insensible to their own futures. Late in 286 BC events took a decisive turn. First, word reached them of the army's involvement in a desperate contest with Agathocles, son of Lysimachus, and Seleucus, far to the east. Then, nearer at hand, a flying column sent by Lysimachus was let inside the walls of Miletus by the townsfolk. The seamen in the port now had to choose; some kept faith with old loyalties and took their ships south to Caunus, in Caria, where there were enough of them to provide Antigonus Gonatus (Demetrius' son) with a considerable fleet in years to come. Others of the captains brought their ships over to Lysimachus as the new power on the spot, while the rest decided their futures were best secured in the south.

It was in this direction that Philocles jumped. The reward for turning his coat and dumping his old chief was installation as commander of the Ptolemaic navy in the Aegean, a post of vice-regal authority that he made his own well into the reign of Ptolemy II Philadelphus (reigned 281-246 BC). The Phoenician cities and squadrons he brought over with him had been the heart of imperial navies since the time of the Achaemenids and their adherence was a coup that pushed the balance of power at sea far in the Ptolemaic direction.

By 285 BC, the strategists in Alexandria were at last convinced that the time was right to act. With Demetrius a dead letter, Philocles was sent in command of a task force to complete the subjection of the Aegean. Now the maritime organisation that had been preparing for so long went over the top. Hundreds of triremes, scores of quadriremes and even larger warships sailed to take the Antigonid arsenal of Caunus in south Anatolia. Then they swept through the Cyclades, finding only a leaderless, confused opposition that was easily evicted from their few remaining military installations.

The island league of Delos that Antigonus Monopthalmus had constructed with so much care years before was now completely subsumed by Ptolemaic influence. Ptolemy's officers patronised the cult centres of Apollo on Delos, as befitted the new rulers of the Greek seas. An altar was established there to the apotheosised Ptolemy and no more was heard of the great religious festivals of Antigoneia and Demetrieia. Bakchon, a Ptolemaic commander, was installed as *nesiarch*, or overseer, of the confederation and others would follow in later years, sent out from Alexandria. A powerbase was developed from which the Lagids could contest control of mainland Greece.

The ministers of the first Ptolemy, looking out seawards from the palace quarter of the dynastic capital, could not ignore the view inland, across the Delta to the land of the red and the black, forty-odd *nomes* (provinces) that were the heart of Egypt. It was an alien landscape, just as Alexandria, very much the Mediterranean city, seemed a profoundly foreign place to most of the indigenous population. The descriptions of the Ptolemies' Egyptian realm are all around a settled theme. The state possessed many advantages, defensible and rich with revenues many times that of Philip II's Macedonia and inhabitants tied down by an intricate and oppressive civilian bureaucracy. The differences between the analysts are over how quickly this condition was imposed and how omnipresent and monopolistic the government really was. The locals were squeezed by an unrelenting taxation system and dragooned into forced labour at the government's whim. Yet this was only the continuation of traditional arrangements. From time immemorial it had required a centrally-planned regime to regulate the flooding of the Nile, a phenomenon that was the foundation of agricultural life and the potential for any sort of civilisation. A battered Pharaonic bureaucracy was taken over by the Hellenistic elite, a pattern of ages within which the requisitioning of great estates for the crown and establishing of government monopolies fitted exactly.

But there was a major difference between the old and the new for the indigenous population. Under Macedonian rule, from the lowliest peasant to the richest landowner, the Egyptians suffered a kind of ancient apartheid, with Egyptian law and judges for them and other codes for the rest; a situation emphasised to great hurt by the refusal to recruit to the royal army from amongst the Egyptian warrior class.

The people of Egypt were far from unsoldierly; at the great battles of Artemisium and Salamis in 480 BC it had been the Egyptian marines who had stood up best against the armoured hoplites of the Greeks. It was a political decision not to use them in the army, though they continued to provide sailors for the fleet; a prevalent neurosis over the prospect of armed and trained Egyptians tearing down the infrastructure of both royal and private Hellenistic exploitation. Ptolemy's vaunted generosity to Macedonians and Greeks defeated in battle or fallen on hard times was born of these circumstances. Only by importing exiled talent could his military establishment be augmented.

There were other Hellenistic towns in Egypt besides Alexandria but the provenance of most of them cannot surely be placed in the first reign. Certainly Ptolemais, down south towards Thebes, was founded at this time and one other, named Menelaus after the king's brother, must have been founded or re-founded then. The rest possibly date to the era of Philadelphus and his descendants, though logic suggests the Hellenes who settled in numbers as landholders under Ptolemy I would have begun the duplication of the urban centres they had been used to in their homelands. Nor was it just Hellenes; we know of Jewish and Samarian villages in the countryside where soldier settlers were attracted by rights of tax exemption and communal privilege. Yet, despite all this, what is indisputable is that there was no kind of city-founding fever so observable in other Macedonian states.

Gross as was the exploitation of Egypt's people, the need to win at least a sullen acquiescence was not ignored and in Ptolemy's early years much had been done to try and make domestic government palatable and effective. Religious ceremonial was at the heart of communal life; the temples and their clerical retinues the receptacles of national tradition. All this had been trampled on by the Persians, in particular, effectively alienating the people and turning the priesthood (always an important component of the political class) into a willing centre of opposition. This was avoided by Ptolemy I; not for him the vandalising of the ancient cult of the Apis bull - in fact he lavished money to repair the desecration of the Persians - and elsewhere he regularised the position of the clergy with land grants.

The modern visitor gazing in well-deserved awe at the mighty Pharaonic temples is usually unaware that they are looking, for the most part, at Ptolemaic restorations. By the time of Alexander many of them, including the unsurpassable Karnak, were already in a state of great dereliction; in part due to depredations of foreign invaders but more through the ravages of time, most having stood for over one millennium already. The same tourist will also see the impressive temples of Dendera, Esna, Kom Ombo and Philae. Whilst they do not quite match the glories of Karnak and Luxor and the melancholy magnificence of the Ramesseum (though this is arguable in the case of Philae), they are still apiece with these wonders. But what they are looking at are places wholly built in the Ptolemaic period, yet which completely fit with a great Pharaonic tradition stretching back to the time of Menes.

Of all the extraordinary archaeological sites of ancient Egypt, Sakkara perhaps deserves primacy. Often overlooked and only recently fully recognised for the variety of its riches, it is a cornucopia of wonders. The sheer diversity of monuments threatens to overwhelm. Famous for the first great building in stone, the step pyramid of Djoser (circa 2600 BC), the site encompasses over 2,000 years of Egyptian history; from the crumbling ruins of the earlier pyramids to the extraordinary Serapeum where the sacred bulls were buried from the time of the Eighteenth Dynasty (circa 1800 BC) through to the Ptolemaic era.

Although the buildings, tombs and vast subterranean chambers were built over a long period of time, in style and content they are almost all of one recognisable culture: testimony to both the stability and apparent fossilisation of ancient Egypt. But there is one glaring incongruity amongst the ruins. Barely 300 yards from the Serapeum there is a semicircular set of statues. Though done no favours by the modern concrete shelter that surrounds them or the very dilapidated state of the sculptures, they are still clearly recognisable as Greek. Comprising eight pieces, they are known as the Philosophers' circle and it is generally considered they were placed there during the reign of Ptolemy I. Set up as a wayside shrine, possibly near a temple that overlaid the Serapeum.

Plato, Heracleitus, Thales, Protagoras, Homer, Hesiod and Pindar are seven of the eight. Whilst pride of place for Plato, Thales and Homer is predictable, the absentees are a surprise. Where is Socrates, for instance? And what of Aristotle, Ptolemy's old pedagogue? We cannot begin to guess the answer of that particular riddle, but it is the identity of the eighth member of this august company that is particularly of interest. It depicts an old acquaintance, Demetrius of Phalerum, who, though best known as Cassander's puppet ruler of Athens from 317 to 307 BC, deserves better from a long, remarkable and productive career. Cicero held him in high esteem, the Athenian being mentioned in no fewer than seven of his works and each time favourably; his orderly administration of Athens appealed to the Roman psyche in a way that the ups and downs of knockabout Classical democracy did not.

Although none of his many works are extant, the list left to us by Diogenes Laertius bears witness to his extraordinary range. As well as memoirs of his time in charge at Athens, there are books on Ptolemy, Socrates, Artaxerxes, Cleon and Dionysius amongst others. He also wrote learned treatises on politics, law, rhetoric and military matters, along with works on the Iliad and Odyssey. And it is almost certainly to him that we owe the collection and naming of the stories that have come down to us as Aesop's Fables.

Allegedly the son of a poor man from a beach suburb of Athens, he was born about 350 BC, making him slightly the junior of Alexander the Great. He shared an education with the playwright Menander at Aristotle's Lyceum and, though he may have studied under the great man himself, it was Theophrastus who was the biggest influence on his career. A pedagogue – old enough to remember Plato – he had taken over from Aristotle as head of his school when the later was exiled to Euboea. His written output was plentiful, too, and of particular interest are thirty brief sketches called the 'Characters' on common types, like the flatterer, the know-it-all, the chatterer and the boaster.

Demetrius had been part of the embassy to Antipater that included Demades and Phocion at the end of the Lamian War. He signed the agreement that handed over for execution not only Demosthenes and Hypereides but his own brother Himeraeus. He took an increasing role in the government of a city learning to live with the humiliation of a Macedonian garrison installed at Munychia until the shifting of fortunes saw him, in 318 BC, on Polyperchon's death list. He fled the city and avoided the fate of his leader, Phocion.

However, finding in Cassander a soul mate of Peripatetic bent, his career was resuscitated when Antipater's son took control.

At the age of thirty-three, with the backing of Macedonian pikes and a receptive population sick of the traumas of recent decades, he instigated an administration that conformed to the ideological framework of Aristotelian thinking. He pushed a moderate oligarchy representing the 'best people', yet one with a considerably broader franchise than that imposed by Antipater after the Lamian War. He revised and codified the laws, but the positives of the regime were compromised by the taint of hypocrisy, easily exploited by his enemies. To prevent the moneyed class ruining themselves with extravagance he legislated against ostentation. Sumptuary laws hit at the excesses of expenditure over funerals (people apparently spent more on their deaths than during the whole of their lives) and over-lavish entertainment at weddings was tackled by restricting guests to no more than thirty people. The history of sumptuary restrictions shows few examples of success and they make almost inevitable a jaundiced look at the lifestyle of their promoter. Stories circulated of Demetrius as sybarite and debauchee, hosting ridiculously-lavish dinner parties, his exhibitionism and favour for partners of both sexes became legend. And, while prohibiting funeral monuments higher than three cubits, he is credited with setting up no less than 360 statues of himself around the city.

When the other Demetrius ousted him from power in 307 BC he headed for Thebes, a city his administration had sent funds to when Cassander re-founded it, continuing on to Alexandria only after Cassander's death in 297. Ptolemy's first choice of intellectual ballast for his new capital was not, in fact, Demetrius; that honour was reserved for Theophrastus, but the old man was in his seventies and did not relish the move.

Much is unclear from the unreliable anecdotes that describe his Egyptian career but Demetrius' impact was undeniable. Early on, his influence was felt at court where he was certainly a prime mover in the foundation of the Museum that was to place Alexandria where Athens had been, at the centre of the cultural world; fame that was worthy of the reputation of its original royal founder.[2] The concept was of a community of learned men whose key methodology was the systematic Aristotelian compilation of knowledge. Many were Peripatetics who had been favoured in Phalerian Athens and came in good hope of employment to Alexandria. It was an experiment in almost-monastic subsidised learning that became the honeypot for men and women of genius from all branches of the sciences and arts.

Perhaps the most famous was Euclid; the bane of schoolboys for over 2,000 years. There is a charming, if rather unlikely, story about the composer of the

Elements and Ptolemy Soter himself. The king, perplexed by Euclid's logic, asked whether there was a shorter way to understanding other than by his methods. The mathematician's retort was sharp and to the effect that there was no royal road to geometry.

The first real advances in anatomy were made at the Museum by Herophilus who championed the brain as the source of intellect against an orthodoxy that held the heart as the fountainhead. Grizzly research by vivisecting prisoners' bodies – donated by Ptolemy – was the means to his conclusions. Military matters stoked engineering advances by men like Strato, successor to Theophrastus at the Lyceum, who was also Ptolemy Philadelphus' tutor. These were but a few of the great scientists who practised under the first Ptolemy and laid the foundations of what was to follow with the glories of Eratosthenes, Aristarchus and Archimedes.

As devotees toiled in the colonnaded passages of the Museum on volumes of Homer and Hesiod (in many cases the versions we know today are those edited by the hard working pedants of Alexandria), a library of books grew that would become the most staggering collection of the ancient world. It became a royal passion, fuelled by the encouragement of Demetrius, and Ptolemy gave responsibility of monitoring the collection of manuscripts to Demetrius. Shipping coming into the port was ransacked for acquisitions and the royal post deluged the powers around with requests for the choicest finds. Two hundred thousand books were reputedly got together by these enthusiastic collectors.

The Phalerian who had done so much to establish the cultural credentials of Ptolemy's state was also prepared to risk his reputation in the cauldron of religious matters. Ptolemy, enthroned as pharaoh, needed a spiritual bridge to encompass the chasm between the old world he came from and the new one he had taken over. Demetrius became the prime publicist for the new deity, Serapis, custom built for the job. It was derived from the cult of the bull, Apis, worshipped at Sakkara. Apis was identified with Osiris, the most ancient god of the dead, and incorporated in its new form shades of both Zeus and Hades to allow both a Hellenistic and indigenous clientele. Demetrius claimed his eyesight had been restored by the intervention of the new deity as its debut miracle, a public relations coup that clearly delivered the goods in launching a new god into the already-saturated landscape of the Egyptian spirit world.

Yet the thinker and religious reformer remained what he had always been, a politician. And, in the court of an old king, politics is always about the succession. Ptolemy had formed some interesting and dangerous relationships in his early days. The incendiary of Persepolis, Thais, who boasted a previous liaison with Alexander, bore him several children and certainly was with him after he arrived in Egypt. Lamia, the ageing flautist, was his mistress before Demetrius the Besieger found her amongst the booty of Salamis and took her up to the glee of Athenian wits. Legitimised relationships were just as numerous. The first wife, Artacama, daughter of Artabazus, from the Susa weddings, was ditched as quickly as the rest and from then on when he donned a wedding tunic it was to his own significant purpose.

High politics in 321 BC, when finding friends against Perdiccas was the priority, had bound him to Antipater's daughter Eurydice. Though the contract with Eurydice was to be significant and long standing, she brought with her from Macedonia a lady-in-waiting destined to become her rival. Berenice, a young widow, who may have been Antipater's great-niece, was certainly related to Eurydice, and already had two children by a previous marriage. By 316 BC, at the latest, the handmaiden had attracted Ptolemy's attention. A number of children resulted from this long liaison, including some of the most extraordinary characters who would burn a trail across the first half of the third century. The future Ptolemy Philadelphus first drew air on the island of Cos in 309 BC as Berenice accompanied the army campaigning in the Aegean. Her importance and influence is graphically attested in 308 BC when Magas, her son by her first husband, was sent as viceroy to Cyrene to win back and rule the province led into rebellion by Ophellas. Despite Berenice's growing influence, for many years the primacy of Antipater's daughter seemed as un-threatened by the pretensions of her old companion as they had been by Ptolemy's relations with Thais and Lamia. But, in the new century, a sea change occurred as radical developments began to shape the domestic firmament at Alexandria. Opposing camps grew in the court around the rival queens and their offspring. In each gathered courtiers who looked for patronage in the next reign. With a faction-riven court and the diadem at stake, Demetrius of Phalerum could not stand aside and when he jumped the direction came as no surprise. He championed the cause of Eurydice, the sister of his old sponsor Cassander, and the man who wrote books of advice to kings pressed her case in an uncompromising manner.

When exactly the process of replacement of Eurydice as senior wife was completed is unrecorded. The relative maturity of these women and their long-standing relations with Ptolemy makes it improbable that the fierce heat of sexual passion brought about the shift of places in the Egyptian seraglio. An explanation lies in the king's long-lived affection for Berenice that changes in the outside world now allowed him to express. Antipater had died in 319 BC but his son, Cassander, Eurydice's brother, had succeeded him and friendship with the ruler of Macedonia was the bedrock of Ptolemaic foreign policy for most of the last twenty years of the fourth century. Eurydice could not be ousted for fear of alienating her brother but in 297 BC Cassander died and Ptolemy was no longer bound to refrain from actions that would reflect on the status of his first Macedonian queen.

The problem was that the confirmation of the primacy of Berenice had ramifications of greater moment than just the clarification of domestic arrangements. To raise up a new queen consort meant her children would become royal heirs. The decision to repudiate the four children Eurydice had borne him was not to be taken lightly and the king took his time in arranging the matter. Finally, around 287 BC, the succession crisis was resolved when Eurydice, in company with her children, hurried into exile. And all questions were finally answered in 285 BC when Berenice's eldest son by Ptolemy was himself crowned as joint king with full ceremony. Demetrius of Phalerum could expect to lose much from his espousal of the wrong side. Retribution against the great courtier did not come immediately, he still had Ptolemy Soter's confidence, but Berenice and her son would not forget. When Ptolemy II came into his full inheritance, Demetrius' star rapidly went into decline. This pillar of the Alexandrian intellectual establishment was shunned, eventually arrested and perhaps murdered in prison.

While in Alexandria enthusiasts gathered to adopt the ceremonial of a new god and courtiers intrigued in a struggle for power centred on Ptolemy's queens, foreign affairs could not long be left out of consideration. The vulnerability of the kingdom, in the person of its chief of state, had been mitigated with the enthroning of the future Philadelphus but this could not gainsay the complexity and danger of the world left with Demetrius Poliorcetes' downfall. The Ptolemies had picked up much but yet again had to deal with the jumble left by a resultant power vacuum. In the recent past, despite the temporary flirtation with Demetrius, the alliance with Lysimachus had been the cornerstone of international policy. Extensive matrimonial connections had reinforced a bond of real self-interest that had lasted fifteen years. But now the spoils of Demetrius' last disastrous war led to something of a collapse of sympathy between the courts of Alexandria and Lysimacheia.

This development was far from total, indeed Lysimachus married one of his daughters to the future Philadelphus at this time, yet stress lines began to appear. Lysimachus had rounded out his domination of ante-Taurean Anatolia and in snapping up Demetrius' coastal possessions had acquired the remnants of a fleet that might contest Ptolemy's newly-won empire of the seas. In the northern Aegean, his conquest of the islands of the Thracian archipelago clearly indicated an intention to dominate the northern seaways that lay between his European kingdoms of Macedonia and Thrace and his lands in Asia Minor.

Lysimachus' power had become dangerous in the eyes of all his peers but his behaviour added a particular personal spice for Ptolemy. He had given refuge to Eurydice and her children when she was driven out of Alexandria and now the exiled queen's eldest son, Ptolemy 'Ceraunus' ('Thunderbolt') was raised to high office in his government. The Lysimachophobe lobby at Alexandria had even more to point at when his new sponsor rapidly became king of all of Macedonia by treading over the rights and interests of Ptolemy's old friend, Pyrrhus of Epirus.

To inaugurate a new set of alliances must have been tempting, but on a large scale it was resisted. Whatever the strains, a complete break with Lysimachus was not to be contemplated while Seleucus remained a deeply dangerous factor. That king had also kept Eurydice's son at his court for a while, an expectant pensioner kept happy with promises of support to regain his rightful place on the throne of Egypt. If Lysimachus was overtly alienated it would be all too possible for him to encourage a Seleucid adventure against Coele-Syria and Palestine, if not against Egypt itself.

Any rapprochement in Seleucus' direction was bedevilled not only by the unresolved question of Coele-Syria but even more by a recent development in the same geographical region. The last great territorial coup of Ptolemy's reign had been snatching control of the string of Phoenician port cities that had since time immemorial been the most prosperous trading communities of the Levant. And in prizing them from Demetrius' grasp he had achieved what had long been Seleucus' cherished ambition.

If no alliance could be achieved with Seleucus, at least the Athenian connection was kept warm. Their embassies were feted in Alexandria and returned with sizeable contributions to the campaign funds and supply dumps being prepared for the fight to liberate Piraeus and the other Attic forts from Antigonus Gonatus. Equally, we only have hints but it is fair to assume that relations with King Pyrrhus were kept well oiled.

Yet, in the end, despite diplomatic activity, during the last eventful years of the first generation of Macedonian kings it is almost as if the Ptolemies did nothing. There is no question the empire had fallen back into a defensive posture around the period of the overlap between the two Ptolemies. But, equally, the entity itself may have reached some sort of natural stasis. It is a fact that during the life of the dynasty, apart from meddling in Syria and some dubious claims to conquest east of the Euphrates River, the Lagids never expanded much beyond the boundaries left by the founder.

To what extent the first Ptolemy was the moving force at all after 285 BC is also open to question. There is a tradition that he actually abdicated when his son took the diadem and only attended the court in retirement as a private citizen. This is surely wrong and instead the arrangement was a partnership intended to assure the succession and formalise the increasing involvement of Ptolemy II and his household in government. Ptolemy Soter was no proto-Diocletian, but a monarch who knew he had other sons who might be eager to contest the succession if it was not cast in stone.

Ptolemy I died in 283 BC. The corpse of this stout, fleshy-faced 84-year-old was interred with great ceremony by his successor in an Alexandria that had become the greatest city of the Hellenistic world. The body would have been carried through the great thoroughfares of the palace quarter, past the disinterested gaze of the extraordinary collection of animals in the palace gardens that were the increasing passion of Ptolemy II, and on to the great Soma that stood at the centre of the new city where Ptolemy was entombed next to Alexander.

The dead king had shown himself to be cautious and cunning, capable of seeing the strategic picture yet still supervising the details. With wide interests outside of warfare and reported as generous and considerate, he was also murderously ruthless when required. A competent soldier, his great strength was a feel for power politics and infinite patience. Brought up in the school of Alexander, he showed little of his mentor's mercurial brilliance or unorthodox thinking. Disinclined to equal Alexander, he used the magic of his name to shore up the realm he marked out for his own in the confusion of Babylon. And nothing could gainsay his eventual success.

The first to seize a province and claim independence, he accepted constraints at the hands of time and distance as Alexander never could. His egotism could be crude and obvious, yet he was admired and loved by many who knew him and, unlike most of his peers, he died peacefully in his bed. In the end, the ups and downs of nearly thirty years bequeathed to Berenice's son an empire that included Egypt itself, the land bulwarks of Coele-Syria and Palestine to the north, Cyrene to the west and a maritime hegemony resting securely on a curve of occupation and alliance stretching from the Cyclades, along the southern shore of Anatolia to Cyprus and down to the towns of Phoenicia. The sphere of influence included parts of mainland Greece and the Asiatic Aegean. He had also battened his clan on a radically different people in a government that was not seriously threatened for nearly 300 years despite the incompetence and viciousness of many of his descendants.

Chapter 11

Lysimachus

And after the death of Alexander when the provinces were divided
amongst his successors, the most warlike nations were assigned to
Lysimachus as the bravest of them all.[1]

When the victors met in Asia Minor after Ipsus, the man who had provided the heart of the coalition army, who had fought Antigonus to a standstill in 302 BC and was commander-in-chief at the final battle, was virtually in a position to dictate his terms. In theory, his portion was all of Anatolia up to the Taurus Mountains, but the reality was much more complicated. Certainly most of the Asian Hellespont was his. Control of Heraclea gave him a power base on the Pontic coast. Garrisons in Lydia and Phrygia provided centres of administration amongst the peoples of the Anatolian plateau. But in much of the interior, with its lack of urban communities and powerful alternative feudal or tribal traditions, the effectiveness of his government was constrained. It is a truism that ancient rulers only really ruled empires of towns and roads. The mountains and forests remained the domains of local aristocrats and tribal chiefs and this certainly applied in the rugged country of western Anatolia, where the king of Thrace claimed to replace the authority of Antigonus. But, if it is unclear how many peoples and cities paid tribute to the court at Lysimacheia, what is not in doubt is that after Ipsus, in Asia west of the Taurus, hardly a foe existed who could contest the authority of Lysimachus in open battle.

Yet one power was still irritatingly present in parts of this newly-claimed domain. Demetrius Poliorcetes retained control of many important cities around the coast. Parium, Lampsacus, Abydos, Clazomenae, Erythrae, Ephesus and Miletus were strongpoints that encircled Lysimachus' holdings, from the Hellespont almost as far as Caria; fortresses with powerful walls that his forces would find difficult to carry by assault and that could not be blockaded into submission while the Antigonids, who still had control of the seas, could revictual them at will.

Between these two that fortune had pushed cheek by jowl there existed a bitter hatred that went well beyond the natural rivalry felt by Macedonian strongmen when they clashed. The provenance of this ill-feeling is difficult to establish. Demetrius had not served under Alexander in Asia so it is not possible that the hostility between them predated the wars of the Successors. A tradition that appealed to Plutarch is that Demetrius was prone to regale his followers with unflattering stories about the other kings' careers under Alexander and assign them nicknames. Lysimachus was always referred to as the treasurer, which, aside from suggesting he was both parsimonious and had taken less of a warrior's part in the Persian wars, could most offensively suggest he was a eunuch. Such men often filled this post in Macedonian court bureaucracy. What is remarkable about these anecdotes is the way they show what a small and intimate group was the Macedonian aristocracy that inherited the world conquered by Alexander. They might rule from Danube to the Indus but they were a sufficiently small, interactive community that such a jibe caused deep and personal antipathy.

Even the satisfaction of disposing of Demetrius' father at Ipsus did not placate Lysimachus' bile. Throughout the following years his agents in Greece could be depended upon to work against Demetrius' interests. In Athens, working through the exile, Philippides, he offered proper burial in Asia for the Athenian dead of Ipsus and arranged for the ransoming of prisoners; an action that no doubt played some part in Demetrius' wife, ships and supporters being driven out of Athens in 300 BC.[2]

Hatred was repaid with interest. Demetrius' feelings had moved from facile contempt to deepest dislike and, after his rebuff by Athens, he took the opportunity to hit back at Lysimachus. Despite Antigonus' final defeat, a great military empire was not destroyed in a day and he assembled a handsome force. From Greece, western Anatolia, Cyprus and Phoenicia, detachments were garnered to augment those regiments that had escaped the field of Ipsus itself. A fine navy was also collected, including 'sevens' and at least one 'thirteen' crammed with marines and missile throwers. Pyrrhus of Epirus, who at Ipsus, when only eighteen, had shown himself an invaluable second, was left to hold the key places like Corinth, Megara and Chalcis while Demetrius sailed in 300/299 BC, as soon as his warships were equipped and his men embarked. His goal was the heart of enemy country; he went straight for the Thracian Chersonese. His forces ravaged the area; Lysimachus, with no fleet of consequence, could not protect a vulnerable coastline and Lysimacheia, the new prestige headquarters, was even under threat.

There had been little enough time for Lysimachus to digest the conquests of 301 BC. Larger territories meant more frontiers to defend as well as more resources to tap. The latter process was abrasive of the old order, leaving a time lag before the benefits won by his army could be fully reaped. He had inherited only problems. Erstwhile allies were cool and far from in a hurry to assist now that the threat from Antigonus was over. Cassander was deeply involved in Greece and Ptolemy prevaricated, despite his promise to send ships that would have been invaluable in defending the towns under attack by Demetrius. So, in this first test after Ipsus, all Lysimachus could do was to wait until his audacious and embittered enemy grew tired of plundering his domains.

Eventually Demetrius withdrew to take up interests in Asia but his attentions had shown Lysimachus needed allies if he was not to remain vulnerable. The long-standing axis with Cassander's Macedonia would stand. The two were temperamentally suited: cautious but determined and capable of brutality when required. Necessity ensured a continuing accommodation with the government at Pella; a hostile Macedonia in his rear could not be contemplated. These two most northerly of the Hellenistic rulers were bound in a historic role: to defend the civilisations of the south from the tribes that jostled for space and power from Illyria to the Danube and always threatened to spill southwards under pressure from their neighbours. Both kings campaigned against Thracians and Illyrians, a bond not shared by their counterparts in Asia and Africa. In the northern lands that were their particular bailiwick, a different people had begun to fracture population patterns settled for generations. At the turn of the century, Celtic tribes were in motion, disturbing the equilibrium around the Danube.

The outer edge of this maelstrom would reach the frontiers of Lysimachus' kingdom. Wild Celts from the Elbe and Rhine rivers, who lived by hunting and slash-and-burn farming, untouched by the influence of more civilised neighbours, had been uprooted and driven towards the west, south and east. It is likely that Germanic peoples from the Baltic coast had been pressing on their tribal lands and, squeezed out, they had migrated. Some travelled to Belgium, to Italy and southeast Britain, but other groups of these ferocious Gauls or Galatians had taken the road to the Balkans. Their vanguard, moving down the Danube, disturbed their more settled cousins and, with numbers swelled by local recruits, they erupted amongst the Illyrian and Thracian neighbours of Lysimachus and Cassander.

The Gauls were not themselves the immediate threat, it was the disturbance caused amongst their neighbours that meant for many years the two kings looked with fear towards their northern frontiers. The Gauls conquered the Pannonian plain to the northwest of Illyria, crushing local opposition with brutal energy. From there columns travelled south towards what are now Bosnia, Serbia and Albania; folk wanderings that stirred the ethnic pool in the Balkans to a considerable degree. The people they displaced looked for new homes and assaulted others in their turn. When they felt this pressure, the Thracian tribes that bordered Lysimachus' territory looked to compensate themselves to the south.

Desultory campaigning had been carried on both before and around the turn of the century but Lysimachus' commitment to the war against Antigonus meant the northern front was inevitably starved of resources. After Ipsus, greater efforts could be brought to bear. The Getae, in particular, were formidable antagonists in this border warfare. Celtic pressure from their rear made them particularly determined in what for them was a battle for survival. The few facts we have suggests that in their home terrain they were more than a match for the mercenary armies Lysimachus sent against them. Numerous and powerful, they ruled much of the lower Danube and what is now northern Bulgaria.

The first decade of the third century saw Lysimachus' armies engaged constantly in efforts to catch and destroy these elusive enemies in their homeland, where few palaces, forts or towns existed as conventional targets for the Hellenistic armies. It was in these hard-fought forays that Agathocles, the king's son and heir, made his reputation as a brilliant and popular commander. In the face of many obstacles, he had some success in overrunning and dominating parts of the northern marches. Yet far from all he touched ended in triumph. Reportedly, on one occasion the prince was captured and his army dispersed.[3] The Thracians who took him prisoner soon sent him back to his father accompanied by rich gifts, hoping this would persuade him to desist from his attacks and encourage the return of the territories already annexed. They misjudged their man; Lysimachus took it for weakness and it only served to encourage him to crush once and for all a people who had humiliated both his armies and his offspring.

In 292 BC the king himself came to the north, bringing the officers and troops with whom he had triumphed so often in the past. These men, some veterans who had marched with Alexander, were considered unlikely to have much trouble in disposing of backward, undisciplined tribesmen. The royal regiments led the way for the border armies, who had been at war with the Thracians for years. Just as if he were invading the kingdom of a rival Macedonian king, Lysimachus pushed his men forward towards where he imagined the capital of the enemy country lay. He crossed the Danube and marched north, failing to realise that the further he progressed into enemy territory the more he would be vulnerable to their hit-and-run tactics. Soon the army found its supply lines cut and the food they carried with them running out. The men were harassed by archers and javelineers on their flanks and rear and they had no way to hit back. Heavily pressured, he was forced to camp his army behind defensive entrenchments which, though it protected them from death or wounding from missile fire, further aggravated the supply problem. Starvation became a real possibility. The Getae controlled the countryside so the troops could not forage and the inability to hit back undermined morale. Too weak to fight his way out, to stay meant a sure death from hunger. The king's senior officers and closest councillors advised him to leave with a few horsemen so he at least would avoid death or capture, but he refused to desert those who had always been loyal to him. Instead, he offered to negotiate. But, having nothing to bargain with, the Macedonians were forced to surrender to the contemptible 'barbarians' whose lands they had entered so light-heartedly at the beginning of the campaign.

Lysimachus was more fortunate in the enemy leader who had worsted him than he had any right to be. Dromichaetes, the Getae prince, was a clear-thinking man, able to overcome blind prejudice against his current enemy when it was in the long-term interests of his people. The captives were taken to the town of Helis, where the aggressors from the south first realised what deep antagonism the policy of continual warfare against their neighbours had engendered. The Getae warriors and their families, gathered in the town, demanded to decide the Macedonians' fate, which, had it been granted, would certainly have led to their instant extinction.

But, at this moment, Dromichaetes' standing was particularly high, having led his people to a great military triumph, and he used his kudos to the limit in saving the lives of the captives. He persuaded the assembled Getae that a mass killing would only ensure the continuance of the war against a new enemy king even more embittered against the people who had slaughtered the current intruders. On the other hand, by sparing them they could turn a deadly foe into a friend who would return the lands and fortresses they had annexed over the years. Without much option, Lysimachus saw the point and a treaty was arranged. It gave the Getae back the regions they had lost in the last decade and incorporated assurances of non-aggression for the future. To seal the pact, Lysimachus gave his daughter in marriage to Dromichaetes and, as further proof of his good intentions, handed over several hostages, including his Heracleian stepson,

Clearchus (though they were subsequently released fairly quickly). With these unusual but effective negotiations completed, the captive army was escorted back to the Danube and released.

If warfare was endemic in the north, in the first decade of the new century, this did not mean other frontiers were neglected by Lysimachus. From soon after 300 BC, the ruler of Egypt was incorporated in the consortium that included Cassander and was dedicated to doing what damage they might to what was left of Antigonid authority. But before these three could really get into their stride the king of Macedonia died. In May 297 BC the greatest stabilising factor in Macedonian Europe was removed forever.

The emphatic competence of Cassander was followed by an eldest son whose health deprived him of the opportunity to rival any of his progenitors. Philip IV was consumptive and destined to reign for barely four months, leaving confusion behind in his wake. The kingmaker left in the country was Thessalonice, the widow of Cassander and daughter of Philip II, a queen whose impeccable lineage had earned her real support and affection during the years of Cassander's rule but who would fail to impose her authority in a ruptured age. She had two sons by Cassander, besides Philip, with claims on the throne, both of whom were inexperienced and probably minors when their elder brother breathed his last. Thessalonice ruled as de facto regent. But, from within the dynastic fortress their father had created, the princes themselves broke down the walls of authority. Each of the foolish young men attracted factions who urged their claims in hope of advancement and each also had international connections who might expect advantage from interfering in the outcome of the probate arrangements. Antipater, slightly the elder, was married to Lysimachus' daughter, while Alexander was the son-in-law of Ptolemy. But Thessalonice, though owning huge prestige as dowager queen and surviving sister of Alexander the Great, did not tread with circumspection in a situation that was both unstable and complicated.

With wolves like Pyrrhus, Demetrius and Lysimachus poised on her borders, strife should have been avoided at all costs. Yet her eventual solution was to divide the kingdom between her sons. Any question of pushing the claims of the elder brother were outweighed by her affection for Alexander, who she was determined should have his share. The kingdom that had shaken the whole world a generation before was divided and suddenly exposed as so much less than it had been. In the carve-up the Queen's influence secured for Alexander the plum prize of the country west of the Axius River, which included the capital, leaving Antipater the rest, on the Thracian march to the east. This attempt to avoid internecine conflict was soon rendered abortive by the murderous intentions of one of its young signatories.

In engineering the downfall of his mother's policy, Antipater acted with the kind of ruthlessness that showed he had inherited something from his father. Knowing he could never claim the whole kingdom while Thessalonice lived, he had her assassinated. That the portion of Macedonia he controlled was proximate to the borders of his father-in-law's state may well suggest the act was matured and executed with support from that quarter. The coup had been planned in detail and in 295 BC, soon after he had rid himself of maternal restraint, Antipater led an army across the Axius River and drove his brother from the other half of Macedonia.

Alexander fled to Epirus and sought assistance at the court of King Pyrrhus. For the price of territorial concessions Pyrrhus agreed to put himself and his army at the disposal of the dispossessed son of Cassander. Antipater had not been able to win wholesale approval, the matricide had offended many of the men of position who had known and respected Thessalonice. He was bundled out of his recently-won kingdom with hardly any effort by Pyrrhus and again an Alexander, in theory, ruled at Pella. Meanwhile, the Epirotes took charge of the western provinces of Tymphaea and Parauaea, as well as the Macedonian satellite states of Acarnania, Amphilochia and Ambracia, which Pyrrhus was soon to re-found as his capital. Such were the wages of intervention. But the plundered carcass of the northern kingdom was too inviting for this latest settlement to remain unchallenged.

These disruptive events to the west of his kingdom were of great concern to Lysimachus. His own candidate and son-in-law had done badly. The violent rupturing of the Thessalonic settlement had ended with Antipater driven out of Pella into impotent semi-exile in an enclave in the far east of Macedonia. Commitments elsewhere had kept Lysimachus from intervening militarily but the matter was important enough to ensure he tried every other way to help his protégé. It is recorded that he attempted to dupe Pyrrhus by sending a forged letter purporting to be from Ptolemy of Egypt, whose close friendship with the Epirote king was well known. This fraudulent correspondence suggested that he make peace with Antipater and allow him to retain the small portion of Macedonia he still controlled. Most importantly, he was to take his army out of Macedonia and back to Epirus, an arrangement that was to be sweetened with a payment of 300 talents. The trick was clumsily executed as the letter commenced with the greeting 'King Ptolemy to King Pyrrhus, greetings', exposing the subterfuge at once as Ptolemy, when writing to Pyrrhus, always started his missives with 'the father to the son, greetings'.

The incident apparently caused Pyrrhus great affront but, fortunately for Lysimachus, he was sufficiently cool-headed to not let it affect his public policy. He wanted no protracted war with Antipater, given that a divided Macedonia suited the book of his smaller state. Negotiations continued and in 294 BC Lysimachus came himself, with Antipater in his train, to meet Pyrrhus and Alexander at Pella. Agreement was reached on the terms of peace with no difficulty: Epirote rule in the western provinces was confirmed and the two kings of Macedonia agreed on a border between the parts of the kingdom, while Lysimachus' money was to help ensure the smooth departure of Pyrrhus' foreign battalions.

The despoiled Alexander had not just looked to Pyrrhus in his time of troubles but had sent a letter to Demetrius Poliorcetes in case his first sponsor proved inadequate. Demetrius was campaigning against the Spartans when he learned of the far greater pickings to be had from the developing power vacuum left by the squabbling of Cassander's heirs. Sparta became a distraction, an entanglement that he soon extracted himself from and marched his army north.

Alexander no longer wanted or needed military aid from this dangerous confederate, having just got rid of one ally for an exorbitant price. Alexander did not lack nerve, even if he was short on sense. He took his court to meet Demetrius at the border city of Dium, hoping to dissuade him from continuing his progress but, if necessary, bent on desperate measures to fend off the new threat. It is not clear what exactly transpired but an orgy of plot and counter-plot is reported. The Antigonid king apparently only just avoided being poisoned by the young Alexander but kept his anger in check and acted as if he did not know of the attempted assassination, though this may well be gloss from Hieronymus to lend legitimacy to his patron's usurpation. Whatever, Demetrius suddenly declared an intention to return south to Greece. Delighted, Alexander escorted him back to Larissa in Thessaly, where, at a banquet, Demetrius had the hapless Alexander executed.

Demetrius was acclaimed king on the following day by those Macedonians who had come down to Larissa. The choice cannot have been an easy one for men who had been fighting the Antigonids for a generation, but Cassander's remaining son, Antipater, was generally hated and Demetrius had the power to do them great damage if they chose the only other option and resisted his claim in arms.[4] And, as a strong and tried soldier, Demetrius might at least solve the problems of chronic instability that had beset their country.

Demetrius' involvement in Greece and Macedonia opened up new opportunities for Lysimachus. With Agathocles a more than competent proconsul on the Danubian march, Lysimachus and his officers could devote their main attention to expanding control over the rich and politically advanced coastal provinces of what is today the west coast of Turkey. This had been his great prize from Ipsus. Here were the cities of the Troad and Lydia with gold mines nearby and, beyond, the pearl cities of the coast from Abydos down to Smyrna, Antigonia, Ephesus, and Miletus and further.

During the campaign of 302 BC many of the cities had fallen to Lysimachus and his capable aide, Prepelaus, but Demetrius had quickly reversed much of this success. Even after his father's downfall the Antigonids' naval might had secured such important coastal prizes as Parium, Lampsacus, Abydos, Clazomenae, Erythrae, Ephesus and Miletus. But Lysimachus made gains inland, Sardis had been captured virtually straight away, its crucial mint taken over and a fortress treasury set up. We hear of Lysimachus' wife, Amastris, being established there prior to her returning to her adopted home of Heraclea after the king's remarriage to Arsinoe. Though there is no direct evidence, control of Sardis indicates that Lysimachus held sway over much of the west Anatolian interior.

Money was spent and influence exerted to build up the position of Lysimachus' partisans in the cities of the Aegean coast. It was a slow, painstaking process but Lysimachus held the coming hand as the man who controlled the hinterland of these towns, able to threaten the citizens' estates almost at will.

The years 295 to 294 BC seem to have been the high time for filching cities from the Antigonids. Plutarch informs us that while Demetrius was marching around Greece and finally winning the kingdom of Macedonia he lost all his Anatolian cites to the king of Thrace. Campaigning must have occurred, but much of this extension of influence would have been done through diplomacy or intimidation by the man who was now by far the greatest warlord in the area.

By the turn of the first decade of the third century we have incontrovertible testimony of Lysimachus' control over the Ionian league. Hippostratus is named in an inscription found at Miletus as Lysimachus' strategos of the thirteen cities of the region, including Ephesus, Smyrna (renamed Eurydiceia after one of Lysimachus' daughters), Teos, Priene, the island of Samos and, of course, Miletus.

Whether this state of affairs spread right down south to Caria is more problematic. As elsewhere in Asia Minor, here quasi-independent dynasts advertised their power. Pleistarchus, Cassander's brother, ejected from Cilicia by Demetrius, had settled there, renaming the spectacularly-sited Heraclea-under-Latmus as Pleistarcheia. According to epigraphic evidence, he appears to have been succeeded by Eupolemus, a character not without interest. Twenty-odd years earlier he had been Cassander's commander in the Carian wars against Antigonus' nephew and had subsequently served as his overlord's general in central Greece in 312 BC. He is also named in the lead curse tablet found outside Athens during the course of the Four Years' war. Presumably he had served under Pleistarchus during and after the Ipsus campaign. Eupolemus ruled in Caria from 294 to 286 BC and possibly longer.[5] Plutarch implies that by 286 BC Lysimachus controlled the region but, in the absence of any other evidence, it may be reasonable to assume Eupolemus was a virtually-independent strategos. The situation is further complicated by Ptolemaic influence in certain areas of Caria such as Iasus, whereas further south Caunus seems to have stayed loyal to Demetrius, as it was there he tried to reach in an attempt to rendezvous with his fleet after his final defeat by Seleucus.

But, though the historical evidence for Lysimachus' control of the Asia Minor seaboard is sparse, paradoxically its effect is very noticeable in the ruins that remain in the area today. Lysimachus and his Anatolian officers and neighbours were great fortress builders and in Ionia and Caria the political fluidity encouraged very special efforts to renew and improve the defences of the cities there.

The visitor to Ephesus, though their eye will be mainly taken by the well-preserved Roman ruins, will notice along the ridge above the town the remains of a long circuit wall built by Lysimachus. It still stands to over twelve feet high in some places with several towers and postern gates. Its construction must have been a prodigious feat as it encloses a far greater area than that of the actual city. The perimeter is over five miles in length and ensures that all the hills around the town are brought within its defences.

Lysimachus had, in fact, undertaken the massive task of re-siting the town itself, a project that has ensured the survival of the magnificent remains we see today. Over a hundred years before, Herodotus had noted the effect of the silting the river was causing and by Lysimachus' time it was clear that the city, though still prosperous, was bound for catastrophic decline. He decided to move both town and harbour to the west and higher ground. Never noted for his tact, Lysimachus compounded the upheaval by forcibly removing the populations of nearby Teos, Lebedus and Colophon to people his grand new city. Lebedus and Colophon were razed to the ground, though both were later restored to some semblance of their former glory. The graves of those Colophonians who resisted are, on the slender authority of Pausanias, still to be seen as tumuli to the north of the modern day village of Cile.

Elsewhere in Turkey are the scattered remnants of walls and fortifications, many of which were built in the time of Lysimachus. The most impressive of these survivals are those of Heraclea-under-Latmus (Pleistarcheia), whose grandeur exceeds even that of Ephesus. Standing almost to their original height, they are some of the finest Hellenistic defences to be seen anywhere in the world and, though this once strategically-situated port now stands on an inland lake, the impression of the mighty ancient walls set in beautiful rugged mountains is unforgettable.

Only seven years after Ipsus, events had placed Lysimachus' most implacable enemy on the throne of the kingdom whose alliance had always been the cornerstone of his security arrangements. The Thracian border was no longer the meeting place of allies but instead the divide between the bitterest of rivals. Yet Demetrius did not straight away assault the Thracian state. Indeed, it is suggested that Lysimachus actually made a formal peace with Demetrius at this time, though any real pacific intent is belied by Lysimachus' harbouring Antipater and marrying Alexander's widow to Agathocles, all potential irons in the fire of Macedonian domestic politics. For the moment, Demetrius turned elsewhere, determined to enforce his prerogatives as successor of Philip II and Alexander the Great in the Greek peninsula.

In autumn 294 BC a military promenade secured hegemony in Thessaly and Boeotia, where the Thebans and others, for the moment, accepted the reality of the new Macedonian king's military strength. But, the following year, resistance south of Thermopylae was given some extra steel by the arrival of a Spartan army and Demetrius found he had a real job on his hands to contain a Theban drive to independence. Yet, when the Macedonians arrived, Cleonymus, the Spartan king, proved a broken reed. He quickly exited the locality and Thebes fell after a siege. Still rooting to win local popularity, Demetrius only punished a few ringleaders and Hieronymus, the historian, was left as governor of this troublesome territory.[6]

By the summer of 292 BC, Demetrius found his very success had raised up a coalition who deeply feared the re-establishment of a strong king in Pella. The Aetolians felt sufficiently threatened to send envoys to Epirus with proposals for an offensive and defensive alliance. Demetrius rushed back to Boeotia, where the Thebans had revolted again, but at least had the satisfaction of finding his son, Antigonus Gonatus, had already routed the Boeotian field army. Yet the stubborn heart of the resistance would not be stilled until the defenders of Thebes were crushed. The Macedonians had settled down to yet another siege when others intervened.

The Aetolians occupied the passes by Delphi that commanded the road west from Boeotia, while Pyrrhus invaded Thessaly and marched his small but well-trained army to Thermopylae to try and drive a wedge between Demetrius and Macedonia. If successful in temporarily distracting him from the siege of Thebes, this Epirote effort achieved little of substance. Demetrius swiftly turned north, drove Pyrrhus away, reoccupied Thessaly with a detachment of 11,000 men and was soon back in front of the walls of Thebes. The siege was drawn out and difficult and the Besieger found it necessary to bring up the famous engines that had won him such a past reputation. Ferocious but costly assaults were pressed and the king himself wounded, yet again, by a bolt from a catapult before the place was captured.

The Trojan enterprise had father and son squabbling over the effort it was costing and sings paeans of praise for the stalwartness of the defenders. A year and more may have been wasted in front of the seven-gated city, depending on what chronological analysis is accepted. Again it seems Demetrius had committed his prestige as at Rhodes years before. And, if he triumphed in the end, the repeated leniency of Demetrius in victory suggests this was something less than unconditional surrender.

These distractions had cost Demetrius years of his time and, what with adventures in Corfu, visits to Athens and the Pythian games of September 290, Lysimachus had been relieved of his greatest enemy's attention for some of the most problematic years of his reign.[7] Even at the start of the second decade of the third century, Demetrius still had his mind only on Greece. It was the Aetolians who now took his attention. They controlled the approaches to Delphi, the traditional home of the Pythian Games, forcing Demetrius to hold an alternative version at Athens. Feted at the games as a god, he was urged to wage sacred war against the Aetolians, a timely and convenient pretext. He mobilised the army in the spring and from Thessaly invaded; the Aetolians did not have the strength to face him in battle and the Macedonians swept through the country with fire and sword, burning their habitations and stealing cattle, the only real wealth of these communities.

Pyrrhus marched to the Aetolians' aid. But, before he arrived, Demetrius, thinking to get between his enemies, struck his blow first. Leaving an army of occupation of 10,000 men in Aetolia, he then led the rest in an invasion of Epirus itself. A confrontation appeared inevitable but somehow the armies missed each other and Demetrius enthusiastically plundered Epirus while

Pyrrhus entered Aetolia and attacked the Antigonid garrison. The Aetolians must have joined Pyrrhus in some numbers as he probably outnumbered the 10,000 who faced him. The Epirote king defeated the enemy commander in personal combat, smashed the Macedonian phalanx, captured over 5,000 men and massively increased his military reputation.

The upshot of this confused campaign was that no overall winner emerged; the Aetolians had survived and the relative positions of the kings of Macedon and Epirus remained unchanged. It was a war that merely confirmed the power of Macedonia; though greater than that of any other Balkan power, it was far from overwhelming when faced with a combination of rivals, a situation unaltered by the events of the autumn of 289 BC, when news of Demetrius being struck down by illness encouraged Pyrrhus to revenge the looting of Epirus in the previous year. The Epirote king crossed the border and advanced as far as Edessa, and on the way not a few Macedonians joined him. But, once Demetrius recovered sufficiently to send out the Macedonian levy, Pyrrhus fell foul of the weakness that bedevilled his plans in Greece, Macedonia, Italy and Sicily. His small kingdom just did not have the manpower to sustain the high-flying ambitions of its extraordinary monarch. The ruler of Macedonia called on his greater resources and drove the Epirote army back with little difficulty, though his generals made no attempt to follow into Epirus.[8]

Lysimachus had, during the vulnerable years of his reverses in the north, been spared the direct attentions of the personal enemy who occupied the throne of Macedonia. Others who equally feared the power of Demetrius had borne the brunt of the fighting. But distraction and difficulty were not the only reason that Lysimachus had been spared the sight of Demetrius leading a Macedonian phalanx on the direct road over his western frontiers. It was not this portion of the realm that Demetrius truly coveted.

Antigonus' old Asian empire was the target of his son's ambition. Lysimachus had eventually become heir to most of it after Ipsus and Demetrius wanted it back. Some sort of peace had been patched up between Demetrius and Pyrrhus by the end of 289 BC and with this any imminent threat to Macedonia's borders was neutralised. The problems his other enemies in Greece might make could not threaten the northern kingdom itself and Demetrius' projected invasion itinerary would ensure all Lysimachus' efforts would be needed for the defence of his Asian holdings. The fleet and army he assembled from the resources of Macedonia and his Greek, Levantine and island empire were prodigious and the fact that he could mount such an effort makes it all the more surprising that he had never been able to thoroughly deal with Pyrrhus, the Aetolians and other local enemies.[9]

The organisational effort needed for the mobilising of 100,000 men, along with the navy required to transport and protect them, was massive. A fleet of 500 ships was to be built, a project of such size that all the great ports of the Greek seaboard had to be utilised. The king had recently founded Demetrias, on the coast of Thessaly, as his capital and from this centrally-located fortress he supervised the preparations and planned the mobilisation of the army intended to sail in 288 BC. As with the navy, the soldiers were too numerous to bring together in one place and several centres were designated as bases for the invasion.

The size and complexity of the enterprise meant there was no possibility of it remaining secret. Lysimachus knew of the preparations by 289 BC and used the months before the commencement of the campaigning season of the following year well. His northern borders were, at last, reasonably quiet, allowing him to concentrate the royal army against the danger, but he knew that alone against Demetrius he was vulnerable. Frenzied diplomatic activity increased the tempo of life at his capital on the Thracian Chersonese. Ambassadors were despatched to all the courts of the kings to orchestrate opposition to the Antigonid. Lysimachus had for some years been close to Ptolemy of Egypt and his help was particularly important as only he had a fleet that could hope to contest Demetrius' route to Asia. Seleucus was brought into the coalition and the Greeks were encouraged to rise against Demetrius.

Yet the key to the coalition's strategy depended on the attitude of Pyrrhus; only his army was sufficient that, in tandem with Lysimachus, it could confront Demetrius before he left for Asia. The other allies, while valuable, were too far away or could not field soldiers of the quality needed to face the Antigonid's Macedonian phalanx and his veteran mercenaries. Pyrrhus had, however, only recently agreed a truce and no effort was spared by Lysimachus and his allies in persuading him to break it. The emissaries raised the spectre of a victorious Demetrius with the resources of Asia behind him, which would undermine that balance of power in the Balkans on which the security of Epirus depended. The Epirote's cupidity was appealed to by the suggestion that, with success, considerable pickings could be had from Demetrius' kingdom. Pledges were swapped and, while Macedonia's king dreamed of wider empire in the newly built halls of Demetrias, a web was spun around him that stretched from Alexandria, through Antioch to Lysimacheia and Ambracia.

The spring of 288 BC was to have seen the commencement of the great enterprise of Asia, but, before it could materialise, the fruits of Lysimachus' diplomacy became apparent. First he committed himself militarily in a manner not attempted since Ipsus. The royal army mustered from the recruiting grounds of the Greek cities of Asia, the Chersonese and the warrior tribes of Thrace marched west from Lysimacheia, along the coast road that Alexander had travelled in the opposite direction so many decades before. He was gambling on the commitment of his ally as any real coincidence of effort was bound to be difficult to arrange. That he was prepared to face Demetrius in this way showed how desperate the threat was considered in the Thracian king's headquarters. We have no idea of the size of Lysimachus' army but its generals would have been well aware that it could be inadequate to face the whole Macedonian national levy.

Demetrius turned on an enemy he had not encountered in person since Ipsus. Antigonus Gonatus was left to guard the dynasty's Greek fortresses while his father led the main army east from Pella. Lysimachus' journey from his capital was considerable but he eventually reached the rich gold-mining border town of Amphipolis. What happened next is disputed, with the sources contradicting each other. Pausanias mentions a battle where Lysimachus nearly lost Thrace, Polynaeus reports the Thracian king capturing Amphipolis by subterfuge and Plutarch claims that Lysimachus ravaged northern Macedonia with Demetrius turning back before he had a chance to engage his deadly foe.

Whatever the truth, events took a different turn when it became known that Demetrius was being threatened from another direction. Pyrrhus had at last begun to play his part. He had crossed into Macedonia from Epirus and encountered little resistance as most of the levy had gone to Amphipolis. He had proceeded, ravaging the country as he went, into the very heart of Macedonia. He halted at the town of Berrhoea on the edge of the Macedonian plain, southwest of Pella and just across the Haliacmon River from Aegae.

When this second assault became common knowledge in the Macedonian army a backlog of resentment against Demetrius began to surface. Despite his recent success, whole units began to talk about going over to the enemy. Demetrius now decided his people might show greater purpose against a man who was not a Macedonian or friend of Alexander the Great so he turned to face the foreign invader, Pyrrhus.

This was desperate behaviour; caught in a pincer, Demetrius was rattling between its closing limbs with no real plan in his head. On coming up to the Epirote army he found the Macedonians were still loathe to fight; it was not the enemy they wanted to change but their own commander-in-chief. Pyrrhus' agents and citizens of Berrhoea, who had committed themselves to the Epirote cause, began to infiltrate Demetrius' camp. There, discontent turned towards mutiny and many soldiers began to drift away to join Pyrrhus. Friends told Demetrius to leave whilst there was still time. The dishevelled monarch, disguised in a shoddy cloak and hat, did just that, losing Macedonia as easily as he had won it.

Meanwhile Lysimachus had been following hard on Demetrius' heels and reached Berrhoea intent on squeezing his share of the spoils out of Pyrrhus. The Axius River again became the border between the two parts of a divided kingdom. The Macedonian army had, in essence, given the country to the two kings but they took no part in its apportioning and, worst of all, they now found their two new rulers regarded the halves of the kingdom as mere provinces to be attached to already-existing states. Neither kept their court in historic Macedonia; Pyrrhus' capital was sited at Ambracia, while Lysimachus saw no reason to move his headquarters from the strategically-placed Lysimacheia, despite its recent devastation by an earthquake. No doubt to seal the pact, the almost-forgotten Antipater, Cassander's son, was quietly disposed of and his wife, Eurydice, Lysimachus' own daughter, imprisoned.

While his enemies were despoiling his Macedonian seisin, Demetrius had taken the back roads to Cassandreia; there he found his wife, Phila, who held Cassander's foundation with a force who remained loyal to her despite the demise of her husband's fortunes. This woman, now into her old age, had been as great a support to her second husband as she had reputedly been to her father, Antipater, in his days of power. She had used her considerable reputation amongst the Macedonians to help Demetrius through all his dramatic changes of fortune. She had tried to mediate where she could in his relations with her brother Cassander. But the latest disaster sustained by Demetrius was apparently too much; with the vision of her husband losing with such facility the kingdom so associated with her family, she took poison. Demetrius' spirits were more robust; he left for Greece to rally support, even giving Thebes back her constitutional freedom to keep them in his camp.

An attempted comeback in Attica showed Demetrius was not yet done and dusted. A reputation such as his was not destroyed overnight and mercenary captains and faction leaders still held to a man whom Tyche had so often favoured in the past. Lysimachus shuddered as the Antigonid concentrated a fleet, boarded an admittedly fairly puny army and made treaties with those enemies who had previously seemed intent on driving him under. The invasion of Asia started well but, due to the efforts of Agathocles and Seleucus, eventually ran out of steam. By 285 BC, Demetrius was finally a spent force, a prisoner who would never know freedom again, and with that fact a very great deal changed for Lysimachus. His kingdom emerged strengthened from the test of Demetrius' invasion and he now found the opportunity to round out his authority on a number of fronts.

Lysimachus felt both strong and secure enough to brush away his neighbour across the Axius. Pyrrhus was no soft target; his empire had hugely expanded with the removal of Demetrius. Not only did he hold the greater Epirus that resulted from his deal with Alexander, son of Cassander, but he held the better part of Macedonia itself, as well as the whole of Thessaly (save Demetrias), which he had overrun in 286 BC, ironically with the encouragement of Lysimachus. Despite this picture of power, Lysimachus knew from contacts in western Macedonia that Pyrrhus' support did not run deep; his popularity had been facile and open to swift erosion from the beginning. When Lysimachus crossed the Axius in force in 285 BC, Pyrrhus retreated westwards from Pella, down what would become in Roman times the Via Egnatia, to Edessa at the base of the mountain ring round the Macedonian plain, where the terrain was more defensible. He had clearly been caught unawares and he can have had little faith in the Macedonian component of his army. Giving up the capital without a fight must have further reduced his credibility in his Macedonians' eyes, but he could not risk being caught in open country. Some suggest he must have suffered defeat and been driven back to have given up Pella, but there is no need to believe this. When he had fought Demetrius he had made his headquarters in Berrhoea, also in the Macedonian foothills above the plain. And Lysimachus was a very old man who might conceivably go away or die whilst Pyrrhus sat tight.

If to wait and see was a seductive strategy, Lysimachus had no intention of allowing it to succeed. He brought his army up the road to the west and comprehensively cut the supply lines to Pyrrhus' camp near Edessa. Pyrrhus' Macedonians would not fight and his perennial weakness – that he just did not have sufficient Epirotes to battle it out – meant that if he stayed he risked starvation. In fact he fled, allowing Lysimachus to take over the whole kingdom, though retaining control of Tymphaea, Parauaea, Ambracia, Amphilochia and Acarnania.

Though hardly documented at all, certain hints suggest a campaign of very different shape and greater length. It is possible that the initial contact and first rounds of the war were fought out in Thessaly where Antigonus Gonatus had lent troops in support of his new ally, Pyrrhus. But, even together, they could not resist Lysimachus and the Epirote king was forced to withdraw to Edessa, where he prepared another defence. Furthermore, it is proposed that after Pyrrhus' failure there, Lysimachus then invaded Epirus itself and in passing desecrated the graves of the Molossian kings.[10]

With Lysimachus now the complete master in the old kingdom, it would have been par for the course that a coalition of Balkan states would rise up against him. But this was not the case. Certainly there were enemies – Pyrrhus and Antigonus Gonatus remained an axis of opposition – but we do not hear of others joining them. Indeed, the new king at Pella even contrived the extraordinary trick of making friends with the Aetolians. This fiercely independent people went to the extent of naming two of their towns after Lysimachus and his wife Arsinoe. The Phocians also joined Lysimachus' team and showed their usefulness by expelling Antigonus Gonatus' garrison from Elatea. A reason for the failure of a hostile coalition to appear in strength was most probably the perceptions of the Greek political elites. To most of these men the existence of the new-model Epirote army of Pyrrhus, and Antigonus Gonatus with his string of strongholds around Greece, were more of a menace than a man at the head of a far-away continental empire, despite the fact of Lysimachus' recent take-over of the kingdom of Macedonia.

Evidence suggests that this Greek ruling class was more discerning in its perceptions than are the histories on which we depend. The sources that survive have incorrectly driven us to the conclusion that Lysimachus' interests were largely Aegean centred, directed either to the Balkans or towards the great ports of Asia Minor. Many Hellenes understood that as an Asian-centred ruler in charge of a weakened Macedonia, Lysimachus might, in fact, be a potential support rather than a threat. He certainly did little to interfere in mainland Greece in his last years and his Aegean interests were only part of the picture for a man whose concerns spun on a fulcrum around the Hellespont.[11] The heartlands of Anatolia were just as important an arena for his ambitions. Much of this was frontier territory, an environment where both threats and opportunities abounded, land where there was room for expansion over peoples whose customs and traditions could be overridden to maximise economic exploitation in a way not possible in old, established subject communities.

But with opportunities came dangers as there were new potential enemies who had to be faced. After Ipsus, Lysimachus found himself face to face with Zipoites of Bithynia, who controlled a considerable realm. Since 315 BC, he had shown a great interest in the Marmaran cities, particularly Astacus and Chalcedon, for whose control he had tussled unsuccessfully with Antigonus' nephew, Ptolemaeus. After Ipsus, Zipoites renewed his efforts and also threatened Heraclea, which was vital for Lysimachus' Pontic ambitions. In this, Zipoites had important allies, especially Byzantium, a city with a tradition of resisting Macedonian hegemony at the hinge of Europe and Asia.

A Bithynian war certainly occurred in the 280s BC. The details and chronology are uncertain but Lysimachus suffered a humiliating reverse (possibly even losing personally in battle).[12] Nicaea was lost and he was forced to destroy most of Astacus to prevent Zipoites occupying it. Heraclea, Lysimachus' staunch ally, also felt the brunt of the Bithynian monarch's power, losing a substantial part of its territory.

In the circumstances, it is not entirely surprising that Lysimachus inclined to take direct control of that city-state. Heraclea had maintained excellent relations with him through the agency of his ex-wife, Amastris. Since 300 BC the government had devolved on her two sons, Clearchus and Oxathres. The former had been on the Getic campaign with his step-father, even serving as hostage with Dromichaetes, but the losses to Zipoites had severely dented their popularity. An opportunity to unseat them came with the death of Amastris in 284 BC. She perished on a sea voyage and word soon got about that her sons were responsible. Lysimachus arrived at Heraclea, gained entry on account of his friendship with the brothers but then promptly arrested them on charges of matricide. The subsequent trials and execution were a foregone conclusion and Lysimachus further increased his standing by restoring the democratic constitution, a state of affairs that only lasted for a few years before the city was handed over to the voracious Arsinoe.

Nor was this the only example of expansion in those last years before the final trauma. In Paeonia, too, he decided direct rule was a safer option than keeping up a buffer state. In this small kingdom to the north of Macedonia, Audoleon, father-in-law of Pyrrhus, had long reigned. He had maintained friendly relations with Alexander (indeed his father may have served with distinction in Asia[13]) and Cassander. He had also given aid to the Athenians in their recent struggle against Demetrius. His death in 284 BC precipitated a dynastic crisis. Audoleon's son, Ariston, fled to Thrace, whereupon Lysimachus decided to restore him

> so that the inhabitants should recognise the royal prince and receive him
> kindly. But when they were washing Ariston in the royal bath and had set
> the royal table beside him according to custom Lysimachus gave the signal
> to disarm them. Ariston escaped on horseback. ...while Lysimachus
> captured Paeonia.[14]

The septuagenarian ex-bodyguard of Alexander the Great now ruled a commonwealth that stretched from the Antigonid outpost of Demetrias, in Thessaly, through Macedonia, northward through Paeonia and Thrace to at least the Haemus range, then over into Asia (with north Aegean islands as maritime barbicans of the Marmaran gateway to the Pontic basin) to take in Hellespontine Phrygia, Heraclea, Aeolia, Lydia, Ionia, parts of Caria, Phrygia and Lycaonia down to the Cilician Gates. This was the size of the estate he had piled up over four decades and the greatest threat to the edifice must have seemed the advanced age of its ruler. Yet he was far from having nobody to carry on after him.

First there was Agathocles, a man of stature and talent sufficient to make him an ideal heir. Yet he was fatally removed in a manner the sources point up in lurid personal and sexual detail. What is less commented on is the political dimension. The heir to the diadem must have been middle aged in the late 280s BC, with an impressive military career of near two decades behind him. In his years of power in Thrace and Anatolia he had appropriated an immense portfolio of patronage in both the military and civil administration to bind key members of the political elite to his person. From Philippopolis to Sardis there were officers and ministers who owed their careers to him; at least one city was founded by Agathocles and many others owed a debt of gratitude.

Others of the Successors had found a way to resolve the problem of an ageing king and mature heir but this pattern was not followed in Lysimacheia. Over the years a solution along the lines tested by Ptolemy and Seleucus – either a partnership system or a division of regional responsibility – must have been pressed by Agathocles and his friends. Yet the old man refused to grasp the nettle, too much used to a monopoly of supreme command. The man who showed such interest in the details of administration in the cities of the Asiatic Aegean could neither bear to share the top seat at the table nor alienate any significant portion of his holdings. Agathocles, back in triumph from driving Demetrius to his ultimate destruction, surely found his father's attitude excruciatingly frustrating. So there remained a king-in-waiting with his own revenue and armed forces, fuelling a paranoia in Lysimachus that finally led to the most radical solution of the problem.

Like many of his peers, Lysimachus had married several times. To his marriage bed had come the daughter of Antipater, the widow of Dionysius of Heraclea and the daughter of Ptolemy of Egypt. Arsinoe was a career ruler not a mere begetter of dynastic continuity. The debates in Lysimachus' council with her present must have been plangent affairs where resentments and wounds might be left that could fester into the crude and murderous solutions that were finally attempted to solve the succession issue. This remarkable woman, daughter of Berenice, had accrued great influence at Lysimachus' court since her marriage to the king in 300 BC. Her mother had been a second stringer who had successfully moved her own family to the top of the dynastic pile in Ptolemaic Egypt and was clearly a model of ambition for her daughter. It is no great surprise she coveted the throne for the oldest of her three sons, Ptolemy Lysimachou, rather than allowing it to fall to the heir apparent, Agathocles, the king's son by Nicaea. For eighteen years or so Arsinoe had worked to increase her influence in the kingdom. She had attained a considerable power base. Apart from her position as Lysimachus' wife, she had accrued the newly re-founded Ephesus, Heraclea and Cassandreia as personal appendages.[15]

The bitterness engendered by this competition for the succession, it is suggested, was exacerbated when Agathocles rejected the sexual advances of Arsinoe. The frustrated queen is accused of pioneering a movement at court to dispose of the second man in the state. Bent on a coup, it seems there now entered a man who would be of great assistance to her plans. This was that demonic character Ptolemy Thunderbolt, the son of Ptolemy and Eurydice, and so half-brother of Arsinoe. This exile had left Egypt with his mother some years before and had spent time at Antioch, hoping for assistance from Seleucus, before arriving at Lysimacheia in 287 BC. He apparently became a key member of the murderous cabal that played on the old monarch in the years between 285 and 283 BC. And this inveterate intriguer, it is suggested, actually carried out the assassination once the old king had given his stamp of approval to Arsinoe's vicious pogrom.

In fact, it is difficult to imagine Arsinoe and her half-brother easily working in tandem after the history of this unforgiving pair. Particularly as, at this time, Lysimachus married his own daughter by Nicaea (also called Arsinoe) to Ptolemy II, the man who had taken the very throne that the Thunderbolt considered his own. The evidence that connects him to the murder is thin – Ptolemy Lysimachou is at least as likely a suspect – and only the symmetry of this political killer being responsible for the end of Agathocles as well as Seleucus and Arsinoe's two youngest sons makes it attractive.[16] It feels right that at the bar of history Ptolemy's brief would have been found asking for this one to be taken into consideration too.

The plot was carried out between 283 and 282 BC. Unfortunately, not only the agent of Agathocles' downfall but also the manner of his going is unclear. The sources, Justin, Memnon and Strabo, are brief and unreliable, suggesting in turn poisoning, imprisonment followed by poisoning and even that Lysimachus carried out the murder himself. Whatever, the deed went off for

Arsinoe with a smoothness that belied its dreadful consequences. Almost immediately, reverberations began to impact in the wider world like the waves from a stone thrown into a pond. Agathocles' wife, Lysandra (another daughter of Ptolemy Soter), and her children fled the court of Lysimacheia and, together with Lysimachus' son, Alexander, went into exile in Seleucus' kingdom at Antioch. They were followed by others who had been known associates of the murdered man or by those who were just terrified by the atmosphere engendered when an infanticide monarch was ruling under the influence of Arsinoe and Ptolemy the Thunderbolt.

Chapter 12

The Final Hand

*Lysimachus was seventy-four years old; Seleucus seventy-seven. But at
this age they both had the fire of youth, and an insatiable desire of power;
for though they alone possessed the whole world, they yet thought themselves
confined within narrow limits, and measured their course of life, not by their
length of years, but by the extent to which they carried their dominion.*[1]

The coalition monarchs had attempted to agree at the outset the details of the
spoliation of the Antigonid empire. Originally, Ptolemy was to have been
rewarded with Coele-Syria for his part in pinning down Antigonid resources
in the Levant. But his efforts had been puny and the rulers who had actually
faced Antigonus in battle were appalled by his lack of resolve. Instead,
Seleucus' share of the carve-up was to be enlarged to include the province.
But, before he could take advantage of the pact he found that Ptolemy had
reoccupied most of Coele-Syria. The only way to win it back was war and he
was not inclined to that step at that time. It is suggested that this unusual lack
of bellicosity was due to a long-standing affection for the king who had put
him on the road to power, just over a decade before. There may have been
something in this sentimental dimension but *realpolitik* also had a role to play.
Ptolemy had thwarted both Perdiccas and Antigonus in his time and, even
after Ipsus, Seleucus could not raise the same military effort as those two
previous enemies of the Lagid king. In any case, he had much to do in
digesting the gains he had already made. Western Mesopotamia and northern
Syria had to be secured and garrisoned. The snout of Seleucus' kingdom that
pushed forward to the Mediterranean Sea, north of Phoenicia, was vulnerable
from all sides. Demetrius held Sidon and Tyre, Ptolemy occupied the country
south of the Orontes valley and in Cilicia, just across the Bay of Issus,
Cassander's brother, Pleistarchus, was establishing his own principality. The
old anti-Antigonid alliance, with no mutual enemy to give it reason, had
sundered into a collection of potential opponents, each intent on gaining at the
others' expense.

Ptolemy, Lysimachus and Cassander were strengthening the ties between
their royal houses by a number of marriages and these developments of

necessity thrust Seleucus into the arms of Demetrius. Ambassadors were sent to Demetrius offering friendship and a marriage alliance in which Seleucus would wed Stratonice, Demetrius' daughter by Phila. The young woman, who must have been well over 30 years younger than the bridegroom, was to be brought by Demetrius to the coast of Syria where both the political and nuptial arrangements were to be consummated.

On the journey, bad weather forced the fleet to put in at Cilicia and Demetrius took the opportunity to raid the treasury at Cyinda, where he purloined 1,200 talents of treasure. Pleistarchus, caught unprepared, was unable to act at all to defend himself. With an abatement in the storm, the much-enriched father of the bride sailed on to Rhosus, a city on the coast just south of Issus, where Alexander had won his victory over Darius. Seleucus and his court were there to meet them and elaborate and lengthy celebrations were laid on to mark the occasion.

This entente caused shock waves to reverberate round the courts of the Macedonian kings; erstwhile allies were thoroughly unsettled by this new alliance. Nor were the fears unfounded, as soon as the celebrations were over, Demetrius invaded Cilicia and threw out the unfortunate Pleistarchus. This was done with Seleucus' connivance, even if he was not actively engaged in the invasion of his neighbour, but, far from turning out to be the first of many joint ventures, the Cilician affair was the beginning of a rift between them. Seleucus had understood that the marriage contract had included a dowry and Cilicia was to be it. He expected the province to be handed over to his officers, on the payment of a sum of money, and was outraged when his father-in-law rebuffed his claim and held the place himself. If he was not to gain territorially in this direction, he still hoped to be compensated elsewhere and, in 295 BC, he proposed that Demetrius should hand over Sidon and Tyre as the price of their marriage alliance. This only worked to deepen the split, as Demetrius felt even the request was an unforgivable slight on his dignity.

After the chaos attendant on the fall of the Antigonid empire, the Seleucid state was one of four major powers. In fifteen years of marching and fighting Seleucus had laid claim to a vast empire but was now faced with the need to rule it. He had no hesitation in deciding the political heart of the empire would be at its westernmost edge. The court was transferred first from Babylonia to Seleuceia in Pieria, a port on the coast north of Laodicea, until he had constructed a purpose-built capital at Antioch on the northern reaches of the Orontes River, close to Antigonia. With his councillors and administrators provided with a home he turned to the permanent establishment of the royal army. In the regions neighbouring the capital he planted garrisons and military colonies. At Apamea, further up the Orontes, the elephant corps was permanently housed, while in Cyrrhus, to the northeast of Antioch, many of his veterans were settled, provided with rich lands for their families in return for producing future recruits for the ranks of the royal regiments.

This western orientation should not suggest that the first Seleucid lost interest in the provinces east of the Euphrates. He, more than anybody, knew the importance of the wealth of Babylonia and Iran. To retain direct control of the upper satrapies from Syria had been a problem Antigonus never solved and now a different king wrestled with it. Only a permanently peripatetic ruler could hope to retain the reins of power in his own hands in a state that stretched from Antioch to Afghanistan, and this would have kept him too often away from the Hellenic west. The solution was to delegate and in his son, Antiochus, he had an agent both competent to carry the responsibility and trustworthy enough not to be tempted to abuse the power that came with it. Sovereignty of the eastern lands was handed over to this viceroy; as with the Roman Empire after Diocletian, a world where facilities for travel were primitive and political power was both personal and dependent on military might, division of power was an answer that had to be accepted.

The year 293 BC saw the administrative division of the empire formalised when Antiochus was made joint king with his father, an event pinpointed by developments that led to Stratonice, the daughter of Demetrius, leaving Seleucus and marrying his son. Antiochus, we are informed by Plutarch, had fallen in love with his father's wife and was pining away because of these unnatural feelings for his stepmother. Seleucus' concern for his heir was such that when the court physician, Erasistratus, guessed the truth and reported it to the king, he divorced his queen and married her to his son. It was during the public ceremonial involved in this remarriage that Antiochus and Stratonice were declared king and queen of upper Asia. These bizarre family arrangements have little, in reality, to do with romance and much more to do with Seleucus' changing relations with Demetrius. Indeed, it is difficult to see how the prince can have formed this infatuation as, during this period, he was far more frequently at Seleuceia on the Tigris than at Antioch. Almost certainly, the arrangement was a device to avoid the embarrassment of having Demetrius' daughter as his queen after he had broken with him; yet, by removing her in this way, he did not drastically damage her status, which might have brought on immediate war with her father.

Details of Antiochus' stewardship in the east are completely unknown but it is reasonable to assume he followed the pattern of government that had served the Achaemenid kings in the past. Spending his summers in the highlands of Iran, he would find the palace of Ecbatana could still be quite tolerable in the hot months when Mesopotamia sweltered in temperatures of well over 100 degrees. The arrival of winter would have brought the court back to Seleuceia on the Tigris, where the heat would have diminished sufficiently to make the business of government possible. On his journeys round the vast hinterland of the upper satrapies, the young king continued to plant Hellenistic cities, many of which were soundly enough based to sustain themselves through the demise of Seleucus' dynasty and the advent of the nomadic Parthians. It was far from being a merely clerical exercise, the personal supervision of the monarch was required for much of the initial construction work. Macedonian rulers were normally extremely interested in techniques of engineering and this is reflected in the fact that one of their most important functions, along with leading their armies in war, was the founding of cities. These cities were monuments to their power and the glory of the dynasty in the way the palaces of the Persians, the pyramids of the Pharaohs and the military friezes of the Assyrians had been for these earlier imperialists.

Seleucus had done much to strengthen his position in the Levant while Antiochus was busy organising the upper satrapies. The alliance with Demetrius was not, in the end, totally fruitless; he eventually did gain possession of Cilicia, either by force or agreement. This greatly strengthened his northern frontier and gave him the rampart of the Taurus Mountains as protection from the west. To the south, he refurbished the towns and forts on his frontier with Ptolemy and new towns were built to guard the roads from the south that an invader might use.

This unspectacular but steady consolidation was interrupted by developments in the world outside of Seleucus' kingdom. The death of Cassander had led to a savage struggle for the throne of Macedonia and, though he had not been involved, the consequences would reverberate almost to the gates of Antioch itself. His former ally, Demetrius, emerged as the new king at Pella but responsibilities for the homeland of Philip and Alexander did nothing to dampen his appetite for adventure and conquest. When it became clear the object of his ambition was in Asia, Seleucus was happy to be part of the reconstituted coalition that aimed to ruin the imperial projects of the son, just as they had the father.

Waiting at Antioch, he could not take part in the active opposition to this dangerous enemy. News reached him that great events had occurred in the Balkans which looked to turn the situation upside down. Demetrius had been driven from Macedonia and fled to his son, Antigonus Gonatus, who was holding on in Greece with the rump of the Antigonid army. Though weakened, he was not tamed by this experience, alive and uncaptured with his fleet intact in their Greek bases and with a small but veteran army of mercenaries, he pressed on with his invasion plans.

In the cold light of day, this was a desperate enterprise. Demetrius only had 11,000 infantry and a few thousand cavalry when he sailed from Greece in this last throw of his career. The beginning of 287 BC was an anxious time for Seleucus when he was still unsure of Demetrius' destination. But relief came when he heard dependable news that the invader had taken the shortest route across the Aegean and had made landfall at Miletus, far from Seleucid turf. It was clear he was confining his aggression to Lysimachus' territory in Caria, Lydia and Ionia where his father had ruled for years and where he might still expect to find friends.

If Demetrius' first season back in Asia had been a considerable success, 286 BC would show the beachhead he had constructed there was built on sand. Agathocles, son of Lysimachus, arrived from the north with a large army and forced him to retreat inland and east into Anatolia. He disappeared with his small force of mercenaries into Phrygia and rumours abounded about his ultimate intentions. Some thought he aimed to march through the mountains of Armenia and set himself up as a king in Media. Unfortunately for any such extravagant hopes, Agathocles pursued him remorselessly. In a series of running fights, Demetrius' men were worn down and, having lost 8,000 since landing the previous year, he turned south towards the Taurus Mountains.

If the condition of Demetrius' army had been known to Seleucus it would have been little enough consolation; he heard the stories of Demetrius' ambitions in the east and each day Agathocles' army was herding the unpredictable king closer to his frontier. His fears were realised when the shattering news arrived that Demetrius had crossed the Taurus passes and was encamped near the town of Tarsus in level Cilicia. The agricultural lands of this coastal plain offered the weary troops the forage and provisions they required. Demetrius had no wish to make an enemy of Seleucus by plundering the province – he was too aware of his own weakness – but he could not deny the men who had stayed loyal during the epic march across Anatolia. Letters arrived at Antioch from the intruder at Tarsus, declaring he had no desire for war and only hoped for aid as a relative by marriage who had fallen on hard times. Seleucus showed either great indecision or Machiavellian subtlety in dealing with this unwanted guest. He first ordered his officials in Cilicia to organise provisions for Demetrius' men and animals and even wrote reassuringly that he forgave the depredations already carried out in the province. He had tried to use Demetrius before as a counter to his other rivals and it was possible he could still be a stick to beat Lysimachus with. But this positive potential had to be weighed against the threat this unstable force might pose to Seleucus' own power.

These issues were hotly debated amongst the king's council at Antioch and the final policy was only decided when Seleucus' trusted general, Patrocles, pointed out that the fugitive's volatile temper, combined with his desperate position, made him far too dangerous to be left at large.[2] Convinced he would be as likely to turn on him as to aid the Seleucid cause, the king took the decision to crush Demetrius. With all precaution, Seleucus led his army into Cilicia to confront the intruder, only to find he had decamped and retreated back into the Taurus Mountains. The king of Asia did not immediately follow on his heels and was even prepared to reopen negotiations when emissaries from Demetrius rode down from the hills to find him. The ambassadors asked first that their leader should be allowed to march away unmolested to find some barbarian lands where he could settle himself and his remaining soldiers. Demetrius was playing for time; it was not believable that this man who had come to conquer Asia would settle for the role of tribal chieftain. Seleucus was prepared to humour him as he made his preparations for the coming contest. He was organising the defences of all the passes south into Syria while negotiations were in progress. A truce was agreed and Demetrius was allowed to spend two months of the winter of 286/285 BC in Cataonia on condition he handed over some officers as hostages.

But, if he did not break the truce by an outright assault, Seleucus had no intention of allowing this breathing space to provide the enemy with room for manoeuvre. He built up his own forces in encampments close to Demetrius' winter quarters to pen them in. But Demetrius would just not lie down even in the face of these odds. Refusing to allow himself to be entrapped, he slipped away from the area allotted to him and overran the rest of Cataonia. This decided Seleucus that he must attack and destroy the interloper. His generals were ordered to winkle out the small and tattered army. In this darkest hour, the fugitive Demetrius showed those reserves of military talent and fortitude in adversity that make his chequered and flawed career such an epic story. Making good use of the difficult terrain, he fought off all attempts to reach him and even scored a minor victory against one of the enemy corps, a combat distinguished by the use of scythed chariots. We know Seleucus had some of these weapons at Ipsus but they do not seem to have been used and on this occasion his officers had no success with this anachronistic armament as the Antigonid veterans avoided their charge with ease and dispersed them with missile fire and counterattacks. Worse was to follow when it became known Demetrius had gained control of one of the roads into northern Syria.

Now Demetrius' luck deserted him as he fell ill. His army lost its impetus and his weary band of followers had the leisure to reflect on the position they were in. Morale plummeted. Many deserted to Seleucus, while others, less sure of their reception at his hands, fled in search of safety elsewhere. Demetrius was disabled by sickness for forty days and by the time he was back on his feet his army was sadly depleted in numbers and his situation more desperate than ever. During this hiatus, Seleucus had not attacked in force; instead he had been content to restrict his enemy ever more closely in his mountain fastness, expecting lack of supplies, disease and desertion to do his work for him.

Antigonus' son was not an easy prey to contain, he still had the rump of his army, the best of his formidable veterans, and with those he struck back. Feinting southwest towards Cilicia, when darkness fell he turned his men east, slipped past the Seleucid armies unnoticed and crossed the Amanus Mountains into northern Syria. He marched hard towards the region of Cyrrhus, where many Macedonians and mercenaries had been settled in military colonies since Alexander's time. There he hoped to find old soldiers who had served with him or his father, who might still have some sentiment for the Antigonid house. Seleucus, at least now knowing which way he had gone, gathered every available soldier and followed close on his heels. Officers were sent to secure the loyalty of the provincial cities and to isolate Demetrius' tiny army in preparation for obliterating it in a final battle. Seleucus caught up with his quarry and camped his men right up by the enemy's position to force him to fight at last. This belated bellicosity almost cost him dear when the resourceful Demetrius attempted a night attack on his sleeping camp. In the nick of time, the Seleucids were warned by deserters of the impending assault and, realising his ruse had been discovered, Demetrius withdrew into the night, swiftly pursued by the awakened Seleucids.

On the following morning both armies were near Cyrrhus, a military foundation of Antigonus and capital of the region. The terrain was rugged hills and narrow valleys and here Demetrius turned to fight, knowing his army was overtaken and battle unavoidable. His hope was that the nature of the country would restrict the deployment of the enemy's greater numbers against his own few thousand weary troops, whom he now drew up in battle array. With virtually no cavalry at all, he deployed his infantry in two wings across a valley where the flanks of the army would be protected by the rough ground on the valley sides. Seleucus approached from the southeast to deny the enemy any possibility of withdrawing eastwards in the direction of the upper satrapies. His army was far larger but the choice of ground denied any chance to deploy his horsemen, though he did find room to bring up a few elephants to decisive effect. When the two armies clashed, Demetrius led his wing with customary élan; taking the initiative, he threw himself on the infantry opposite and drove them back. The other flank had less success; here the Seleucid troops pressed so hard that Demetrius had to send reinforcements from his wing so they could hold their line. Both sides seemed for the moment evenly matched when Seleucus risked a dangerous manoeuvre to break the deadlock.

It had been reported to Seleucus that a small pass led around the flank of the enemy line and through this ravine he led eight elephants and a unit of royal guards. Arriving on the enemy's exposed flank, he did not attack at once. He knew Demetrius' men must have been affected by the desperate nature of their predicament, exposed as they were in the heart of enemy country and exhausted by the ordeal of the last months. Judging they had lost the will to resist, the king of Asia dismounted, took off his helmet so he could be recognised, and with only a small shield for protection approached the enemy battle line. He shouted to them 'how long will your madness continue, staying with a famished pirate chief, when you could earn your pay with a rich king, and have a share in a kingdom which is a reality, not a dream?'[3] The action exposed him to considerable danger; these were men who had stayed loyal to the son of Antigonus through thick and thin, who could have deserted before but had not. Demetrius' soldiers, exposed, outnumbered, threatened on their flank by crack troops and fearsome beasts and with nowhere to retreat, proved to have had enough.

Demetrius fled with a few companions away from the battlefield. Reaching the Amanus Mountains by nightfall, they tried to hide from Seleucus' pursuit. A thorough manhunt was got under way and orders sent to guard all the routes that refugees from the battle might take. Demetrius' aim was to make his way back to his fleet at Caunus, a difficult journey across half of Anatolia. The futility of this hope became clear in the night, when he could see the campfires of his pursuers all around his forest refuge. With no possibility of slipping through this cordon, he finally accepted defeat and emerged to throw himself on the mercy of an opponent who had at last brought an end to his amazing career of triumph and disaster.

The sequel to this drama is quickly told. Despite an offer of 2,000 talents by Lysimachus to have him killed, which was indignantly refused by Seleucus, Demetrius was kept in comfortable confinement near Antioch for a few years before he drank himself to death in early middle age.

For thirty years Seleucus Nicator ('the Victorious') had ruled the Macedonian empire east of the Euphrates (Babylonian chronicles date the start of his reign from 312 BC). For nearly two decades of the new century his kingdom had included the lands of the Levant, except for Coele-Syria and Phoenicia. In extent and potential wealth his domain was far greater than those of his peers, who had also fought with Alexander. The innovative form of government he had developed with his son had stood the test of time, with the joint monarchs essentially independent in the two halves of the kingdom. Subject to the two main centres at Antioch and Seleuceia on the Tigris, there were seventy-two satrapies, each ruled by a strategos, and by far the majority of these were directly subservient to Antiochus in the east. Apart from these bare bones, the methods of government of the two kings are a closed book.

The years since the downfall of Antigonus had not seen either of the Seleucid kings embark on major campaigns of expansion. They rounded out their possessions where the opportunity arose, Cilicia was picked up from Demetrius in the west and the Sogdian frontier extended to improve its defensibility in the east. Wars with the other Macedonian kings had been avoided, except where Demetrius' eruption across the Taurus had forced Seleucus to defend himself. Now, at over seventy years of age, Seleucus abandoned this non-combative approach to his peers and decided on an aggressive campaign against Lysimachus. Part of the motivation behind this change of policy was opportunist; intrigues at the court of Lysimachus offered an almost irresistible opening.

Agathocles, Lysimachus' eldest son, was murdered on his father's orders and the dead man's wife and children fled to Antioch looking for refuge. The assassination of the popular and competent heir to the throne had thrown the court and army high command of Lysimachus' kingdom into turmoil. Friends and dependants of the dead prince feared for their lives and fled from the murderer's court, many of them, following Agathocles' family, made their way to Seleucus. The welcome they received from the ruler of Asia encouraged others in defection and even Alexander, another son of Lysimachus, fled east to escape from the power of his dangerous father. Most encouraging for Seleucus was the news of the dislocation these events had caused in the ranks of Lysimachus' army. The murdered man had been their commander on many campaigns over the previous two decades and the manner of his death had shocked and distressed them.

For Seleucus the opportunity offered by the murder of Agathocles had coincided with an imperative that each year was becoming more pressing. The old man knew he could not live much longer and, while he was still able, intended to try and ensure the security of his empire where it was most vulnerable. It was from the west that recent history showed an Asian empire must anticipate the most serious danger. Invaders backed by disciplined European troops would always feel the temptation to plunder the riches of the East and Lysimachus alone was in a position to attempt this.

The whole of the military forces of the Seleucid west were mobilised for what was the last great enterprise of his life. The royal regiments and elephants at Apamea were placed on a war footing, the military colonists from Syria and Mesopotamia called up to provide the heavy infantry and Macedonian-style cavalry that were the hard core of the army. Iranian troopers were recruited to supplement this cavalry, but in limited numbers as the best Persian, Median and Bactrian horse were required by Antiochus to defend the eastern frontier. Ceremonial leave was taken of the court at Antioch and Seleucus led his large and formidable invasion force on the historic road that led through the Cilician Gates and up onto the Anatolian plateau. Little is known of the campaign except its most general outline. Lysimachus did not go to meet the invader but waited in western Asia Minor so he could fight his enemy on home ground without his lines of communication being too extended. It is also possible he was reluctant to ask his soldiers to do any hard marching, since the loyalty of many had been suspect since the affair of Agathocles.

Alexander, the exiled son of Lysimachus, had command of one column of the Seleucid army. He overran much of Phrygia, taking the town of Cotiaeum in person, while Seleucus led the main force that attacked the key citadel of Sardis, in Lydia. With the intruders as far west as Lydia, Lysimachus could no longer delay offering battle and he drew up his men on the plain of Corus in central Lydia. The Battle of Corupedium that occurred when the two armies collided was the last great set-piece encounter fought between Alexander's old generals. The details are unrecorded but Seleucus emerged as victor and his enemy was killed in battle; one tradition envisages the two old warriors fighting hand to hand at the climax of the combat.

Though almost certainly untrue, this suggestion does have a pleasing symmetry with these geriatrics, who had both followed Alexander in their youth, acting out this last dramatic episode in front of followers for whom those campaigns against the Persians must have seemed part of the remotest history. Even in death, Lysimachus did not rest easy. Agathocles' wife, Lysandra, was determined to avenge her husband's murder beyond the bitter end and refused to allow his body to be buried. It was only with great difficulty that Alexander, despite fighting on Seleucus' side, managed to retrieve his father's corpse (guarded by Lysimachus' own dog) and buried it near Lysimacheia.

Lysimachus' achievements would evaporate like morning mist in the sunshine. No descendant of his dodged in skirmishes with Galatian looters, sponsored great libraries or had to put up with the ignorant arrogance of Roman proconsuls. This insubstantiality might seem to have been predestined by geography, with the Hellenistic world falling into Egyptian, Asian and Macedonia spheres. But this is hindsight; Lysimachus' kingdom physically prefigured a Byzantine state that came in to being almost 1,000 years later and showed the kind of endurance that would be the envy of any civilisation. For half a long lifetime, Lysimachus' empire had filled that Balkan-Anatolian niche that under the later Romans would hold its own against Huns, Goths, Bulgars, Avars, Magyars, Arabs, Turks, Cathars, Russ and many, many more.

Now Seleucus was a unique remnant, the last of the successors who had been contemporaries of Alexander the great and, at 77 years old, the only ruler left in the Hellenistic world who had actually marched in that king's conquering army. Lysimachus was gone and the towns and provinces in Europe and Asia that he had ruled were open to his conqueror. The army he had brought from Antioch had been joined by the numerous survivors of the enemy that fought at Corupedium and now nowhere in the world was there a land power that could offer him any great threat. It was autumn 281 BC by the time the takeover of Lysimachus' empire was begun, agents were sent to the cities of the Aegean coast and the Hellespont to announce his victory and the great inland fortresses, such as Sardis and Ancyra, were secured with garrisons. Local aristocrats and administrators offered their submission and were confirmed in possession of their estates or replaced according to their merits.

Minor problems still rankled, due to the activities of certain remnants of the old order. Arsinoe, who had been Lysimachus' queen, was a remarkable woman who would later have a great influence in the world as the consort of Ptolemy II. At this time, she refused to accept the end of her dynasty merely because of her husband's death and had set herself up in the recently heavily-fortified city of Ephesus. The citizens did not share her priorities and on hearing of Seleucus' victory they looked to their own interests, driving Arsinoe and her retinue out to avoid the imminent prospect of a siege. If control of the Aegean coast of Asia Minor had come easy enough, in other areas Seleucus had not only inherited his dead rival's possessions but the inconvenience of his enemies as well.

Zipoites, king of Bithynia, may well have initially given aid to Seleucus to discomfit his old enemy, but, now that the invader had replaced Lysimachus as an even greater power in northwestern Anatolia, this local potentate turned against him. Others also disliked the substitution of an even more formidable state north of the Taurus. Heraclea, on the Black Sea coast, had been released from subjection by Lysimachus' defeat and now looked to gain friends to protect her new-found independence. The towns of Byzantium and Chalcedon joined her in an alliance and they won the support of Mithridates of Pontus to form the northern league that at least ensured Seleucus did not have untrammelled power in that part of Anatolia.

Whatever the developments in the northern periphery, they were not central to the old king's plans. He had decided to invade Europe and acquire both Thrace and Macedonia, spear-won lands he felt entitled to after his victory over Lysimachus. His extraordinary success, so far, was such as to encourage almost any ambition. It is suggested that the king could not resist the lure of his homeland and that this drove him to disregard the advice of the Didyma oracle that he ought not to return to Europe. Once in Pella, he could leave his Asian possessions to be ruled by Antiochus while he lived out his days on the throne of Philip and Alexander. Sentiment may have had some influence on his policy; it had been fifty years since he had seen the green hills of his birthplace and none of these Successors forgot the tribal pride of their Macedonian origins.

By the winter of 281/280 BC, the army had been concentrated and was ready to move to the Hellespont. There was no hint of opposition but the crossing was time consuming because of the huge numbers of men and animals that had to be ferried over to the European side. The invaders travelled the coast road that hugged the eastern shore on the way to Lysimacheia where the old court had been quartered.

Travelling in the king's entourage was Ptolemy the Thunderbolt, the dispossessed heir of the first Macedonian monarch of Egypt. He had fled from his father's court years before, first to Seleucus and then to Lysimachus, where he allegedly had a considerable hand in the murder of Agathocles. Eventually he switched his allegiance back to Seleucus' side although the sources are ambiguous on the timing. Whatever the exact circumstances, his high birth guaranteed a warm reception and he was soon holding commands that kept him close to Seleucus' side.

Ptolemy the Thunderbolt had designs of his own on the throne of Macedonia. He had built up a considerable faction since joining the Seleucids, finding fertile ground amongst Lysimachus' followers who were concerned what the future would bring with Seleucus at an advanced age and his natural heir thousands of miles away to the east. A candidate on the spot who was of high birth and prestige would have attracted not a few who held a pragmatic approach to their own long-term futures. When he reached Lysimacheia, Ptolemy felt he had sufficient support to make his move. A coup would be risky but his career showed a man who was impetuous and to whom precipitate action was second nature.

The king left Lysimacheia looking forward to an easy conquest of Macedonia; the army was relaxed and anticipated no action. An atmosphere of security permeated the whole high command surrounding Seleucus who, himself, was in the mood for sightseeing. This was a common diversion for the Macedonian aristocracy and he had heard about a rough monument situated near the line of march that, according to local legend, commemorated the passing of Jason and his Argonauts. Determined to halt and see it, the king strayed away from the close attention of his bodyguard and Ptolemy and his henchmen were able to ensure they were closest to the old tourist when they reached the object of his search. They cut him down with their swords in a matter of seconds and the ease with which they accomplished the assassination suggests the blight of treachery had bitten deep amongst Seleucus' followers. Security was a high priority amongst the great men of this epoch, normally a king's bodyguard would confiscate the weapons of any who came into their master's presence, so it is difficult to believe that Seleucus would have voluntarily trusted this prince so close to his undefended person. Key officers responsible for his safety must have been implicated and it is a rare tribute to Ptolemy's talents as an intriguer that he could have subverted those close to such an eminently successful leader.

This suspicion is supported by the sequel, none of the dead king's men tried to arrest the assassins, no hue and cry was raised, the body was left in the dust as his assailants pushed on with their coup. Wearing the diadem stolen from the corpse, Ptolemy returned to the camp of the main army where he was promptly acclaimed king in place of the man he had murdered.

Demetrius Poliorcetes called Seleucus 'commander of the elephants' in derision, but it cannot be denied that the appellation had a real aptness for the last of the *Diadochi*. He came to prominence in India where the Macedonians first fought, and then incorporated into their armament, this fearsome yet fragile weapon. The only recorded compact made by Seleucus on his anabasis that marked out the eastern half of his empire was drawn up with Chandragupta Maurya and sealed with a gift of 500 war elephants; beasts that at Ipsus ensured Seleucus' place at the table of the great eastern Mediterranean powers at the beginning of the third century. A few animals were still, almost a generation later, fit enough to scare Demetrius' ragtag mercenaries into surrender in the hills of Northern Syria. The family connection with these creatures was kept up by his son, Antiochus, who established his prestige in the west, after his father's death, by defeating a band of Galatian marauders in Anatolia in a battle known as the elephant victory.

He may not have been the most talented or impressive of his peers but Seleucus is certainly one of the most sympathetic, an adventurer who rode his share of luck but also one with a basic decency unusual for the time. He refused to sell Demetrius' life for Lysimachus' gold and also seems to have had more empathy with his non-Hellenic subjects than any of the other Successors. His achievement was not negligible, he left an empire that survived, in part, for over two hundred years and, perhaps more importantly, provided for the permanent transmission of Hellenistic values and culture to the East.

The final irony was that we hear of Seleucus, at the last, in connection with one whose successors would deeply impinge on his legacy. Philetairos of Pergamum (a castrati bureaucrat who had deserted Lysimachus and taken his fortress and the bulging treasure trove it protected over to Seleucus before Corupedium) was the man who retrieved the last *Diadochi*'s murdered corpse and sent the ashes to Antiochus. After this act of piety he returned to Pergamum to start, through the blood of his nephew, the Attalid dynasty that would eventually supplant the Seleucids in most of Anatolia. And it was Attalid Pergamum, in tandem with the Rhodians, that brought into the Hellenistic orbit the Roman armies that would finally deprive Seleucus' descendants of any real power on the world stage.

Epilogue

Assassination thus brought to an end the last of the original *Diadochi*; a denouement unleashed by one of the most dangerous characters of the era. In the Middle Ages this bloody and inveterate intriguer would undoubtedly have been named Ptolemy the Bad but the Hellenistic age had less use for these simplistic pejoratives. This son of Ptolemy had been denied the opportunity for legitimate power in Egypt that he felt himself entitled to and the few dynamic years of his adult life suggest the experience had unhinged an already brutal personality. His reign as king of Macedonia did not last long, brought to an end as it was in defeat and death. It was a regnal career that conformed to type with the murder of his half-sister Arsinoe's children before he lost his head, severed to adorn the spearhead of a Galatian warlord.

Forty years of fighting had done much to mould the world Alexander left in such a fluid state on his demise. Uncertainty and anxiety is the common experience of the majority in any age of great historical change and this was certainly the case in the time of the first Successors. More cities were taken and regions ravaged than had been the case for generations. Warfare had been the backdrop of many an ancient civilisation but in this time its effects became quantifiably greater and more widespread, a bellicosity that was funded by the great release of treasures piled up in the empires of the east.

This disruptive uncertainty was compounded immediately on the death of Alexander's last general by barbarian incursions from central Europe. In 279 BC Galatian hordes broke through the northern marches of the littoral world in a way that Illyrian or Thracian raiders had never previously done. Their reign of terror was short lived but the trauma was considerable. The Hellenistic world eventually found the vitality and military power to rebuff or redirect these physically powerful but unsophisticated gatecrashers; but their impact was potent and reflected in the art and politics of the civilisation they had assaulted. As the great frieze at Pergamum reflects their impact on the aesthetic, the way the second generation of Hellenistic kings chose to eschew complete devotion to military aggression indicates another effect. Their comparative quiescence allowed the Hellenistic kingdoms to drop into the pattern that lasted till the Romans came and the reason can be traced to the strains wrought psychologically and physically by the Galatian invasions.

Not that military activities entered a complete decline (indeed the Gauls themselves in the guise of cheap and available mercenaries added a new dimension to it), but the scale tended to be less total than before 280 BC.

Antigonus Gonatus was content with establishing his place on a small Balkan stage and his campaigns remind us more of the wars of classical Greece than the Macedonian-world wars of his predecessors. His restraint of ambition would not have been considered by either his father or his grandfather. The heirs of Ptolemy Soter could be acquisitive of Coele-Syria and in reclaiming the naval position lost at Salamis, but no Macedonian pharaoh ever aimed to unite the Hellenistic world under the banner of the Lagids. Seleucus' successors found the task of digesting the Galatian remnants into their Anatolian state, of combating the centrifugal tendencies of local administrators and containing an aggressive Parthian dynasty in Iran quite sufficient to absorb their talents and resources without harbouring ambitions of world supremacy.

Certainly Pyrrhus – the very archetype of hero king – by 280 BC still had almost a decade of his career to run. But it was westwards against Rome and Carthage that his best efforts were expended and his last campaign in Macedonia and the Peloponnese altered nothing, ending when an old woman in Argos closed the Epirote king's life with a well-aimed roof tile. As a man and leader contemporaries regarded Pyrrhus highly. Hannibal (the greatest tactician of the ancient world) placed him in the very highest category of commanders. But his return from Italy only served to prove how much he had outlived his time, an unpredictable giant who did not fit a smaller time.

Notes

Abbreviations

ABSA	*Annual of the British School at Athens*
AJP	*American Journal of Philology*
CA	*Classical Antiquity*
CQ	*Classical Quarterly*
GRBS	*Greek, Roman and Byzantine Studies*
HSCP	*Harvard Studies in Classical Philology*
JHS	*Journal of Hellenic Studies*
LCM	*Liverpool Classical Monthly*
YCS	*Yale Classical Studies*
ZPE	*Zeitschrift für Papyrologie und Epigraphik*

Introduction

1   Plutarch, *Moralia III*, translated by F C Babbitt (London and Cambridge, Massachusetts, 1931) 177 C.
2   Alexander created a special disciplinary unit, called the Disorderlies, to which he drafted all Macedonians known to be critical of the disposal of Parmenion.

Chapter 1: Babylon

1   Quintus Curtius Rufus, *The History of Alexander*, translated by John Yardley (London 1984), 10.5.5.
2   Significantly, the story of the ring, whilst it appears in Curtius, Justin and Diodorus, is not mentioned in Arrian's *Anabasis*. Arrian's source, Ptolemy, did not wish to advertise Perdiccas' pre-eminence at Babylon.
3   For what follows, see R M Errington, 'From Babylon to Triparadeisos 323-320 B.C.' in *JHS*, 90 (1970), pp 49-77 and his excellent account. For another view, and alternative use of the sources, see N G L Hammond and F W Walbank, *History of Macedonia*, vol. 3 (Oxford, 1988), pp 95-106; and A B Bosworth, *The Legacy of Alexander* (Oxford, 2002).
4   According to the Alexander Romance, Alexander not only bequeathed his ring to Perdiccas, but also Roxanne, instructing him to marry her. Some, most notably W M Heckel in *The Marshals of Alexander's Empire* (London and New York, 1992), have seen this as a plausible suggestion. The part of the Romance this comes from is the *Last Days and Testament of Alexander*, which appears to be a pamphlet written soon after Alexander's death for propaganda purposes. It is a curious mixture of romance and history. W M Heckel, in 'The Last Days and Testament of Alexander the Great', *Historia Einzelschriften*, 56 (1988), has produced an excellent account of its provenance and purpose, though his conclusion that it was written as propaganda for Polyperchon is open to question.
5   The true identity of Quintus Curtius and the date of his writing are unknown. However it is generally believed that he lived in the first century AD. Evidence for this can be adduced from Book 10 where he compares the succession crisis at Babylon to events at Rome. Here he is clearly paralleling Perdiccas with Tiberius' reluctance to accept the imperial purple. See W M Heckel (1988), pp 1-4.
6   J R Ellis, 'The Assassination of Philip II', in *Studies in Honour of Charles Edson* (London, 1981) pp 135-6, disputes the veracity of this tale which only occurs in Plutarch, *Alexander*, 10, though the exile is mentioned in Arrian, *Anabasis*, 3.6, but giving five names instead of four.
7   Quintus Curtius, *History of Alexander*, 10.7.18-19.
8   *Ibid*, 10.9.15-18.
9   The plans also included the building of a massive pyre to Hephaistion, a pyramid to the memory of Philip and six huge temples. A thousand ships were to be constructed for the campaign against Carthage and new cities to be founded with a mixture of European and Asian settlers. The authenticity of these plans has been questioned but there seems no good reason to reject them. Perdiccas' intention was to forestall any exploitation of the plans by Craterus and he used the assembly to kill them off once and for all. See E Badian, 'A King's Notebooks' in *HSCP* 72 (1968), pp 183-204; R Lane Fox, *Alexander the Great* (London, 1973) 477 and R M Errington, 'From Babylon to Triparadeisos', p 59.

Chapter 2: The Perdiccas Years

1   Suidas, 27.
2   Indeed, a Macedonian general, Iollas, is mentioned in Thucydides, 62.1, as deputy to Perdiccas II. He may well have been Antipater's father.
3   In the 390s BC, Orestes, the young legitimate king, was killed by his regent, Aeropus.

Aeropus claimed the throne and was succeeded briefly by his son Pausanias. At the same time, another scion of the royal house, Amyntas II, also claimed the throne. Both were murdered and Amyntas III succeeded in 393/2 BC. He ruled shakily for twenty-four years, at one point being restored to the kingdom by dint of Spartan arms. Alexander II inherited the mantle in c.370 BC but only survived two years before being assassinated by his brother-in-law, Ptolemaeus. Alexander's brother, Perdiccas III, killed Ptolemaeus three years later only to perish at the hands of the Illyrians in 360 BC.

4   Craterus did not approve of some of Alexander's policies in the East and his departure opened the way for Hephaistion's ultimate advancement. The idea that Antipater intended to rebel against Alexander has had many adherents over the years. However, there is no evidence for this supposition and two telling points against it. Cassander was sent to try to change the king's mind and, if Antipater was distrusted, Alexander was hardly likely to ask his viceroy to bring troops over in person.

5   The Harpalus affair led to a major trial of Demades and Demosthenes amongst others; Hypereides being one of their prosecutors. The chronology and implications of the whole episode are hotly disputed. See E Badian, 'Harpalus', in *JHS* 81 (1961), pp 16-43; and N G Ashton, 'The Lamian War: a False Start', in *Historia*, 30 (1983), pp 117-120.

6   Plutarch, *Phocion*, 22, translated by I Scott-Kilvert and published in *The Age of Alexander* (London 1973).

7   Presumably the Greeks left a small force to prevent Antipater leaving Lamia too quickly. Diodorus, 17.15, notes the shortage of manpower the allied army had faced with the desertion of the Aetolians and others.

8   He is usually called Cleitus the White to differentiate him from Cleitus the Black (who Alexander killed in a drunken brawl). He commanded an infantry battalion in India but later became a cavalry *hipparch*, serving as such at Sangala and in the Mallian campaign. He was sent home with Craterus and Polyperchon but was probably instructed to help in the construction of the fleet in Cilicia. There is no evidence that he was ever an admiral of Perdiccas (and subsequent defector) as is often suggested.

9   The course of the naval battles, so vital to the ultimate Macedonian success, is unfortunately little understood. Diodorus' account is brief and confused and it is unsure whether there were two, three or even four battles which took place. See Diodorus, 18.15.8-9, and note N G Ashton, 'The *Naumachia* near Amorgos in 322 BC' in *ABSA*, 72 (1977), pp 1-11; and 'How Many Penteris' in *GRBS*, 20 (1979), pp 327-42; and for widely different interpretations: Hammond and Walbank, *History of Macedonia*, pp 113-122 and Heckel, *Marshals of Alexander's Empire*, pp 373-7.

10   There is a marked similarity between the brief description of Crannon and the preceding battle involving Leonnatus. The suspicion lingers that Diodorus has muddled them up. Plutarch, *Phocion*, 26, attributes the defeat at Crannon to inexperienced leadership and Antipater bribing certain partners of the allied cause. The latter charge may have some substance but the former cannot be substantiated and seems to have been used by Plutarch in order to point up the qualities of Phocion.

11   The Samian question was referred by Antipater to the kings in Asia, i.e. Perdiccas. This use of correct protocol by Antipater argues that he and Perdiccas were, at this time, still on good terms.

12   Arrian, *Events After Alexander*, 1.11, which is preserved only in the works of Photius, states that Perdiccas fought Ariarathes in two battles and, having finally defeated him, had him hanged.

13.   Plutarch, *Eumenes*, 4.1, translated by B Perrin and published in *Parallel Lives VIII* (London and Cambridge, Massachusetts, 1919).

14   Cited in Justin, *Epitome of the Philippic History of Pompeius Trogus*, 13.4.

15   For a good summary of the arguments about where Alexander was to be buried see E Badian, 'A King's Notebooks'.

16   Plutarch, *Eumenes*, 5.4.

17   While there is every reason to believe that Craterus was popular with the rank and file Macedonians, our sources tend to overstate it. Ultimately dependent on the eye witness accounts of Eumenes' fellow Cardian, Hieronymus, this alleged popularity was used to point up Eumenes' cleverness. Uncritical acceptance of Hieronymus is all too often the case. He had his biases too, as pointed out by S Hornblower, *Hieronymus of Cardia* (Oxford,1981).

18   Pharnabazus had a very interesting past. Son of Artabazus, one of Darius' nobles, he was the brother of Barsine, Alexander's mistress. After the death of Memnon, he took command of the naval war in the Aegean until captured in 332 BC. He later escaped but seems to have been forgiven and welcomed (like his father) by the Macedonians. Phoenix is hitherto unknown.

19.   Mentioned in Cornelius Nepos' *Lives: Eumenes*, 4. According to Plutarch, *Eumenes*, 7, Eumenes found Craterus still alive and mourned over him as he lay dying. This seems a highly romanticised account. Diodorus, 19.59.3, is different again: Eumenes apparently entrusted the bones of Craterus to an officer, named Ariston, who eventually handed them over to Phila for burial in 315 BC.

20 Philotas was removed from the satrapy of Cilicia for being too friendly with Craterus, later serving under Antigonus. He was replaced by Philoxenus.

21 See Diodorus, 18.35.1-6.

22 Diodorus Siculus, *Universal History, IX*, translated by R M Geer (London and Cambridge, Massachusetts, 1947), 18.33.3.

23 The pro-Ptolemaic source in Diodorus has not been identified. P A Stadter, *Arrian of Nicomedia* (Chapel Hill NC, 1980), pp 148-9, offers the intriguing, but plausible, explanation that Ptolemy himself carried on his history of Alexander to the events after his death.

24 According to Arrian, *Events After Alexander*, 1.34, both Philip Arrhidaeus' secretary, Asclepiodorus, and Attalus made speeches supporting Eurydice at Triparadeisus. The presence of Attalus seems intrinsically unlikely, given his close Perdiccan links, but he may well have sent agents.

25 Indicative of Antipater's skill at political balance is the appointment of four bodyguards for Philip Arrhidaeus at Triparadeisus. The four chosen were the brother of Lysimachus; the brother of Peucestas (the Persian satrap); Alexander, the son of Polyperchon; and Ptolemaeus, the nephew of Antigonus.

Chapter 3: The Struggle for Macedonia

1 Athenaeus, *The Deipnosophists*, translated by C B Gulick (London and Cambridge, Massachusetts, 1928), Vol. II, iv.155.

2 Hammond and Walbank, *History of Macedonia*, p 130, maintain that the decision to appoint the 'manager of the kings' lay with the assembly and that Cassander failed even to get elected as number two to Polyperchon, which is why he fled to seek Antigonus' help. The sources, in our opinion, do not bear out this analysis.

3 This is from Quintus Curtius, 8.5.22-6.1. However, Arrian, *Anabasis*, 4 12.2, has a similar story but names Leonnatus as the 'offender'.

4 Justin, 13.4, mentions Cassander as having been appointed as commander of the king's guards and attendants by Perdiccas at Babylon. This seems inherently unlikely, given Justin's notorious unreliability and the fact that Cassander had no status with the army in Asia.

5 There are four different references to Demades' demise: Diodorus, 18.48.4; Arrian, *Events After Alexander*, 1.15; Plutarch, *Demosthenes*, 31; and Plutarch, *Phocion*, 30. Diodorus makes no mention of Cassander being involved and Arrian merely says Cassander had Demades put to death. However, the Plutarch references are contradictory and confusing, with Cassander killing Demades with his own hand in one version (*Phocion*) and having him executed in the other (*Demosthenes*).

6 One of many Nicanors, it is unclear who he was. He has been identified as Aristotle's son-in-law, who announced the Exiles Decree at the Olympic Games in 324 BC. However, recent scholarship has suggested that this Nicanor was the son of Balacrus, the satrap of Cilicia, and Phila, the daughter of Antipater, who subsequently married Craterus and then Demetrius. See, for example, A B Bosworth, 'A New Macedonian Prince', in *CQ*, 44 (1994), pp 57-65.

7 In some respects, Polyperchon's decree harked back to Alexander's Exiles Decree. But, it was purely an expedient move against the allies of Cassander. See R H Simpson, 'Antigonus the One-Eyed and the Greeks', in *Historia*, 8 (1959), in particular pp 388-9.

8 There is some doubt about this as only Polynaeus, *Stratagems*, 4.11.2, which describes Cassander arresting Nicanor by trickery, mentions an assembly. Diodorus, 18.75.1, simply refers to him as being assassinated.

9 For the intriguing possibility that Olympias' tomb might yet be found see C F Edson 'The Tomb of Olympias', in *Hesperia*, 18 (1949), 84-95.

Chapter 4: The Rise of Antigonus

1 Plutarch, *Moralia* VIII, translated by P A Clement and H B Hoffleit (London and Cambridge, Massachusetts, 1969), 633 C.

2 Ptolemaeus was left as a garrison commander in Caria in 334 BC. Together with Asander, he later won a famous victory over Orontobates, capturing several towns near Halicarnassus. He then disappears from history, until his death in 313 BC. R A Billows' *Antigonos the One-Eyed and the Creation of the Hellenistic State* (Berkeley, 1990), p 426, plausibly suggests he was ill for much of the time. His son, and namesake, was to prove an able, if ultimately flawed, lieutenant for Antigonus.

3 For Marsyas, see W M Heckel, 'Marsyas of Pella: Historian of Macedon', in *Hermes*, 108 (1980), pp 444-62.

4 Asander is not named in the meagre sources but Antigonus is described as in charge of Lydia, whilst, in fact, Asander was. The whole sequence of events is controversial. Some maintain that the three battles are, in fact, the three campaigns of Calas, Balacrus and Antigonus, whilst others claim that Antigonus was given temporary command of the whole of Asia Minor. For a wide range of

interpretations, see Billows, *Antigonos the One-Eyed*, especially pp 43-45; A R Burn, 'Notes on Alexander's Campaigns 332-330', in *JHS*, 72 (1952), pp 81-91 and E M Anson, 'Antigonus, the Satrap of Phrygia', in *Historia*, 37 (1988), pp 471-7.

5   Plutarch, *Eumenes*, 3.3.

6   For details of a possible illustrated amphora relating to the Carian campaign see H Hauben, 'An Athenian Naval Victory in 321 B.C.', in *ZPE*, 13 (1974), 56-67.

7   W M Ramsay, 'Military Operations on the North Front of Mount Tarsus', in *JHS*, 43 (1923), pp 1-10, suggests a location for Nora, near the modern town of Eregli, in southeast Turkey. To our knowledge, this has never been followed up.

8   Polemon was the younger brother of Attalus. Both had been unsuccessfully sent by Perdiccas to retrieve the corpse of Alexander from Ptolemy. But his main claim to fame was running away at the trial of Philotas. For details, see Quintus Curtius, 7, and Arrian, *Anabasis*, 3.27.

9   E M Anson, 'The Siege of Nora: A Source Conflict', in *GRBS*, 18 (1977), pp 251-6, points out the discrepancy in the two sources (Plutarch, *Eumenes*, 12, and Diodorus, 18.50.4 and 18.53.5) on how Eumenes secured his release. Plutarch suggests that Eumenes cleverly amended the oath of loyalty to include both kings and Olympias. Anson rightly rejects this.

10   Antigenes had been an officer under Philip. He had been awarded a prize for bravery by Alexander and also featured in the Battle of the Hydaspes, leading a heavy infantry battalion, possibly the Silver Shields. He was later one of the leading assassins of Perdiccas. Nothing is known about Teutamus.

11   R M Errington, 'Diodorus Siculus and the Chronology of the Early Diadochoi 320-11 BC', in *Hermes*, 105 (1977), pp 478-504, has argued forcefully for a different chronology of the years 320-311 BC. He would put back these events by a year, with Antigonus wintering in Mesopotamia in 317/6 not 318/7. The new chronology, however, creates more problems than it solves; having said that, the whole problem is perhaps insoluble with neither chronology being entirely satisfactory.

12   The Median empire was in existence from circa 750 BC. It had continuous clashes with the Assyrians, until finally defeating them in 612 BC (with the aid of Babylonia). Persia was a vassal state until Cyrus rebelled in the 550s BC and founded the more famous Persian empire.

13   Diodorus Siculus, *Universal History IX*, 19.43.9.

14   This is from Plutarch, *Eumenes*, 16, whose whole narrative of the two battles is somewhat confused and should be treated with caution.

15   Plutarch, *Eumenes*, 17.7.

16   *Ibid*, 18.1.

17   *Ibid*, 18.2.

18   Antigenes is usually regarded as having been executed in this cruel way because of his treachery to Eumenes. However, this is far from clear as Heckel has so eloquently pointed out in *Marshals of Alexander's Empire*, pp 315. Teutamus, according to one source, led the negotiations with Antigonus after the battle. Antigenes was renowned for his trustworthiness, having dissuaded Teutamus from treachery before (Diodorus 18.62.6), and may well have been killed because of his loyalty to Eumenes. It is significant that the fate of Teutamus is unknown; perhaps he entered Antigonus' service as a reward for his disloyalty.

Chapter 5: Stalemate

1   Pausanias, *Guide to Greece*, translated by P Levi (London, 1971), Vol. I, *Central Greece*, 1.6.7.

2   Mentioned in Athenaeus, *Deipnosophists*, I. 18A.

3   Peucestas is mentioned as part of Demetrius' court in Athenaeus, *Deipnosophists*, VI 614F. A Peucestas is mentioned in an inscription from Theangela in Caria detailing a treaty between them. It is thus feasible that Peucestas acted as an Antigonid officer during the Carian campaign, although there is no other evidence.

4   No fewer than four of our sources use Cassander when they quite clearly refer to Asander as satrap of Caria. Quintus Curtius. 10.10.2; Justin, 13.4; and Arrian, *Events After Alexander*, 5, are all guilty, as is Diodorus on at least three occasions: 18.3.1, 18.39.6 and 19.62.6. Our case rests.

5   Billows, *Antigonos the One-Eyed*, p 110, argues that Antigonus had a substantial fleet after his victory over Cleitus and the subsequent defection of Sosigenes' ships in 317 BC but that it was lost to Ptolemy, in Phoenicia, and to Cassander, in Cyprus. However, there is no hard evidence for this and it presupposes that Antigonus had a standing navy, a dubious assumption.

6   The most substantial discussion of this decree is in Simpson, 'Antigonus the One-Eyed and the Greeks'.

7   Telesphorus is often assumed to be Antigonus' nephew. There is no evidence for this assumption, only a stray reference to a Telesphorus in Diogenes Laertius, V.79. When, in Athens, Menander, the famous playwright, was in danger of being brought to trial as a close friend of the disgraced Demetrius of

Phalerum, a man called Telesphorus interceded on his behalf. He is described as a cousin of Demetrius but which Demetrius is not specified. However, as the anecdote appears in the life of the Phalerian there is no real reason to assume an Antigonid connection or that it is the same Telesphorus. If the officer Telesphorus was Antigonus' nephew it is somewhat strange that nowhere does Diodorus mention this fact.

8   Asander had agreed to hold his satrapy as vassal to Antigonus, surrendering his brother as good faith to his intentions. However, he repented of this quickly and, rescuing his brother, reverted to his previous alliance, approaching Ptolemy and Seleucus for aid (Diodorus, 19.75.1).

9   We know the name of a Thymochares from an Athenian inscription (IG 2.1.682) which names him as Athenian naval strategos.

10   The date of the Battle of Gaza, which has aroused much debate, we place in autumn 312 BC. See L C Smith, 'The Chronology of Books 18–20 of Diodorus Siculus', in *AJP*, 82 (1961), pp 288-90; H. Hauben, 'On the Chronology of the Years 313-311 B.C.', in *AJP*, 94 (1973), pp 258-61 and P V Wheatley, 'The Year 22 Tetradrachms of Sidon and the Date of the Battle of Gaza', in *ZPE*, 144 (2003), pp 268-76, contra A B Bosworth, *Legacy of Alexander*, pp 225-31.

11   There is no actual evidence that Antigonus intended to invade Egypt but it is difficult to see the campaign against the Nabataeans in any other context.

12   In 1899 a marble stele was found at Scepsis containing a letter from Antigonus announcing the peace treaty, probably similar letters were sent to other Greek cities. Seleucus was not mentioned, nor the defeat at Gaza. Interestingly, Polyperchon is noted; presumably he still had some influence in the Peloponnese. See C B Welles, *Royal Correspondence in the Hellenistic Period* (London, 1930). For the best discussion of the peace in general, see R H Simpson, 'The Historical Circumstances of the Peace of 311', in *JHS*, 74 (1954), pp 25-31.

13   Diodorus Siculus, *Universal History X*, translated by R M Geer (London and Cambridge, Massachussetts, 1954), 19.105.1.

Chapter 6: Ptolemy

1   Diodorus Siculus, *Universal History X*, 19.86.3. See Chapter 2, note 23, above.

2   The dichotomy between the glamour of Egypt and the intelligence of Greece is more apparent than real. M Bernal, in his invigorating book, *Black Athena: The Afroasiatic roots of Classical Civilisation* (London, 1987), has argued that Ancient Greece was extensively colonised and 'civilised' by the Egyptians and Phoenicians. The orthodox view, seeing Greece as a European/Aryan civilisation, is, Bernal maintains, an essentially nineteenth-century racist invention.

3   Until fairly recently, Ptolemy was regarded as an unimpeachable source for Arrian, as evidenced, for instance, in the many works of Tarn. It was only in the 1960s and 70s that this view was challenged, most notably by R M Errington, 'Bias in Ptolemy's History of Alexander', in *CQ*, 19 (1969), pp 233-42. Now this view is the new orthodoxy, despite a spirited defence of Ptolemy by J Roisman, 'Ptolemy and his rivals in his history of Alexander', in *CQ*, 34 (1984), pp 373-85, and more feebly by W M Ellis, *Ptolemy of Egypt* (London and New York, 1994).

4   A Ptolemy, who may have been the son of Lagus, is mentioned mopping up enemy survivors after the battle at the Persian Gates (Arrian, *Anabasis*, 3.18.9) but it is far from clear which of the many Ptolemies in the army it is. See Heckel, *Marshals of Alexander's Empire*, p 223.

5   See P Harding, *From the end of the Peloponnesian War to the battle of Ipsus, Translated Documents of Greece and Rome, No 2* (Cambridge, 1985) p 159-61.

6   It was thought that Diodorus had confused Nicocles of Paphos with Nicocreon of Salamis. However, Nicocles ruled from the other side of the island and started minting his own coins during his hapless revolt against Ptolemy. Polynaeus, 8.48, confirms his separate identity.

7   Our only source for the siege is Plutarch, *Demetrius*, 7. The context is unclear, only stating that Demetrius was on his way back from Syria. The episode could, in theory, as easily be placed after Demetrius' abortive attack on Babylon following the Nabataean campaign in 311 BC. However, it makes more sense of Ptolemy's activities in Cilicia and Caria to plump for 309 BC.

8   Whose garrison it was at Andros is unknown. The most likely candidate is Antigonus, though Billows, *Antogonos the One-Eyed*, p 225 (among others), argues that it could have been Ptolemaeus.

9   Diodorus Siculus, *Universal History X*, 20.37.1.

10   *Ibid*, 20.37.2, only mentions food and money.

11   Mentioned in Diodorus, 20.50.5.

12   H Hauben, 'Antigonos' Invasion Plan for his Attack on Egypt in 306 BC', in *Orientalia Lovaniensia Periodica*, 6/7 (1975), pp 267-71, describes this invasion.

13   Diodorus Siculus, *Universal History X*, 20.76.3.

14   For a detailed chronology of Ptolemy's assumption of the kingship, see A E Samuel,

Ptolemaic Chronology (Munich, 1962), 3-24.

15   It is not attested, but still very likely, that in the campaigning season of 301 BC Ptolemy once more advanced into Coele Syria. But any impact on the Antigonid enemy was negligible. No reinvestment of Sidon is reported and reinforcing the defences of the newly-filched territories seems to have been the extent of his efforts for the coalition.

Chapter 7: Seleucus

1   Plutarch, *Moralia X*, translated by H N Fowler (London and Cambridge, Massachusetts, 1936), 790.

2   Appian, *Roman History*, translated by H White (London and Cambridge, Massachusetts, 1912), Book XI (*The Syrian Wars*), 56.

3   There are several versions of this story. In some an unnamed sailor retrieves the diadem and puts it on his head to prevent it getting wet but is executed for his pains. Arrian, *Anabasis*, 7.22.5, and Appian, *The Syrian Wars*, 56, discuss both versions.

4   This episode comes from the so-called royal journals, a subject of much debate as to their veracity in Alexander scholarship. The shrine was to Serapis, which poses another problem as the god was invented by Ptolemy and Demetrius of Phalerum several years later. J D Grainger, *Seleukos Nikator* (London and New York, 1990), pp 218-19, rather curiously, sees the whole story as Antigonid propaganda against his enemies.

5   Cornelius Nepos, *Eumenes*, 5, also says Antigonus was the other assassin.

6   Grainger, *Seleukos Nikator*, suggests there may have been fighting between Docimus and Seleucus. However, this is based on a line in the Babylonian Chronicles (10 Obverse 8/9) which has been translated either as: 'after it was destroyed fire consumed it', in A K Grayson, *Assyrian and Babylonian Chronicles* (Locust Valley, NY, 1975), p 116; or as 'after they sank, fever consumed him', in S Smith, *Babylonian Historical Texts* (London, 1924) p 143. It could be construed as relating to Antipater dying (Smith) or a battle between Docimus and Archon or Docimus and Seleucus. In reality, evidence of seven words will hardly bear the weight of any interpretation!

7   Babylonian Chronicle 10 Obverse 5 in Smith, *Babylonian Historical Texts*, p 142.

8   Appian, *The Syrian Wars*, 53, records that Antigonus dismissed the hitherto unknown Blitor as governor of Mesopotamia for allowing Seleucus to escape.

9   Diodorus, 19.55.5, suggests that Ptolemy's reputation for cordiality and kindness were the reason Seleucus fled to him. In reality, Egypt was the nearest major satrapy and did not involve traversing any Antigonid-controlled lands.

10   The previous satrap of Babylon, Pithon, had been killed at Gaza, fighting alongside Demetrius. There presumably was now something of a power vacuum in the province.

11   Diodorus Siculus, *Univeral History X*, 19.100.6.

12   In 1924, S Smith was the first to publish the chronicle in *Babylonian Historical Texts*; see also Grayson, *Assyrian and Babylonian Chronicles* for a more modern (1975) interpretation. Errington's 'Diodorus Siculus and the Chronology of the Early Diadochoi' uses the chronicle as the basis of his revised and controversial chronology (see Chapter 5, note 11, above) with some limited help from the *Marmor Parium*. But, apart from the chronicle's extremely fragmentary nature there are extraordinary problems in trying to match three different sources, all of which have a different calendar system. The Greek year starts in June, the Macedonian in October and the Babylonian in April!

     Billows, *Antigonos the One-Eyed*, pp 141 ff, has an extremely odd interpretation of the Chronicle arguing that Antigonus was not personally involved in the war, being too busy founding cities in Hellespontine Phrygia. The evidence for this is meagre, to say the least, and seems to be used to pin the blame for the defeat by Seleucus on Demetrius.

13   Hornblower, *Hieronymus of Cardia*, pp 97-98 argues, somewhat unconvincingly, that Diodorus chose to omit Hieronymus' version of the war 'which was not enlivened by Hieronymus' personal observation'.

14   A Persian satrap called Evager was killed in this battle. He is generally assumed to be Evagoras, the Antigonid satrap of Aria.

15   Diodorus Siculus, *Universal History X*, 19.92.5.

16   Smith, *Babylonian Historical Texts*, p 143, translation of Reverse, lines 10-11.

17   *Ibid*, pp 138-140.

18   *Ibid*, p 144, translation of Reverse, lines 26-9.

19   See Polynaeus, 4.9.1.

20   This story is retailed by Plutarch, *Alexander*, 62. Justin, 15.4, has Chandragupta offending Alexander and barely escaping with his life. However, these smack of later interpolation as Chandragupta's early career is well known from Indian sources and these do not mention him meeting Alexander.

21   Asoka ruled from 273 to 236 BC. After a victorious war in which he killed many people, he became convinced that war was wrong and professed the idea of non-violence. He vowed to 'conquer by right

conduct alone'. 'Right conduct' was graphically explained by the inscriptions he had set up all over India. They espouse secular and humanistic ideas based on the Buddhist eight-fold path of right thinking. Asoka also instituted a massive programme of social and welfare legislation. Asoka's lion from the pillar at Sarneth was adopted as the emblem of India at independence in 1948.

22 Exactly what provinces Seleucus ceded is not clear. Strabo, *Geography*, 15.2.9, claims that Aria, Gedrosia, Arachosia and Parapamisadae were given up, as does an Asokan inscription. However, Antiochus was active in Aria not long after the treaty. In Arachosia that remarkable survivor, Sibyrtius, was still in office twenty-odd years after Alexander's death, for he played host to Seleucus' ambassador to India, Megasthenes (see note 23, below). Perhaps only parts of the provinces were taken up by Chandragupta.

23 Megasthenes' accounts of India, now lost, were used extensively by subsequent writers. Arrian rated him highly whereas Strabo and Pliny are somewhat less complementary. The extent and dates of his ambassadorship to Chandragupta are unknown, though they presumably belong to the period after the treaty.

Chapter 8: Ebb tide

1 Plutarch, *Moralia III*, 182.
2 Plutarch, *Alexander*, 77, makes Perdiccas an accomplice in this murder, though the whole story seems somewhat fanciful.
3 Hammond and Walbank, *History of Macedonia*, pp 167–8, argue that Alexander IV was killed two years later, after the assassination of Heracles. But there is no real evidence for this assertion. See P Green, *Alexander to Actium* (London, 1991), pp 28 and 747.
4 Diodorus Siculus, *Universal History X*, 19.105.3-4.
5 See W W Tarn, 'Heracles, Son of Barsine', in *JHS*, 41 (1921), pp 18–28.
6 Diodorus Siculus, *Universal History X*, 20.28.2.
7 Plutarch, *Demetrius*, 2, translated by Scott-Kilvert in *The Age of Alexander*.
8 For details of Demetrius of Phalerum's subsequent career see Chapter 10, pp 176–80.
9 Plutarch, *Demetrius*, 9.
10 There were other Antigonias as well, but they are not well attested, being mentioned only in Strabo or Stephanus of Byzantium. For a full, if somewhat biased, discussion of Antigonus' city-founding activity, see Billows, *Antigonos the One-Eyed*, pp 292–305.
11 Antigonia was actually five miles northeast of Antioch. Seleucus levelled Antigonus' city, though it was still in existence, presumably as a village, three hundred years later.
12 Diodorus Siculus, *Universal History X*, 20.53.2.
13 The assumption of the kingship by the Antigonids was tinged with sadness as Demetrius' younger brother died at about this time and was buried with royal honours. Philip is a shadowy figure; being sent to the Hellespont in 310 BC to deal with the revolt of Phoenix is the only other noteworthy mention of him. For other dubious anecdotes about him, see Billows, *Antigonos the One-Eyed*, pp 420–1.
14 Every book on this period has different and various theories about the assumption of kingship by the *Diadochi*. Most see it as an epochal moment when the various Hellenistic monarchies came into being. But it was the natural extension of what had been happening since, at the latest, Antipater's death.
15 Cassander had sent 10,000 measures of barley and Lysimachus 40,000 measures of barley and the same amount of wheat.
16 For a good account of the Colossus, see P Clayton and M Price (eds), *The Seven Wonders of the Ancient World* (London and New York, 1988).
17 The Athenian electorate was 20,000 plus and the quorum required to elect key officers was 6,000. Clearly, mass participation was the norm, though there was the inducement of an attendance fee.
18 Athenian classical democracy has been criticised on a number of counts, most notably its exclusion of women and slaves from the electorate. But this is to judge Athens by modern standards. The much-vaunted British parliamentary system did not give the vote to any sizeable proportion of the population until the 1832 Reform Act and, of course, women had to wait until 1928 for the dubious privilege of the same voting rights as men.
19 Amongst the inscriptions belonging to this period are ones that tell of artillery being placed on the acropolis and temples being used as arsenals.
20 For discussion of the tablet and its provenance see R A Billows, 'Anatolian Dynasts', in *CA*, 8 (1989), pp 173–206.
21 Pleistarchus' defeat is only recorded in Pausanias, 1.15.1.

Chapter 9: Ipsus

1 Plutarch, *Phocion*, 29.

2   Diodorus Siculus, *Universal History X*, 20.106.2.
3   Heckel, *Marshals of Alexander's Empire*, p 274, argues that Lysimachus was a bodyguard under Philip, due to lack of evidence for his career under Alexander, though there is similarly no evidence to justify this claim!
4   Plutarch, *Alexander*, 46, translated by Ian Scott-Kilvert in *The Age of Alexander*.
5   The incident is mentioned by both Curtius, 8.2.35, and Justin, 15.3.12, though the emphasis is slightly different. The ever-unreliable Justin prefaces the story with an almost identical tale only involving Lysimachus, where Alexander inadvertently wounds him and has to staunch the wound with his diadem. This is clearly a late invention (paralleled in Appian *Syrian Wars*, 64) intended as propaganda for Lysimachus' rise to kingship. There are several similar anecdotes about Seleucus.
6   Justin, 15.3, (as opposed to Plutarch, *Alexander*, 55) puts a much better gloss on Lysimachus' part, claiming he had actually put a broken Callisthenes out of his misery, after Alexander had entertained himself by mutilating the philosopher and shutting him in a cage with a dog. Lysimachus' later relationship with the Indian sage, Calanus, gives some support to this view. Unfortunately, as with all these incidents, the situation is even more complicated; several scholars claim that the Lysimachus mentioned by Plutarch is the king's old Macedonian tutor and not Agathocles' son, though the evidence is ambivalent at best.
7   His interest in matters philosophical seems to have continued in later life, with Hipparchia, Theodorus and, most notably, the Athenian Crates, being entertained at his court; though, contrarily, there is also a report that he expelled all philosophers from his kingdom.
8   The marriage could also have taken place after Seuthes' defeat in 313 BC. The evidence is not compelling for either date.
9   Antipater may have tried to help Lysimachus out with troops, as Diodorus, 18.18.4, mentions the possible resettlement of twelve thousand disenfranchised Athenians in Thrace, as part of the terms of the Lamian War settlement. It is not clear, however, whether they all went to Thrace.
10   Nevertheless, Seuthes survived; his kingdom was still in existence at the turn of the century as witnessed by the find of the so called Great Inscription found at Seuthopolis, which indicates that a local dynast, Spartocus, was in charge at Cabyle, eighty miles to the west. Both Spartocus and Seuthes issued coins, though their distribution is very localised. For details of the excavations at Seuthopolis see M Cicikova and D P Dimitrov, 'The Thracian City of Seuthopolis', *British Archaeological Reports (BAR)*, Supplement Series No.38 (1978).
11   Lysimachus also recruited Docimus' personal eunuch, Philetaerus, the later treasurer and founder of Pergamum. At some point during Docimus' rollercoaster career(whether before or after Ipsus is unknown) he founded a town called Docimeium, a place later renowned for its red-veined marble, called docimite by the local inhabitants and much prized by the Romans. See R H Simpson, 'A Possible Case of Misrepresentation in Diodorus XIX', in *Historia*, 6 (1957), pp 504–5.
12   Most commentators assume Seleucus wintered in Cappadocia on the basis of Diodorus, 20.113.4. Whilst this is possible, it seems to us that Seleucus, having already come so far, would have wanted to join Lysimachus for the winter and avert the possibility of Antigonus picking them off singly in a surprise attack. A lesser, if related, problem is when Prepelaus joined Lysimachus. There is no mention in the sources but *pace* Billows, *Antigonos the One-Eyed*, p 177, it was probably at Synnada.
13   Dionysius had allied himself to Antigonus by marriage of his daughter to Ptolemaeus (see Chapter 6). He had also fought under Antigonus in Cyprus.
14   Athenaeus, *Deipnosophistae*, XIII, 578 B, refers to a mistress of Demetrius with whom Antigonus fell in love, but it is generally assumed that this anecdote refers to Antigonus Gonatas.

Chapter 10: Lagid Revival

1   Plutarch, *Moralia III*, 189.
2   The Alexandria that Ptolemy cultivated also produced one of the Seven Wonders of the World. He already had an indirect association with another, the Colossus of Rhodes, and like that wonder the great Pharos or Lighthouse of Alexandria no longer exists in any semblance whatsoever. Although completed during his son's reign, the Lighthouse was Ptolemy's original conception, intended to crown the glory of Alexandria. If not the world's first lighthouse, it was certainly the largest. The Pharos' exact form is unknown but appeared to have consisted of three tiers, being over 300 feet high and crowned by a statue of Zeus. Like the Colossus, it was severely damaged by earthquake and was in ruins in the fourteenth century. Now the site is covered by an Islamic fort built from the debris. Several scholars have seen in the Pharos the original inspiration for the minaret.

Chapter 11: Lysimachus

1   Justin, *Epitome of the Philippic History of Pompeius Trogus*, translated by J S Watson (London, 1853), 15.3.

2   Later Lysimachus was to send corn and offer a new mast and sail for the festival ship of 298 BC.

3   Agathocles' capture is attested to in a fragment of Diodorus. However, Pausanias, 1.9.7, considers it a doublet of Lysimachus' later capture by Dromichaetes and thus ahistorical.

4   What happened to Antipater at this point is unknown. As he is next heard of at Lysimachus' court, he presumably fled there.

5   For the arguments on Eupolemus and his dates see Billows, 'Anatolian Dynasts'.

6   According to various stories in Polyaenus, that inveterate troublemaker Lachares was at Thebes. He escaped to Lysimachus after hiding in a sewer for several days and, incredibly, was still fomenting intrigues as late as 279 BC, when he attempted to betray Cassandreia to Antiochus. However, Pausanias claims that he was murdered for his ill-gotten gold soon after fleeing Athens.

7   The chronology of the siege of Thebes and the various campaigns Demetrius waged after seizing the throne of Macedonia is disputed. Green, *Alexander to Actium*, Hammond and Walbank, *History of Macedonia* and H S Lund, *Lysimachus* (London and New York, 1992) all offer different views. Thankfully, the Pythian Games of 290 BC provide a *terminus post quem*.

8   If on land a balance was retained, at sea Demetrius was unassailable. A short time earlier he took from Pyrrhus the important island of Corfu. It had been joined to Epirus as a dowry when Pyrrhus married Lanassa, daughter of Agathocles, the Tyrant of Syracuse. But she became disenchanted when Pyrrhus took an Illyrian princess as another wife and in pique offered herself and her dowry to Demetrius. He did not hesitate for an instant but wed the woman and sent his navy to take over the island.

9   Plutarch almost certainly exaggerated the number of troops Demetrius raised. It was just not possible to maintain huge armies in Greece in the same way it was in Asia.

10 Pausanias (1.10.2) is the source for the Thessalian campaign but is brief and cursory. However, there is tantalising evidence for the alliance between Pyrrhus and Gonatus. Fragments of a play by Phoenicides called *The Flute Players* refer to a secret treaty between the two. The play, a comedy, was performed in Athens at about this time. As for the desecration of the Epirote graves, this is again from Pausanias (1.9.10), but even he doubts the historicity of the incident.

11 This is not, of course, to say that Lysimachus did not protect his interests. Philippides, a leading Athenian who had spent seventeen long years in exile at Lysimachus' court, returned to his native city and became prominent in political affairs, as did Bithys, Lysimachus' so-called parasite. Both could be relied on to promote Lysimachus' view in the city. An even more outstanding political returnee was Demochares, the nephew of Demosthenes. Exiled in 303 BC, he also came home after the final defeat of Demetrius. Though not exiled at Lysimachus' court, he was chosen to head two embassies to Lysimachus which returned with subsidies of 130 talents.

12 Evidence for the campaign comes from a few fragments of Memnon. The defeat Lysimachus is said to have suffered at the hands of Zipoites may well be referring to the Battle of Corupedium, where the Bithynian fought alongside Seleucus.

13 The commander of the Paeonians under Alexander was called Ariston. He is mentioned several times, most notably in slaying a Persian noble in single combat and for his part in the victory at Gaugamela. His name and status suggests he may have been the father of Audoleon. See Heckel, *The Marshals of Alexander's Empire*, pp 354-5.

14 Polyaenus, *Stratagems*, translated for the authors by B Polack, 4.12.3. The anecdote may well have compressed the time scale between his restoration and subsequent eviction by Lysimachus.

15 Though this is debated by some scholars. See, for instance, Lund, *Lysimachus*, p 194.

16 Only Memnon suggests Ptolemy Thunderbolt's involvement in the murder of Agathocles. It has been plausibly suggested that he has confused the Thunderbolt with Ptolemy Lysimachou, who had much more to gain from Agathocles' death. To confuse matters even more, some commentators claim that the Thunderbolt was innocent of any plotting and fled to Seleucus after Agathocles' demise. For opposed views on this matter see, for instance, Green, *Alexander to Actium*, pp 132-3, contra Hammond and Walbank, *History of Macedonia*, pp 239-40. As for Ptolemy Lysimachou, he remarkably survived the fall out from both Agathocles' and his father's death. After Corupedium he escaped to Illyria and skirmished unsuccessfully with both Ptolemy Thunderbolt and Antigonus Gonatus before ending up in Telmessus in Lycia. Here he and his descendants apparently ruled as independent dynasts.

Chapter 12: The Final Hand

1   Justin, *Epitome*, 17.1.

2   Patrocles had ably defended Babylon against Demetrius in 312 BC and was still in service to the dynasty in 280 BC, when he was in command of Antiochus' army in Asia. In addition, at some point during Seleucus' reign he was sent to investigate the Caspian Sea. He evidently wrote a book full of geographical information as he is cited frequently by Pliny and Strabo. Unlike his contemporary Megasthenes, Patrocles met with Strabo's approval.

3   Polyaenus, *Stratagems*, 4.9.3.

Bibliography

Ancient Sources

Appian, *Roman History*, translated by H White (London and Cambridge, Massachusetts, 1912).

Athenaeus, *The Deipnosophists*, II, translated by C B Gulick (London and Cambridge, Massachusetts, 1928).

Diodorus Siculus, *Universal History IX*, translated by R M Geer (London and Cambridge, Massachusetts, 1947).

Diodorus Siculus, *Universal History X*, translated by R M Geer (London and Cambridge, Massachusetts, 1954).

Justin, *Epitome of the Philippic History of Pompeius Trogus*, translated by J S Watson (London, 1853).

Pausanias, *Guide to Greece, Vol. I Central Greece*, translated by P Levi (London, 1971).

Plutarch, *Alexander*, translated by I Scott-Kilvert and included in *The Age of Alexander* (London, 1973).

Plutarch, *Demetrius*, translated by I Scott-Kilvert and included in *The Age of Alexander* (London, 1973).

Plutarch, *Eumenes*, translated by B Perrin and included in *Parallel Lives VIII* (London and Cambridge, Massachusetts, 1919).

Plutarch, *Moralia VIII*, translated by P A Clement and H B Hoffleit (London and Cambridge, Massachusetts, 1969).

Plutarch, *Moralia X*, translated by H N Fowler (London and Cambridge, Massachusetts, 1936).

Plutarch, *Phocion*, translated by I Scott-Kilvert and included under the title *The Age of Alexander* (London, 1973).

Polyaenus, *Stratagems*, translated for the authors by B Polack.

Quintus Curtius Rufus, *The History of Alexander*, translated by John Yardley (London 1984).

Modern Authors

Adams, W L, 'The Dynamics of Internal Macedonian Politics in the time of Cassander', in *Ancient Macedonia*, 3 (1983), pp 2-30.

Anson, E M, 'The Siege of Nora: A Source Conflict', in *GRBS*, 18 (1977), pp 251-6.

Anson, E M, 'Antigonus, the Satrap of Phrygia', in *Historia*, 37 (1988), pp 471-7.

Ashton, N G, 'The *Naumachia* near Amorgos in 322 B.C.', in *ABSA*, 72 (1977), pp 1-11.

Ashton, N G, 'How Many Penteris', in *GRBS*, 20 (1979), pp 327-42.

Ashton, N G, 'The Lamian War a False Start' in *Historia*, 30 (1983) pp 117-120

Austin, M M, *The Hellenistic world from Alexander to the Roman conquest, A selection of ancient sources in translation* (Cambridge, 1981).

Austin, M M, 'Hellenistic Kings, War and Economy', in *CQ*, 36 (1986), pp 450-466.

Badian, E, 'Harpalus', in *JHS*, 81 (1961), pp 16-43.

Badian, E, 'The Struggle for the succession to Alexander the Great', in *Gnomon*, 34 (1962), pp 381-7.

Badian, E, 'A King's Notebooks' in *HSCP*, 72 (1968) pp 183-204.

Badian, E, 'A Comma in the History of Samos', in *ZPE*, 23 (1976), pp 289-94.

Bernal, M, *Black Athena: The Afroasiatic roots of Classical Civilisation* (London, 1987).

Bevan, E R, *The House of Seleucus* (London, 1902).

Bevan, E R, *A History of Egypt under the Ptolemaic Dynasty* (London, 1927)

Billows, R A, 'Anatolian Dynasts', in *CA*, 8 (1989), pp 173-206.

Billows, R A, *Antigonos the One-Eyed and the Creation of the Hellenistic State* (Berkeley, 1990).

Bosworth, A B, 'The Death of Alexander the Great: Rumour and Propaganda', in *CQ*, 21 (1971), pp 112-36.

Bosworth, A B, 'The Government of Syria under Alexander', in *CQ*, 24 (1974), pp 46-64.

Bosworth, A B, 'Eumenes, Neoptolemus and PSI 12.1284', in *GRBS*, 19 (1978) pp 227-37.

Bosworth, A B, 'Alexander and the Iranians', in *JHS*, 100 (1980), pp 1-21.

Bosworth, A B, 'The Indian Satrapies under Alexander', in *Antichthon*, 17 (1983), pp 37-46.

Bosworth, A B, *From Arrian to Alexander* (Oxford, 1988).

Bosworth, A B, *Conquest and Empire - The Reign of Alexander the Great* (Cambridge, 1988).

Bosworth, A B, 'A New Macedonian Prince', in *CQ*, 44 (1994), pp 57-65.

Bosworth, A B, *The Legacy of Alexander* (Oxford, 2002).

Burn, A R, 'Notes on Alexander's Campaigns, 332-330', in *JHS*, 72 (1952), pp 81-91.

Chaniotis, A, *War in the Hellenistic World* (Oxford, 2005).

Champion, J, *The Strategy of Antigonus Monopthalmus 315-301* (unpublished thesis).

Cicikova, M and Dimitrov D P, 'The Thracian City of Seuthopolis', in *British Archaeological Reports (BAR)*, Supplement Series No.38.

Clayton, P, and Price, M (eds.), *The Seven Wonders of the Ancient World* (London and New York, 1988).

Edson, C F, 'The Tomb of Olympias', in *Hesperia*, 18 (1949), pp 84-95.

Ellis, J R, 'The Assassination of Philip II', in *Studies In Honour Of Charles Edson* (London, 1981), pp 99-137.

Ellis, W M, *Ptolemy of Egypt* (London and New York, 1994).

Errington, R M, 'Bias in Ptolemy's History of Alexander', in *CQ*, 19 (1969), pp 233-42.

Errington, R M, 'From Babylon to Triparadeisos 323-320 BC', in *JHS*, 90 (1970), pp 49-77.

Errington, R M, 'Alexander in the Hellenistic World', in *Entretiens Hardt*, 22 (1976), pp 137-79

Errington, R M, 'Diodorus Siculus and the Chronology of the Early Diadochoi 320-11 BC', in *Hermes*, 105 (1977), pp 478-504.

Errington, R M, *History of Macedonia* (Berkeley, 1989).

Grainger, J D, *Seleukos Nikator* (London and New York, 1990).

Green, P, *Alexander to Actium* (London, 1991).

Grayson A K, *Assyrian and Babylonian Chronicles* (Locust Valley, NY, 1975).

Hadley R A, 'Hieronymus of Cardia and early Seleucid Mythology', in *Historia*, 18 (1969), pp 142-52.

Hadley, R A, 'The Foundation Date of Seleucia-on-the-Tigris', in *Historia*, 27 (1978), pp 227-30.

Hammond, N G L, and Walbank, F W, *History of Macedonia, vol.3* (Oxford, 1988).

Harding, P, *From the end of the Peloponnesian War to the battle of Ipsus*, Translated Documents of Greece and Rome, No 2 (Cambridge, 1985).

Hauben, H, 'On the Chronology of the Years 313-311 BC', in *AJP*, 94 (1973), pp 256-67.

Hauben, H, 'An Athenian Naval Victory in 321 BC', in *ZPE*, 13 (1974), pp 56-67.

Hauben, H, 'Antigonos' Invasion Plan for his Attack on Egypt in 306 BC', in *Orientalia Lovaniensia Periodica*, 6/7 (1975), pp 267-71.

Heckel, W, 'Marsyas of Pella: Historian of Macedon', in *Hermes*, 108 (1980), pp 444-62.

Heckel, W, 'Some Speculations on the Prosopography of the Alexanderreich', in *LCM*, 6 (1981), pp 63-9.

Heckel, W, 'The Last Days and Testament of Alexander the Great', in *Historia Einzelschriften*, 56 (1988).

Heckel, W, *The Marshals of Alexander's Empire* (London and New York, 1992).

Hornblower, J, *Hieronymus of Cardia* (Oxford, 1981).

Lane Fox, R, *Alexander the Great*, (London, 1973).

Lund, H S, *Lysimachus* (London and New York, 1992).

Parker, R A, and Dubberstein, W H, *Babylonian Chronology* (Chicago, 1945).

Ramsay, W M, 'Military Operations on the North Front of Mount Tarsus', in *JHS*, 43 (1923), pp 1-10.

Roisman, J, 'Ptolemy and his rivals in his history of Alexander', in *CQ*, 34 (1984), pp 373-85.

Rosen, K, 'Political Documents in Hieronymus of Cardia', in *Acta Classica*, 10 (1967), pp 41-94.

Rostovtzeff, M, *Social andEconomic History of the Hellenistic World*, 3 Vol. (Oxford, 1953).

Samuel, A E, *Ptolemaic Chronology* (Munich, 1962).

Shipley, G, *The Greek World after Alexander* (London and New York, 2000).

Simpson, R H, 'The Historical Circumstances of the Peace of 311', in *JHS*, 74 (1954), pp 25-31.

Simpson, R H, 'Ptolemaeus' Invasion of Attica in 313', in *Mnemosyne*, 8 (1955), pp 34-7.

Simpson, R H, 'A Possible Case of Misrepresentation in Diodorus XIX', in *Historia*, 6 (1957), pp 504-5.

Simpson, R H, 'Antigonus the One-Eyed and the Greeks', in *Historia*, 8 (1959), pp 385-409.

Simpson, R H, 'Abbreviation of Hieronymus in Diodorus', in *AJP*, 80 (1959), pp 370-9.

Smith, L C, 'The Chronology of Books 18-20 of Diodorus Siculus', in *AJP*, 82 (1961), pp 283-90.

Smith, S, *Babylonian Historical Texts* (London, 1924).

Stadter, P A, *Arrian of Nicomedia* (Chapel Hill, NC, 1980).

Tarn, W W, *Antigonus Gonatas* (Oxford, 1913).

Tarn, W W, 'Heracles, Son of Barsine', in *JHS*, 41 (1921), pp 18-28.

Tarn, W W, and Griffith, G T, *Hellenistic Civilisation* (London, 1952).

Tritle, L A, *Phocion the Good* (London, 1988).

Walbank, F W, *The Hellenistic World* (London, 1981).

Welles, C B, *Royal Correspondence in the Hellenistic Period* (London, 1930).

Welles, C B, 'The Discovery of Sarapis and the Foundation of Alexandria', in *Historia*, 11 (1962), 273-4.

Welles, C B, *Alexander and the Hellenistic World* (Toronto, 1970).

Westlake, H D, 'Eumenes of Cardia', in *Bulletin of The John Rylands Library*, 37 (1954), pp 309-327.

Wheatley, P V, 'The Year 22 Tetradrachms of Sidon and the Date of the Battle of Gaza', in *ZPE*, 144 (2003), pp 268-76.

Woodhead, A G, 'Athens and Demetrius Poliorketes at the end of the Fourth Century BC', in *Studies in Honour of Charles Edson* (London, 1981), pp 357-67.

Index

The
CHANCTONBURY
crashes

The story of
five German aircraft that never returned from
the Battle of Britain

MARTIN F. MACE

HISTORIC MILITARY PRESS